100

SMART Board™

LESSONS

TERMS AND CONDITIONS

IMPORTANT - PERMITTED USE AND WARNINGS - READ CAREFULLY BEFORE USING

Minimum specification:
- PC/Mac with a CD-ROM drive and at least 128 MB RAM
- Microsoft Office 2000 or higher
- Adobe® Reader®
- Interactive whiteboard
- Notebook™ software
- Facilities for printing and sound (optional)

PC:
- Pentium II 450 MHz processor
- Microsoft Windows 2000 SP4 or higher

Mac:
- 700 MHz processor (1 GHz or faster recommended)
- Mac OS X.4 or higher

For all technical support queries, please phone Scholastic Customer Services on 0845 6039091.

YEAR

3

Scottish Primary 4

CREDITS

Authors
Jon Audain (foundation subjects and science), Rhona Dick (history), Eileen Jones (English), Ann Montague-Smith (mathematics), Alan Rodgers and Angella Streluk (geography)

Development Editor
Niamh O'Carroll

Assistant Editor
Nicola Morgan

Illustrators
Andy Keylock (book illustrations), Jim Peacock (book and Notebook file illustrations), Chris Saunderson (additional Notebook file illustrations), Ian Hunt (additional book illustrations).

Series Designer
Joy Monkhouse

Designers
Rebecca Male, Allison Parry, Andrea Lewis and Melissa Leeke

CD-ROM developed in association with
Q & D Multimedia

ACKNOWLEDGEMENTS

SMART Board™ and Notebook™ are registered trademarks of SMART Technologies Inc in Canada, the United States, the European Union and other countries.

Microsoft Office, Word and Excel are either registered trademarks or trademarks of Microsoft Corporation in the United States and/or other countries.

With grateful thanks for advice, help and expertise to Angus McGarry (Trainer) and Fiona Ford (Education Development Consultant) at Steljes Ltd.

All Flash activities designed and developed by Q & D Multimedia.

Interactive Teaching Programs (developed by the Primary National Strategy) © Crown copyright.

With thanks to Mike Longden for the use of various photographs, and T-Mobile for the use of and image of a Motorola mobile phone www.t-mobile.co.uk.

The publishers gratefully acknowledge:
Articles of Faith for the use of an image of Lakshmi © 2005, Articles of Faith www.articlesoffaith.co.uk.
Jackie Andrews for the use of 'The Story of Lakshmi' by Jackie Andrews © 2006, Jackie Andrews, from *100 Activprimary Whiteboard Lessons: Year 3* (2006, Scholastic Ltd)
Caroline Binch for the use of illustrations from *Down by the River* by Caroline Binch © 2001, Caroline Binch (2001, DK Publishing) and *Silver Shoes* by Caroline Binch © 1996, Caroline Binch (1996, Heinemann).
The Royal Mint for the use of images of coins © Crown copyright.
SNTE (Societe Nouvelle d'Exploitation de la Tour Eiffel) for the use of an image of the Eiffel Tower © SNTE; Photo: Bertrand Michau.

Every effort has been made to trace copyright holders for the works reproduced in this book, and the publishers apologise for any inadvertent omissions.

Designed using Adobe InDesign.

Made with Macromedia is a trademark of Macromedia, Inc. Director ®
Copyright © 1984-2000 Macromedia, Inc.

Published by Scholastic Ltd
Villiers House
Clarendon Avenue
Leamington Spa
Warwickshire CV32 5PR
www.scholastic.co.uk

Printed by Bell and Bain Ltd, Glasgow

1 2 3 4 5 6 7 8 9   7 8 9 0 1 2 3 4 5 6

Text © 2007 Jon Audain (foundation subjects and science), Rhona Dick (history), Eileen Jones (English), Ann Montague-Smith (mathematics), Alan Rodgers and Angella Streluk (geography)

© 2007 Scholastic Ltd

British Library Cataloguing-in-Publication Data
A catalogue record for this book is available from the British Library.

ISBN 978-0439-94539-4

The rights of the authors of this work have been asserted by them in accordance with the Copyright, Designs and Patents Act 1988.

Extracts from the Primary National Strategy's *Primary Framework for literacy and mathematics* (2006) www.standards.dfes.gov.uk/primaryframework © Crown copyright. Reproduced under the terms of the Click Use Licence.

Extracts from The National Literacy Strategy and The National Numeracy Strategy © Crown copyright. Material from the National Curriculum © The Queen's Printer and Controller of HMSO. Reproduced under the terms of HMSO Guidance Note 8.

Extracts from the QCA Scheme of Work © Qualifications and Curriculum Authority.

CONTENTS

100 SMART BOARD™ LESSONS

Interactive whiteboards are fast becoming the must-have resource in today's classroom as they allow teachers to facilitate children's learning in ways that were inconceivable a few years ago. The appropriate use of interactive whiteboards, whether used daily in the classroom or once a week in the ICT suite, will encourage active participation in lessons and should increase learners' determination to succeed. Interactive whiteboards make it easier for teachers to bring subjects across the curriculum to life in new and exciting ways.

'There is a whiteboard revolution in UK schools.'

(Primary National Strategy)

What can an interactive whiteboard offer?

For the **teacher**, an interactive whiteboard offers the same facilities as an ordinary whiteboard, such as drawing, writing and erasing. However, the interactive whiteboard also offers many other possibilities to:
- save any work created during a lesson
- prepare as many pages as necessary
- display any page within the Notebook™ file to review teaching and learning
- add scanned examples of the children's work to a Notebook file
- change colours of shapes and backgrounds instantly
- use simple templates and grids
- link Notebook files to spreadsheets, websites and presentations.

Using an interactive whiteboard in the simple ways outlined above can enrich teaching and learning in a classroom, but that is only the beginning of the whiteboard's potential to educate and inspire.

For the **learner**, the interactive whiteboard provides the opportunity to share learning experiences, as lessons can be delivered with sound, still and moving images, and websites. Interactive whiteboards can be used to cater for the needs of all learning styles:
- kinaesthetic learners benefit from being able to physically manipulate images
- visual learners benefit from being able to watch videos, look at photographs and see images being manipulated
- auditory learners benefit from being able to access audio resources such as voice recordings and sound effects.

With a little preparation all of these resource types could be integrated in one lesson, a feat that would have been almost impossible before the advent of the interactive whiteboard!

Access to an interactive whiteboard

In schools where learners have limited access to an interactive whiteboard the teacher must carefully plan lessons in which the children will derive most benefit from using it. As teachers become familiar with the whiteboard they will learn when to use it and, importantly, when not to use it!

Where permanent access to an interactive whiteboard is available, it is important that the teacher plans the use of the board effectively. It should be used only in ways that will enhance or extend teaching and learning. Children still need to gain practical first-hand experience of many things. Some experiences cannot be recreated on an interactive whiteboard but others cannot be had without it. *100 SMART Board™ Lessons* offers both teachers and learners the most accessible and creative uses of this most valuable resource.

About the series

100 SMART Board™ Lessons is designed to reflect best practice in using interactive whiteboards. It is also designed to support all teachers in using this valuable tool by providing lessons and other resources that can be used on a whiteboard with little or no preparation. These inspirational lessons cover all National Curriculum subjects. They are perfect for all levels of experience and are an essential for any SMART Board users.

Safety note: Avoid looking directly at the projector beam as it is potentially damaging to eyes, and never leave the children unsupervised when using the interactive whiteboard.

Introduction

About the book

This book is divided into four chapters. Each chapter contains lessons and photocopiable activity sheets covering:
- English
- Mathematics
- Science
- Foundation subjects.

At the beginning of each chapter a **planning grid** identifies the title, the objectives covered and any relevant cross-curricular links in each lesson. Objectives are taken from the relevant Primary National Strategy, National Curriculum Programmes of Study (PoS), or the QCA Schemes of Work. All of the lessons should therefore fit into your existing medium-term plans. The planning grids have been provided in Microsoft Word format on the CD-ROM for this purpose.

Lesson plans

The lessons have a consistent structure with a starter activity, activities for shared and independent work, and a plenary to round up the teaching and learning and identify any assessment opportunities. Crucially, each lesson plan identifies resources required (including photocopiable activity sheets ▣ and Notebook files that are provided on the CD-ROM ●). Also highlighted are the whiteboard tools that could be used in the lesson.

Photocopiable activity sheets at the end of each chapter support the lessons. These sheets provide opportunities for group or individual work to be completed away from the board, but link to the context of the whiteboard lesson. They also provide opportunities for whole-class plenary sessions in which children discuss and present their work.

Two general record sheets are provided on pages 170 and 171. These are intended to support the teacher in recording ways in which the interactive whiteboard is used, and where and how interactive resources can be integrated into a lesson.

What's on the CD-ROM?

The accompanying CD-ROM provides an extensive bank of Notebook files. These support, and are supported by, the lessons in this book. As well as texts and images, a selection of Notebook files include the following types of files:
- Embedded Microsoft Office files: These include Microsoft Word and Excel documents. The embedded files are launched from the Notebook file and will open in their native Microsoft application.
- Embedded interactive files: These include specially commissioned interactive files as well as Interactive Teaching Programs (ITPs) from the Primary National Strategy.
- Printable PDF versions of the photocopiable activity and record sheets, as well as the answers to the mathematics activities, are also provided on the CD-ROM.
- 'Build your own' file: This contains a blank Notebook page with a bank of selected images and interactive tools from the Gallery, as well as specially commissioned images. It is supported by lesson plans in the book to help you to build your own Notebook files.

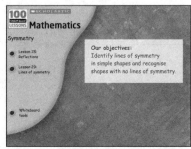

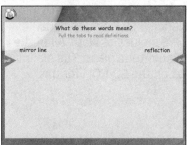

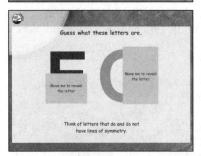

The Notebook files
All of the Notebook files have a consistent structure as follows:

Title and objectives page
Use this page to highlight the focus of the lesson. You might also wish to refer to this page at certain times throughout the lesson or at the end of the lesson to assess whether the learning objective was achieved.

Starter activity
This sets the context to the lesson and usually provides some key questions or learning points that will be addressed through the main activities.

Main activities
These activities offer independent, collaborative group, or whole-class work. The activities draw on the full scope of Notebook software and the associated tools, as well as the SMART Board tools.

What to do boxes are also included in many of the prepared Notebook files. These appear as tabs in the top right-hand corner of the screen. To access these notes, simply pull out the tabs to reveal planning information, additional support and key learning points.

Plenary
A whole-class activity or summary page is designed to review work done both at the board and away from the board. In many lessons, children are encouraged to present their work.

Whiteboard tools page
The whiteboard tools page gives a reminder of the tools used in the lesson and provides instructions on how they are used.

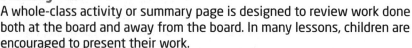

HOW TO USE THE CD-ROM

Setting up your screen for optimal use
It is best to view the Notebook pages at a screen display setting of 1280 × 1024 pixels. To alter the screen display, select Settings, then Control Panel from the Start menu. Next, double-click on the Display icon and then click on the Settings tab. Finally, adjust the Screen area scroll bar to 1280 × 1024 pixels. Click on OK.

If you prefer to use a screen display setting of 800 × 600 pixels, ensure that your Notebook view is set to 'Page Width'. To alter the view, launch Notebook and click on View. Go to Zoom and select the 'Page Width' setting. If you use a screen display setting of 800 x 600 pixels, text in the prepared Notebook files may appear larger when you edit it on screen.

Viewing the printable resources
Adobe® Reader® is required to view the printable resources. All the printable resources are PDF files.

Visit the Adobe® website at **www.adobe.com** to download the latest version of Adobe® Reader®.

Introduction

Getting started

The program should run automatically when you insert the CD-ROM into your CD drive. If it does not, use My Computer to browse to the contents of the CD-ROM and click on the *100 SMART Board™ Lessons* icon.

When the program starts, you are invited to register the product either online or using a PDF registration form. You also have the option to register later. If you select this option, you will be taken, via the Credits screen, to the Main menu.

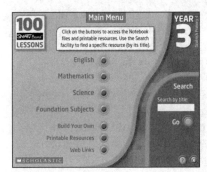

Main menu

The Main menu divides the Notebook files by subject: English, mathematics, science and foundation subjects. Clicking on the appropriate blue button for any of these options will take you to a separate Subject menu (see below for further information). The 'Build your own' file is also accessed through the Main menu (see below). The activity sheets are provided in separate menus. To access these resources, click on Printable resources.

Individual Notebook files or pages can be located using the search facility by keying in words (or part words) from the resource titles in the Search box. Press Go to begin the search. This will bring up a list of the titles that match your search.

The Web Links button takes you to a list of useful web addresses. A help button 🔘 is included on all menu screens. The Help notes on the CD-ROM provide a range of general background information and technical support for all users.

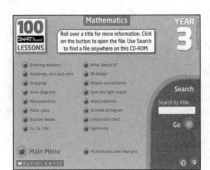

Subject menu

Each Subject menu provides all of the prepared Notebook files for each chapter of the book. Roll over each Notebook file title to reveal a brief description of the contents in a text box at the top of the menu screen; clicking on the blue button will open the Notebook file. Click on Main menu to return to the Main menu screen.

'Build your own' file

Click on this button to open a blank Notebook page and a collection of Gallery objects, which will be saved automatically into the My Content folder in the Gallery. You only need to click on this button the first time you wish to access the 'Build your own' file, as the Gallery objects will remain in the My Content folder on the computer on which the file was opened. To use the facility again, simply open a blank Notebook page and access the images and interactive resources from the same folder under My Content. If you are using the CD-ROM on a different computer you will need to click on the 'Build your own' button again.

Printable resources

The printable PDF activity sheets are also divided by chapter. Click on the subject to find all the activity sheets related to that subject/chapter. The answers to Chapter 2, mathematics, are also provided.

To alternate between the menus on the CD-ROM and other open applications, hold down the Alt key and press the Tab key to switch to the desired application.

English

The lessons in the English chapter match the objectives in the Primary National Strategy's *Primary Framework for literacy*. These objectives are listed in the curriculum grid below, along with the corresponding objectives from the medium-term planning in the National Literacy Strategy. The curriculum grids in this book are also provided on the accompanying CD-ROM, in editable format, to enable you to integrate the lessons into your planning.

The interactive whiteboard offers pace and visual excitement to the lessons. Words can be made to appear or disappear, text can be manipulated, the children can see sentences being constructed, and they will watch paragraphs and stories emerging.

Be generous with the wonderful powers of the whiteboard and involve the children as much as possible in operating the board's tools. This will bring special benefits to children with dominant visual and kinaesthetic styles of learning. Above all, use the interactive whiteboard as another resource for the teaching of English. The whiteboard should support the interaction between you, the children and literacy.

Lesson title	PNS objectives	NLS objectives	Expected prior knowledge	Cross-curricular links
Lesson 1: Marking sentences	**Sentence structure and punctuation** • Compose sentences using adjectives, verbs and nouns for precision, clarity and impact.	**S11**: To write in complete sentences. **S12**: To demarcate the end of one sentence with a full stop and the start of a new one with a capital letter.	• A group of words can form a sentence.	**History** QCA Unit 6 'Why have people invaded and settled in Britain in the past?'
Lesson 2: Setting and atmosphere	**Creating and shaping texts** • Select and use descriptive vocabulary.	**T11**: To develop the use of settings in own stories by writing short descriptions of known places.	• Children should have had opportunities to express personal opinions about a story.	**Geography** QCA Unit 6 'Investigating our local area'
Lesson 3: Verbs	**Sentence structure and punctuation** • Compose sentences using adjectives, verbs and nouns for precision, clarity and impact. **Creating and shaping texts**	**S3**: To know the function of verbs in sentences. **S5**: To use the term *verb* appropriately.	• Experience of sentence construction.	**ICT** QCA Unit 3A 'Combining text and graphics'
Lesson 4: High frequency words	**Sentence structure** • Compose sentences using adjectives, verbs and nouns for precision, clarity and impact.	**W17**: To generate synonyms for high frequency words.	• Some words have similar meanings.	**Speaking and listening** Objective 31: To actively include and respond to all members of the group.
Lesson 5: Story planning in paragraphs	**Text structure and organisation** • Group related material into paragraphs.	**T16**: To begin to organise stories into paragraphs.	• Experience of story writing.	**ICT** QCA Unit 3A 'Combining text and graphics' **Speaking and listening** Objective 29: To choose and present poems or stories for performance, identifying appropriate tone, volume and use of voices and other sounds.
Lesson 6: Direct speech	**Sentence structure and punctuation** • Clarify meaning through the use of speech marks.	**S7**: To know the basic conventions of speech punctuation. **S8**: To use the term *speech marks*.	• Understanding of *spoken* and *unspoken*.	**Speaking and listening** Objective 28: To present events and characters through dialogue to engage the interest of an audience.
Lesson 7: Prefixes	**Word structure and spelling** • Recognise a range of prefixes, understanding how they modify meaning and spelling.	**W10**: To recognise and spell common prefixes and how these influence word meanings. **W11**: To use their knowledge of prefixes to generate new words from root words, especially antonyms.	• Words may be linked to one another.	**History** QCA Unit 6A 'Why have people invaded and settled in Britain in the past? A Roman case study.'

Lesson title	PNS objectives	NLS objectives	Expected prior knowledge	Cross-curricular links
Lesson 8: Verbs and tenses ◉	**Sentence structure and punctuation** • Compose sentences using verbs for precision.	**S4**: To use verb tenses with increasing accuracy. Use past tense consistently for narration.	• Understanding of the concept of time.	**History** QCA Unit 6 'Why have people invaded and settled in Britain in the past?'
Lesson 9: Reviewing a website (1) **P**	**Understanding and interpreting texts** • Identify how different texts are organised, including reference texts on screen.	**T20**: To compare the way information is presented	• Experience of reading non-fiction texts in different forms.	**Geography** QCA Unit 6 'Investigating our local area' **ICT** QCA Unit 3A 'Combining text and graphics'
Lesson 10: Reviewing a website (2) **P**	**Understanding and interpreting texts** • Identify and make notes of the main points of section(s) of text. • Identify how different texts are organised, including reference texts, on screen.	**T20**: To compare the way information is presented. **T21**: To read information passages, and identify main points or gist of text.	• Completion of previous lesson.	**Geography** QCA Unit 7 'Weather around the world'
Lesson 11: -le words ◉	**Word structure and spelling** • Spell words using known conventions.	**W9**: To investigate and learn to use the spelling pattern le.	• Some words have similar spelling patterns.	**Science** QCA Unit 3A 'Teeth and eating'
Lesson 12: Using commas **P**	**Sentence structure and punctuation**	**S13**: To use commas to separate items in a list.	• Punctuation marks help the reader.	**Speaking and listening** Objective 29: To identify appropriate expression, tone, volume and use of voices.
Lesson 13: Using adjectives ◉	**Creating and shaping texts** • Make decisions about form and purpose. **Sentence structure and punctuation** • Compose sentences using adjectives for precision, clarity and impact.	**S2**: To know the function of adjectives within sentences.	• Sentences use different types of words.	**Citizenship** QCA Unit 6 'Developing our school grounds'
Lesson 14: Story planning (2) ◉	**Text structure and organisation** • Signal sequence, place and time to give coherence.	**T7**: To sequence key incidents in a variety of ways, for example, by making simple storyboards. **T9**: To write a story plan for own fable.	• Stories are told in a deliberate order.	**Speaking and listening** Objective 29: To choose and prepare poems for performance, identifying appropriate expression, tone, volume and use of voices and sounds.
Lesson 15: Silent letters **P**	**Word structure and spelling**	**W10**: To investigate, spell and read words with silent letters.	• Letter sounds.	**Geography** QCA Unit 6 'Investigating our local area'
Lesson 16: Essential words ◉ **P**	**Creating and shaping texts** • Make decisions about form and purpose, identify success criteria. **Sentence structure and punctuation** • Compose sentences using adjectives, verbs and nouns for precision, clarity and impact.	**S9**: To experiment with deleting words in sentences to see which are essential to retain meaning and which are not.	• Sentences vary in length and detail.	**Science** QCA Unit 3A 'Teeth and eating'
Lesson 17: Writing instructions **P**	**Understanding and interpreting texts** • Identify how different texts are organised, on paper and on screen. • Explore how different texts appeal to readers using varied sentence structures and descriptive language. **Creating and shaping texts** • Use layout, format, graphics and illustrations for different purposes.	**T16**: To write instructions.	• Some points are more important then others.	**Science** QCA Unit 3A 'Teeth and eating' **ICT** QCA Unit 3A 'Combining text and graphics'
Lesson 18: Singular and plural ◉ **P**	**Word structure and spelling**	**W9**: To investigate and identify basic rules for changing the spelling of nouns when s is added. **W11**: To use the terms singular and plural appropriately.	• The words singular and plural.	**Citizenship** QCA Unit 11 'In the media – what's the news?'
Lesson 19: Compound words ◉	**Word structure and spelling** • Spell unfamiliar words using known conventions including morphological rules.	**W12**: To recognise and generate compound words.	• Everyday vocabulary	**History** QCA Unit 6A 'Why have people invaded and settled in Britain in the past? A Roman case study.'

▭ **9**

Lesson title	PNS objectives	NLS objectives	Expected prior knowledge	Cross-curricular links
Lesson 20: Alphabetical texts 💿	Word structure and spelling	T24: To make alphabetically ordered texts.	• The order of the alphabet.	Art and design QCA Unit 9 'Visiting a museum, gallery, or site'
Lesson 21: Conjunctions 💿 🅿	Creating and shaping texts Sentence structure and punctuation • Show relationships of time, reason and cause through subordination and connectives.	S5: How sentences can be joined in more complex ways through using a widening range of conjunctions.	• Not every sentence is short.	Citizenship QCA Unit 6 'Developing our school grounds'
Lesson 22: Speech and narrative 💿 🅿	Sentence structure and punctuation • Clarify meaning through the use of speech marks.	S4: To use speech marks and other dialogue punctuation appropriately in writing, and to use the conventions which mark boundaries between spoken words and the rest of the sentence.	• The term direct speech.	History QCA Unit 6A 'Why have people invaded and settled in Britain in the past?'
Lesson 23: Story planning (3) 💿 🅿	Creating and shaping texts • Use beginning, middle and end to write narratives in which events are sequenced logically. Text structure and organisation • Signal sequence, place and time to give coherence.	T10: To plot a sequence of episodes modelled on a known story, as a plan for writing. T13: To write more extended stories based on a plan of incidents and set out in simple chapters with titles and author details.	• Experience of longer stories.	Speaking and listening Objective 25: To explain a process or present information, ensuring items are clearly sequenced, relevant details are included and accounts ended effectively.
Lesson 24: Apostrophes (contractions) 💿	Creating and shaping texts • Make decisions about form and purpose. Sentence structure and punctuation	W11: To use the apostrophe to spell further contracted forms.	• Recognition of an apostrophe.	Geography QCA Unit 6 'Investigating our local area'
Lesson 25: Pronouns 🅿	Sentence structure and punctuation	S2: To identify pronouns and understand their functions in sentences.	• Recognition of nouns.	Speaking and listening Objective 26: To follow up others' points and show whether they agree or disagree in a whole-class discussion.
Lesson 26: Perspective and character 💿 🅿	Engaging with, and responding to, texts • Empathise with characters. Creating and shaping texts	T12: To write a first person account. T5: To discuss (i) characters' feelings; (ii) behaviour; (iii) relationships, referring to the text and making judgements.	• To consider story characters as well as events.	History QCA Unit 7 'Why did Henry VIII marry six times?'
Lesson 27: Homonyms 💿	Word structure and spelling	W14: To explore homonyms which have the same spelling but multiple meanings and explain how the meanings can be distinguished in context.	• Some words look the same, but do not always mean the same.	Art and design PoS (5a) Exploring a range of starting points for practical work.
Lesson 28: IT publishing 💿	Understanding and interpreting texts • Identify how different texts are organised, on paper and on screen. Creating and shaping texts • Use layout, format and graphics for different purposes. Presentation • Develop accuracy and speed when using keyboard skills to type, edit and re-draft.	T21: To use IT to bring to a published form.	• Awareness of school notices.	ICT QCA Unit 3A 'Combining text and graphics'
Lesson 29: Words within words 💿 🅿	Word structure and spelling • Spell unfamiliar words using known conventions including morphological rules.	W8: To identify short words within long words as an aid to spelling.	• Everyday vocabulary.	Mathematics Understanding shape: Read and record the vocabulary of position, direction and movement.
Lesson 30: Time signals 💿	Text structure and organisation • Signal sequence, place and time to give coherence. Sentence structure and punctuation • Show relationships of time, reason and cause through subordination and connectives.	S6: To investigate through reading and writing how words and phrases can signal time sequences.	• Words can be used to connect ideas.	Speaking and listening Objective 34: To identify key sections of an informative broadcast, noting how the language used signals changes or transitions in focus.

Marking sentences

Learning objectives
PNS: Sentence structure and punctuation
● Compose sentences using adjectives, verbs and nouns for precision, clarity and impact.

Resources
'Sentences' Notebook file; individual whiteboards and pens; exercise books/paper and pencils; printout of page 6 from the 'Sentences' Notebook file, one copy per child.

Links to other subjects
History
QCA Unit 6 'Why have people invaded and settled in Britain in the past?'
● Relate texts to history topics.

Whiteboard tools
Write on a Notebook page with a Pen from the Pen tray. Use the Pen tool or a Highlighter pen to highlight different parts of a sentence in different colours. Add text with the On-screen Keyboard and amend existing text by double-pressing. Alternatively, add text using your computer keyboard and the Text tool.

 Pen tray

 Pen tool

 Select tool

 Highlighter pen

 Delete button

 On-screen Keyboard

 Text tool

Starter
Ask the children to make sentences using the subjects on page 2 of the 'Sentences' Notebook file. Invite some children to say and write their examples on the board. Go to page 3. Write one of the previous sentences on the board, as a stimulus, and discuss what makes it a sentence. Write a class definition of a sentence.

Whole-class shared work
● Say two collections of words. Ask the children to decide which collection is a sentence, and write the corresponding number on their individual whiteboards. For example:
    1. *The dog barked.* 2. *The broken door* (answer: 1).
● Discuss how the children identified which was a sentence.
● Use the On-screen Keyboard to type some correct sentences onto page 4. Through discussion, establish that each sentence is about someone or something (the subject) and an action (the verb). Introduce these terms *subject* and *verb*. Drag the labels out of the boxes *label 1* and *label 2*.
● Circle the subjects and verbs in each sentence with a matching colour or highlight the words with the appropriate colour .
● Demonstrate extending the sentence with more information. For example: *The dog barked at the cat.* Ask the children in pairs to repeat this for the other sentences.
● Drag the final label, *ending*, from the box *label 3*.
● Highlight or circle the sentence endings with a matching colour.
● In pairs, ask one child to write a subject, then the other child to write a verb and ending. Write up some of their completed sentences. Repeat, reversing roles.
● Ask the children what is wrong with the short piece of text on page 5. Read the words aloud, with and without an appropriate pause. What, do the children think, can you do to show that there are two sentences here? Correct the sentences.

Independent work
● Show the text on page 6, and give out a copy of the page to each child. Explain that the writer has forgotten to mark the sentences. Read out the text to the class and tell them that they must add the capital letters and full stops to their copy of the text.
● The number of missing full stops is hidden in the Hint panel. Support less confident learners by using the Eraser from the Pen tray to reveal the hint.
● Challenge more confident learners to prepare a similar test for classmates.

Plenary
● Ask the children to take turns reading parts of the text aloud. Do others agree about how a line is read?
● Ask volunteers to drag the capital letters and full stops to the correct places. Delete the panel on the left to reveal the correctly punctuated version.
● On page 7, review the main features of a sentence to assess the children's learning and review any common misunderstandings. Press the *Check features* box to confirm.

Setting and atmosphere

Learning objective
PNS: Creating and shaping texts
● Select and use descriptive vocabulary.

Resources
'Settings' Notebook file; individual whiteboards and pens; exercise books/paper and pens.

Links to other subjects
Geography
QCA Unit 6 'Investigating our local area'
● Ask the children to compare the street picture to their local area.

Starter
Talk to the children about the familiar places in which stories are often set, such as a school, a home or a town. Point out that the places are often ordinary. Ask: *How does the writer give them a special atmosphere?* Share views, emphasising the importance of the author's choice of words. Show page 2 of the 'Settings' Notebook file and ask the children for some words to describe the elements in the picture.

Whole-class shared work
● Explain that the photograph on page 3 shows a setting for a story.
● Question the children about the picture. For example: *What is shown in the photograph? Who is in the picture? What are they doing?*
● Use the Spotlight tool to focus on aspects of the photograph and ask: *What word describes this person? How does the setting make you feel? What time of year is it?*
● Pull out the different descriptive words hidden in the picture (by pulling the Christmas tree tabs at the side of the picture).
● Agree on a collection of descriptive words that describe the scene, taking into account different viewpoints. For example, some people find shopping interesting, while others think that it is boring. Write or type about 12 of these in the box next to the picture.
● Copy and paste these words onto page 4 (select the words, select Copy from the dropdown menu, then Paste onto the next page).
● Explain that you are going to write the opening description to a story. You want your reader to form a good mental picture. Demonstrate how to construct up to four sentences about the photograph. Remind the children about the different parts of the sentence - subject, verb and ending - and highlight each part in different colours if necessary.
● Ask the children to close their eyes as you read your description aloud. Invite them to form a picture in their minds. Return to the image on page 3 for the children to compare it with their mental picture.
● Now ask the children to think about their classroom. It is going to be the setting for a story. First they must give the reader a vivid picture.
● Share some descriptive words about objects and the children's feelings about the classroom. Write some ideas on page 5 of the Notebook file.

Independent work
● Ask the children to jot down additional, atmospheric words about the classroom. Invite them to use these words, and some from page 5, to write a description of the classroom in four to six sentences.
● Prompt less confident learners with questions about the classroom. Press the *Hints* box on page 5 to show suitable words.
● Challenge more confident learners to describe a contrasting classroom.

Plenary
● Invite children to read their descriptions to the class. Challenge the others to identify the descriptive words used. Add any new words to page 5.
● Type some of the descriptions on the board onto page 6 and save them for future lessons.

Whiteboard tools
Use a Pen from the Pen tray or the On-screen Keyboard to add text. Convert handwritten words to text by selecting them and choosing the Recognise option from the dropdown menu. Use the Spotlight tool to focus on aspects of the photograph, adjusting the transparency to 50% through the dropdown menu.

 Pen tray

 Select tool

 Spotlight tool

 Highlighter pen

 On-screen Keyboard

Verbs

Learning objective

PNS: Creating and shaping texts

PNS: Sentence structure and punctuation

● Compose sentences using adjectives, verbs and nouns for precision, clarity and impact.

Resources

'Build your own' file; photocopiable page 41 'A mixed menagerie' for each child.

Links to other subjects

ICT

QCA Unit 3A 'Combining text and graphics'

● Ask the children to use computers for their polished poems, selecting font, graphics and layout to complement the text.

Starter

Open the 'Build your own' file, which contains a blank Notebook page and a selection of Gallery resources. Remind the children of the work on building sentences (Lesson 1). Ask: *What was needed in each sentence?* (Capital letter, full stop, subject, verb.)

Focus on the verb. Define a verb as a *doing* or *being* word and write this on the whiteboard. A verb can express an action, a happening, a process or a state. Every sentence needs a verb. Display the picture of a dog, from the English folder under My Content in the Gallery [icon], on the board and ask for some suitable *doing* words for the dog (barked, walked and so on). Write these words underneath the picture. Repeat for other examples (using, for instance, the images of a boy or a baby from the English folder in the Gallery); no more than two per page.

Whole-class shared work

● Write the following sentence on the board: *The dog barked.* Ask the children to identify the subject and the verb.
● Progress to longer sentences, such as: *The kite flew into the air.* Ask a child to identify and highlight the verb.
● Explain that a verb can be a chain of words. Provide examples such as: *The dog is escaping.* Work together to change the verbs on the board into *chains*.
● Discuss how verbs may have similar meanings. Establish that it is important to select the right one for meaning and impact.
● Encourage the children to substitute new verbs in some sentences on the board. Give the children prompts such as: *A verb to express height* – 'The kite soared into the air.'
● Demonstrate these substitutions on the board by typing or writing over the verbs.
● Ask a child to cross the room. Write up the sentence: *Harry __ across the room.*
● Ask the other children, on individual whiteboards, to write an appropriate verb in the gap (such as *Harry rushed across the room*). Share answers, typing the most appropriate verbs.
● Repeat the game. Progress to other actions such as *talking, looking* and *writing.* Draw attention to particularly expressive verbs and write them on the board.

Independent work

● Explain that you want the children to write a poem on the theme of animals. Say that the verbs must be chosen carefully to suit the animals.
● Ask the children to finish the poem on photocopiable page 41. Tell them to treat it as a first draft which they will try to improve, particularly the verbs, before writing a final version.
● Support the children by helping them with their choice of animal and appropriate verbs.
● Challenge the children to identify verbs in a given text.

Plenary

● Let the children read drafts to the class. Select and praise appropriate verbs.
● Write these verbs on a new page on the board and add them to some of the pictures on the board if appropriate. Explain that you are starting a class collection of expressive verbs.
● Save this Notebook file, and return to it in later lessons.

Whiteboard tools

Select images from the English folder in the Gallery (under My Content). Add new pages by pressing on the Blank Page button.

 Pen tray

 Select tool

 Highlighter pen

 On-screen Keyboard

 Blank Page button

 Gallery

High frequency words

Learning objective
PNS: Sentence structure
● Compose sentences using adjectives, verbs and nouns for precision, clarity and impact.

Resources
Photocopiable page 42 'High frequency words' for each child. Choose eight to ten high frequency words (such as: *good, big, nice, horrible, great, terrible, mean, lovely*). Create a Notebook file using each word in a pair of phrases (*good weather; a good book*). Make a randomly-ordered list of appropriate synonyms for your words (*sunny, exciting*).

Links to other subjects
Speaking and listening
Objective 31: To actively include and respond to all members of the group.
● Encourage oral participation by everyone in the class.

Starter
Write these words on a blank Notebook page: *nasty, unpleasant, awful*. Ask: *What do they have in common? When would you use them?* Stress the similarity of meaning between the words. Ask for other examples of words with similar meanings and write these on the board.

Whole-class shared work
● Say a few lines about your weekend. Deliberately use high frequency words and add them to the whiteboard. For example:
> *The weather was awful this weekend. I stayed in and had an awful time. One nice thing was that I cooked myself a nice meal.*
● Question the children about what was said. Why were the words bad choices? (Their meaning was vague. The words are overused.)
● Type the paragraph on the board and highlight the high frequency words.
● Ask: *What words would have been better?* Type up the suggestions, highlighting the new words. For example:
> *The weather was wet this weekend. I stayed in and had a boring time. One interesting thing was that I cooked myself a delicious meal.*
● Let the children try the same oral experiment with a partner. What words did they overuse? Share findings.
● Discuss why high frequency words are often a poor vocabulary choice. As we become used to hearing them, they lack much meaning. Someone may describe a football game as *awful*. Does this mean that the game is *boring* or *of a low standard*?
● Let the children repeat their conversations, coming to the board to replace high frequency words with informative ones. Encourage them to spot the need for replacements and write these alongside the high frequency words in a simple table format on the whiteboard. (Use the Lines tool to create a table.)
● Introduce and define the term *synonym*. Explain that they have just been using synonyms for high frequency words.
● Display your prepared screen. Explain that you have made a list of synonyms for the high frequency words that are in each phrase. Which synonym fits which phrase?
● Work together, replacing high frequency words with their synonyms. Discuss improvements.

Independent work
● Introduce photocopiable page 42. Ask the children to identify the high frequency words and replace them with synonyms.
● Suggest that the children write the phrases containing the word and its synonym on the back of the sheet.
● Support less confident learners in the identification of the high frequency words and supply a range of synonyms from which to select.
● As an extra challenge, ask the children to identify and replace high frequency words in their own recent written work.

Plenary
● Compare results and discuss the synonyms. Are all the replacements appropriate?
● Review what the children have learned. Ask for a class definition of a synonym and write this on the board.
● Save the Notebook file for future reference.

Whiteboard tools
Use the On-screen Keyboard to type. Draw a simple two-column table using the Lines tool.

 Pen tray

Select tool

Highlighter pen

Lines tool

 On-screen Keyboard

Story planning in paragraphs

Learning objective
PNS: Text structure and organisation
● Group related material into paragraphs.

Resources
'Build your own' file; a copy of photocopiable page 43 'Story planning in paragraphs' for each child; individual whiteboards and pens; individual exercise books. Prepare a scene on the board taken from Red Riding Hood using images from the English folder in the 'Build your own' file (under My Content in the Gallery). Start with the background road scene and add images, resizing as necessary.

Links to other subjects
Speaking and listening
Objective 29: To choose and present poems or stories for performance, identifying appropriate tone, volume and use of voices and other sounds.
● Groups of three make an audio recording of one of their completed stories. Suggest that they use a different voice for each paragraph to emphasise a change in the story.
ICT
QCA Unit 3A 'Combining text and graphics'
● Children use computers for a final version of a story, combining text with complementary graphics.

Whiteboard tools
Use the Shapes tool to make boxes. Clone text and images by pressing on them and then selecting Clone from the dropdown menu. Then drag onto the relevant page in the Page Sorter.

 Pen tray

 Gallery

 Select tool

 Highlighter pen

 Shapes tool

 Blank Page button

Starter
Open the 'Build your own' file, which contains a blank Notebook page and a selection of Gallery resources located in the My Content folder. Display a piece of text that incorporates at least three paragraphs. Highlight where each paragraph begins. Explain that a paragraph is a group of sentences that fit well together. Discuss the benefits of paragraphs to the reader and writer. Read through the example on the board.

Whole-class shared work
● Show the prepared picture of Little Red Riding Hood (see Resources). Write single words about the setting and characters.
● Explain that you want to write a shortened version of the story in three planned paragraphs.
● Move to a blank page and create three rectangles, one under the other. Number them 1, 2 and 3. Type a short planning sentence in the first box. For example: *Red Riding Hood made a journey.*
● On individual whiteboards, ask the children to write short planning sentences for the other two paragraphs (for the next stages in the story).
● Compare results. Finalise your three planning sentences and type them in the boxes.
● Stress that this is the plan, not the story. Ask: *What does the plan tell you?* (To write three paragraphs; what to write about in each paragraph.)
● Choose a title for the story. Model writing paragraph one. Use an opening phrase and write approximately three sentences. Clone the title and the first paragraph and drag to a new page (see Whiteboard tools, below).
● Ask the children, with partners, to write part of the second paragraph on individual whiteboards. Assign the first, second and third sentences to different groups of children.
● Listen to the children's ideas and type in sentences for paragraph two. Clone the paragraph plan and put it in place on the second page. Emphasise that the new paragraph begins on the next line, its first word indented.
● Repeat the process for paragraph three. Stress that the planning numbers for the paragraphs are left out on the second page; this is the proper story.
● Read the story aloud. Ask questions such as: *Does it sound right? Is a finishing phrase needed? Are there linking words at the start of paragraphs two and three?*
● After any necessary changes, incorporate additional images from the Gallery and print the page.

Independent work
● Invite the children to plan a story for a Year 2 group. Share ideas for uncomplicated stories with familiar settings.
● Give each child a copy of photocopiable page 43 and invite them to complete the *Ideas* section and the three planning sentences.
● Support less confident learners by providing three pictures from the Gallery.
● Encourage more confident learners to begin to write the stories.

Plenary
● Ask some children to demonstrate their planning on the whiteboard. Refer back to the Red Riding Hood story and discuss how helpful it was to plan the story in paragraphs.

Direct speech

Starter
Go to page 2 of the 'Direct speech' Notebook file. Focus on the sentence:
Cinderella said, "Why do I always have to work?"

Ask the children to comment on the punctuation. What is special about it? (Marks separate some words from the rest of the sentence. The marks are used to indicate direct speech.) Reveal the words *direct speech* in the speech bubble and ask for some examples of sentences that include direct speech, either from the children's own ideas, or taken from a class text. Pull the tab to reveal the definition of the term *direct speech*.

Whole-class shared work
● Ask the children to look in a reading book to investigate the rules for direct speech. Encourage them to make notes on their findings.
● Display page 3 and tell the children that there are six rules about direct speech. Ask the children for these and write their suggestions on the board. Reveal one at a time by dragging the rules from the bucket of water.
● The rules include:
  ● All spoken words are enclosed in speech marks
  ● Speech marks work in pairs
  ● Spoken words are separated from non-spoken
  ● A comma usually separates spoken words from non-spoken words
  ● A capital letter shows the start of direct speech
  ● Each speaker has a new line.
● Show the extract from the story of Cinderella on page 4. Are the rules of direct speech applied? Discuss. Highlight where the rules apply.
● Invite children to come to the board and drag the punctuation marks and capital letters into the correct places.
● Drag down the Screen Shade on the left to reveal the correct punctuation for direct speech.
● Discuss what each character on page 5 might be saying. Reveal each of the speech bubbles in turn using the Eraser. Point out that speech bubbles are ideal in picture books but they are not practical in narrative stories.
● Demonstrate converting a speech bubble into a narrative sentence with direct speech. Look at the example on page 2 of the Notebook file.
● Invite a child to do this on the board using one of the other speech bubbles on page 5. Check with the class if the rules were followed and repeat for the other two speech bubbles.

Independent work
● Ask the children to complete the pictures on the photocopiable page. Each picture needs text to fill a speech bubble.
● Underneath the boxes ask the children to write a narrative sentence with the words inside the speech bubble repeated inside speech marks.
● Provide support by asking the children to write speech bubbles and supply skeletons of narrative sentences with some punctuation already in place.
● Challenge more confident learners to use sentences to create a passage of dialogue, reminding them to remember all the rules.

Plenary
● Add some of the results to the Notebook file on page 6. Emphasise how speech marks have replaced speech bubbles.
● Ask the children for some more narrative sentences related to the Notebook file. If a microphone is available, you could record the children's script and add to it in subsequent lessons.

Prefixes

Learning objective
PNS: Word structure and spelling
● Recognise a range of prefixes, understanding how they modify meaning and spelling.

Resources
Photocopiable page 45 'Prefixes' for each child; individual whiteboards and pens. Type and save the words from the photocopiable sheet onto a Notebook file. Use the Shapes tool to create boxes with the prefix headings at the top. Press the Right Mouse button and select Clone to create multiple copies of the prefixes within the boxes. Make new words by adding words to the prefixes. Use a Highlighter pen to highlight the prefixes in a separate colour.

Links to other subjects
History
QCA Unit 6A 'Why have people invaded and settled in Britain in the past? A Roman case study'
● Use etymological dictionaries to research Latin prefixes in today's English (*cent, aqua, ped, corp, oct*).

Whiteboard tools
Clone text by pressing on it and selecting Clone from the dropdown menu.

 Pen tray

 Select tool

 Highlighter pen

 Shapes tool

 On-screen Keyboard

Starter
Write on a blank Notebook page: *unwell, unhappy, untidy.* Allow one minute's thinking time as the children decide on two characteristics that the words share. Listen to their ideas. Characteristics to highlight are: they all begin with *un*; when *un* is removed, the opposite meaning is left.

Whole-class shared work
● Introduce and define the term *prefix* (a group of letters, with a meaning, at the start of a word).
● Type or write these words on the whiteboard: *cycle, fill, caution, turn, historic, angle.* Away from the words, type or write these prefixes: *re, tri, pre.*
● Involve the children as you demonstrate, by dragging the words, how a prefix can join to a word to create a new word. The resulting words are: *tricycle, refill, precaution, return, prehistoric, triangle.*
● Ask the children to try to work out the meaning of the prefixes (*pre* means 'before'; *re* means 'again'; *tri* means 'three').
● Look again at your original example words. Ask: *What is the prefix?* (un) *What does the prefix mean?* (not) *Un* is used to create a word's opposite.
● Demonstrate removing the prefixes, leaving words of opposite meaning. Repeat the demonstration with other words that form opposites with *un*, for example: *pleasant, usual.*
● Introduce and define the term *antonym* (a word with the opposite meaning). Revise *synonym* (a word with the same meaning).
● Play a game in which you provide a word and the children make its antonym, orally or by writing answers on individual whiteboards. For example: *comfortable, tidy, selfish.*
● Now provide an example which breaks the rule: *visible.* Does anyone know the correct answer? Write it on the whiteboard, highlighting its prefix: *invisible.*
● Continue the game, slipping in other words that will not take *un*, for example: *like* (dislike), *sense* (nonsense).
● List the prefixes you have found for creating antonyms.

Independent work
● Ask the children to complete photocopiable page 45 'Prefixes'. Let them use dictionaries where necessary.
● For further support, reduce the list of words. Let the children work with partners.
● As a further challenge, ask the children to add extra words to the groups and think of new prefix groups.

Plenary
● Use your prepared Notebook file (see Resources) to model correct answers.
Ask: *Can you identify any patterns?* (such as *im* before words starting with *p*).
● Make a separate list of all the prefixes used in this lesson on separate pages and start a word list of words that include these prefixes.

Verbs and tenses

Learning objective
PNS: Sentence structure and punctuation
● Compose sentences using verbs for precision.

Resources
'Verbs and tenses' Notebook file; individual whiteboards; exercise books/paper. Prepare a *Today* and *Yesterday* label for each pair.

Links to other subjects
History
QCA Unit 6 'Why have people invaded and settled in Britain in the past?'
● Link text to history topics.

Starter
Remind the children that verbs are *doing* or *being* words. Stress the need for a verb in a sentence. Give quick oral practice in identifying verbs, using shared work from the *Verbs* lesson (see page 13). Go to page 2 of the 'Verbs and tenses' Notebook file and read the sentences on the page.

Work together to identify and highlight the verbs. Explain that verbs can be used to express time, informing the audience when things happen. Pull out the definition of *verbs* at the bottom of the page.

Whole-class shared work
● Ask the children to read the sentences on page 3. When, can they tell you, are events happening? Introduce the *Today* and *Yesterday* labels on the whiteboard. Move the labels to the appropriate sentences.
● Provide pairs with one *Today* and one *Yesterday* label. Say a number of sentences, using past and present tense verbs. For example: *I booked a holiday; He looks scared.* After each sentence, ask the children to hold up the correct label. Sometimes use a verb in both forms: *I long to go home; I longed for a hot meal.*
● Introduce the terms *past* and *present*. Explain that a verb indicates time. The tense of the verb is the time.
● Use page 4 to demonstrate changing present into past by the regular addition of *-ed.*
● Let the children practise changing three of these regular verbs on their individual whiteboards before revealing them on the Notebook page by dragging the white circle to the end of the verbs.
● Explain that not all verbs form past tenses in this regular *-ed* way. Do the children know any irregular past forms? Reveal the examples on the whiteboard.
● Play a game in which one child tells a one-minute story about something that happened. Invite the other children to write the past tense verbs on their whiteboards.
● Pool the results, recording these on page 5. Examine the proportion of regular *-ed* past forms to other past forms. Highlight regular and irregular past forms in different colours.
● Read the *Vikings* text (page 6) with the children, highlighting the verbs. Agree on the tense used in this passage (all past tense).

Independent work
● Ask the children to convert the *Vikings* text into a live commentary, on their individual whiteboards, as if everything is happening now.
● Suggest to less confident learners that they prepare orally with a partner. Does the verb sound right?
● Extend by asking the children to add a new paragraph of their own, first in the past and then in the present.

Plenary
● Ask the children to provide the answers as you make changes on the whiteboard. Pull down the Screen Shade to check they have identified all of the present tense verbs correctly.
● On page 7, recap the differences between the past and present tense of verbs.

Whiteboard tools
Amend existing text by double-pressing on it and typing. Pull down the Screen Shade to reveal a present-tense version of the text in the independent work.

 Pen tray

 Select tool

 Highlighter pen

 Screen Shade

Reviewing a website (1)

Learning objective
PNS: Understanding and interpreting texts
● Identify how different texts are organised, including reference texts on screen.

Resources P
Access to the internet; individual whiteboards and pens; photocopiable page 46 'Website review sheet' for each child or group. Have website **www.channel4.com/essentials** (last accessed 12 March 2007) open on its title page.

Links to other subjects
ICT
QCA Unit 3A 'Combining text and graphics'
● Suggest that the children share their reports with other groups using email.
Geography
QCA Unit 6 'Investigating our local area'
● Use this lesson as a preliminary step to investigating the local area.

Starter
Launch Notebook. Minimise it and display the home page of the website. Tell the children that for this year's geography unit, *Investigating our local area*, you are considering using this website. Ask the children to talk to a partner about how useful this site might be, and how it might present information. Share ideas.

Whole-class shared work
● Talk about starting points for this geography unit. Stress the need to think about what must be investigated and how to do the work. What should be the first step on this website?
● Collaborate on how to proceed and the links to follow on the website. For example, on the home page you must select geography. Ask: *What should we do next?*
● At each stage, ask the children to discuss the navigation and the clarity of the instructions on the website. Ask: *Could you use this site on your own or would you need help?*
● Try out some activities. View the A–Z glossary. Check if your queries are in the FAQs for a particular section. Investigate a worksheet and consider if it would be suitable.
● Focus on presentation. Are the children happy with a page's layout? Do they find information easy to access and understand? Discuss the design of individual pages, and save and annotate any special features.
● Try out the quiz for a particular section. Is the game presentation useful? At which stage in your work would the quiz be useful? (Used initially, it would inform teachers about what the class needed to learn. Used at the end of the topic, it would assess children's learning.)
● Examine a page with plenty of text, for example *What's the big idea?* Ask questions that can be answered by the text, such as: *What is difficult about living in a rural area? What is happening in some city centres? Where do most people live?*
● Discuss how quickly information was found. Emphasise the reading skills of scanning and using key words to extract information easily.
● Move out of the site. Hold a discussion on the website's presentation of information. Record brief comments on a new page on the interactive whiteboard. Emphasise that not everyone has to have the same viewpoint.

Independent work
● Ask the children, in groups, to become judges in a website presentation competition.
● Set the task of writing a report on the way this site presents information using the 'Website review sheet' (photocopiable page 46).
● Encourage less confident learners to work with a partner, expressing ideas orally before recording them in writing.
● Challenge more confident learners to produce a guide to this website.

Plenary
● Share some of the reports, by typing the information or viewing scanned images on the whiteboard.
● Ask: *Would the creators of the website be pleased with the reviews? Why?* Discuss any possible improvements identified by the children.

Whiteboard tools
Minimise Notebook and use the Floating tools to annotate features of the website. The Floating toolbar can be customised to include any tools. Use the Capture tool to take snapshots of webpages when discussing the presentation. Upload scanned reports or images by selecting Insert, then Picture File, and browsing to where you have saved the images.

 Pen tray

 Floating tools

 Capture tool

 On-screen Keyboard

Reviewing a website (2)

Learning objectives
PNS: Understanding and interpreting texts
● Identify how different texts are organised, including reference texts on screen.
● Identify and make notes of the main points of section(s) of text.

Resources ℗
Access to the internet; individual whiteboards and pens; photocopiable page 46 'Website review sheet' for each child. Have website **www.bbc.co.uk/schools/ whatisweather** (last accessed 12 March 2007) open.

Links to other subjects
Geography
QCA Unit 7 'Weather around the world'
● Use the BBC schools website to ask geographical questions and encourage the children to use appropriate geographical vocabulary.

Whiteboard tools
Use the Shapes tool and the Lines tool to create a table. Use the Floating tools to annotate features of the website. The Floating toolbar can be customised to include any tools, including the Screen Shade. The Gallery includes a range of appropriate weather icons and images, found in the Earth Sciences folder.

 Pen tray

 Lines tool

 Shapes tool

 Floating tools

 Screen Shade

Starter
Remind the children of the website about the local area from the previous lesson. Pose one or two questions: *Did you think the site presented information well? Would you recommend the site to another Year 3 class?* Write the questions on a blank Notebook page. Record the results to the questions in an unusual and interesting way. For example, a *For* and *Against* table; ticks and crosses; arrows or a pictogram.

Whole-class shared work
● Tell the children they will be thinking about the geography topic *Weather around the world.* Invite them to assess the value of a website you have found on this topic. The website is an educational resource specially created for their age group.
● Minimise Notebook and open the BBC schools website. Guided by the children, move through its pages. Encourage comments, questioning reactions. *Do the graphics and animation distract you or help you to concentrate? Is information too difficult or too easy? Is the layout good?*
● Move to a page with a reasonable amount of text such as *Weather and people.* Allow the children one or two minutes to read the page. Activate the Screen Shade to hide the page. Ask the children to record four or five key words and one fact from the page, on their individual whiteboards.
● Compare the results; the facts may vary. Did the children have reasons for their selections?
● Look again at that website page. Did many people select words in capitals? Were their facts taken from bullet points?
● Discuss the use of bullet points to attract attention and emphasise importance; capital letters and font changes have the same effect.
● Give time for close reading. What can the children discover about the presentation? Guide them towards these points: question and answer format; variety in layout; information easy to find; capitals and enlarged font; key words.
● Share ideas for alternative layouts. Give the children, in pairs, two minutes to plan a new way to present this page.
● Compare ideas: sections for different climates, charts, additional graphics, and speech bubbles are all possibilities.

Independent work
● Ask the children to complete the 'Website review sheet' (photocopiable page 46) by writing a summary of the website. Tell them that their views must be clear and easy to understand.
● In the final section, let the children choose their preferred website.
● Less confident learners may prefer to rely on the presentation devices used in the Starter section.
● Challenge more confident learners to create a chart of key geographical words from both websites.

Plenary
● Scan and view some completed review sheets.
● Consider future work: the children, in pairs or small groups, could plan their own web page of information for a geography topic (perhaps weather or the local area).

-*le* words

Learning objective
PNS: Word structure and spelling
● Spell words using known conventions.

Resources
'-*le* words' Notebook file; individual whiteboards and pens.

Links to other subjects
Science
QCA Unit 3A 'Teeth and eating'
● Ask the children to make a poster of healthy and less healthy -*le* words such as: *vegetable, apple; pickle; raspberry ripple; crumble.*

Starter
Display the list of -*le* words on page 2 of the Notebook file. Ask the children what the words have in common. When they spot the pattern, select the dark blue panel at the top, and increase the transparency to reveal the answer. Explain that -*le* is a common spelling pattern in English.

Ask: *Can you spot any examples around the classroom? Does anyone's name end in -le?* Add examples to the board and highlight the -*le* endings.

Whole-class shared work
● Consider the words on the board. Does -*le* always have the same sound? Mention words such as *mile* and *whole*, where -*le* is not a separate syllable and has no sound of its own.
● Move on to page 3. Tell the children that you are holding a *spelling bee*, setting familiar words for children to say or write on their individual whiteboards. Press the red buttons to hear the words.
● Invite the children to spell the words and use the Eraser to reveal the correct answers.
● View the correct spelling of the words that don't end in -*le*. Point out that their final letters produce the same sound as -*le*. Ask: *How can you know which letters to use?* Share ideas.
● Suggest some pointers to help the children with spelling. Page 4 offers a useful classroom poster with three such spelling conventions, which can be discussed, highlighted and added to.
● Go to page 5. Explain that answers to this crossword are all -*le* words. Allow thinking time before filling in an agreed answer. If necessary, prompt the children with further clues. For example, *4 across is a speech __?*
● Use the Eraser to reveal the letters in the crossword.
● Explain that the crossword answers show some examples of -*le* words. Ask the children if they can spot any with similar endings.
● Display the chart on page 6, which contains headings representing the main -*le* family groups: -*able*, -*ckle*, *double letter + le*, -*dle*, -*cle*, -*ble*, -*ible*, -*ple*. Drag the words to the correct columns.

Independent work
● Ask the children to copy the -*le* chart into their books. Challenge them to use a current reading book or notices around the room to add new words to these family groups. Suggest a minimum of six words per family.
● Support less confident learners by directing them towards suitable resources for finding words.
● Extend the activity by inviting the children to highlight words that are new to them and ask them to find out their meanings.

Plenary
● Compare results. Use the whiteboard to create a class -*le* chart, which can be saved for future use.
● Review any common difficulties with spelling individual words with reference to the chart where necessary. Use this as a starting point for creating a *Difficult -le words* list on page 7 to come back to in subsequent lessons.

Whiteboard tools
Use the Transparency tool to reveal the answer in the Starter. Use the Eraser from the Pen tray to remove the annotations covering each word in the *Spelling bee*, and to reveal the answers on the crossword.

 Pen tray

 Select tool

 Transparency tool

 Highlighter pen

Using commas

Learning objective
PNS: Sentence structure and punctuation

Resources
Photocopiable page 47 'Using commas' for every child.

Type the following text into a new Notebook page, keeping the background white: *Fox, Hare, Rabbit and Squirrel held an emergency meeting. They talked, listened, argued and agreed. They had food, water, warmth and shelter. They faced one problem.*

Type the text in a colour that will show up clearly on both a black and a white background (blue works well) and set the font size to at least 24. Double-press on the text and change the commas and full stops to white, so that they cannot be seen. The punctuation is revealed when background colour is set to black.

Links to other subjects
Speaking and listening
Objective 29: To identify appropriate expression, tone, volume and use of voices.
● Speakers use intonation to interpret punctuation; listeners hear where commas are required.

Whiteboard tools
Use the On-screen Keyboard to type the text. Alternatively, use your computer keyboard with the Text tool selected. Press the Right Mouse button in the Pen tray to set the background colour.

 Pen tray

 On-screen Keyboard

 Text tool

 Select tool

 Highlighter pen

Starter
Revise the terms *noun* and *verb* using earlier Notebook files if necessary. (A noun is a name of *somebody* or *something*; a verb is a *doing* or *being* word.)

Display (without punctuation) the prepared text. Ask the children to identify the nouns and verbs. (Nouns: *fox, hare, rabbit, squirrel, meeting, food, warmth, shelter, water, problem.* Verbs: *held, talked, listened, argued, agreed, had, faced.*)

Highlight the nouns and verbs in different colours as they are identified; then erase the highlighting after they have all been identified.

Whole-class shared work
● Ask the children to look again at the text. Is there anything strange?
● Focus on full stops. Four full stops are missing. Where are they needed? Agree and add them.
● Ask the children how they worked out where to place full stops. Did they read *aloud* in their heads?
● Let one child read the text to the class. What do others notice about the reading? Did the child have particular stopping places? (At full stops.)
● Ask someone else to read the text aloud. Did this child stop at extra places?
● Explain that this text needs pauses that are not marked by full stops, in order to make sense. *How can we mark a pause?* (A comma.)
● Demonstrate what a comma looks like on the board and explain its function: a punctuation mark to help the reader to separate parts of a sentence; it sometimes corresponds to a pause in speech. Write the definition on the board.
● Admit that you know that this text needs six commas. They are already in place, hidden. Challenge the children to work out where. Try one sentence at a time, allowing the children two minutes to decide if and where commas are needed. Then experiment with the children's suggestions, using the black Pen.
● Press the Right Mouse button and select Set Background Colour. Change the background to black to reveal the correct punctuation.
● Talk about the positions of the commas. Emphasise that these commas have been used in lists. The last two items in each list do not need separating by a comma as they are separated by *and*.

Independent work
● Ask the children to write sentences containing lists using photocopiable page 47, which supplies both pictures and sentence starters. Leave the example text on display as a model.
● Support children with ideas for nouns or verbs to include in their lists.
● Extend the activity by asking the children to add new sentences of their own.

Plenary
● Share some of the children's sentences. As the children read their sentences aloud, let the others decide where commas are needed. Does the written version match the spoken version?

Using adjectives

Learning objectives
PNS: Creating and shaping texts
● Make decisions about form and purpose.
PNS: Sentence structure and punctuation
● Compose sentences using adjectives for precision, clarity and impact.

Resources
'Adjectives' Notebook file; individual whiteboards and pens; a collection of different objects (such as colourful toys, little and big objects, coloured pencils and crayons) for each group of children.

Links to other subjects
Citizenship
QCA Unit 6 'Developing our school grounds'
● Encourage the children to think of adjectives to describe the school grounds. Are the adjectives positive or negative? Ask the children to think of adjectives that would describe their ideal school grounds.

Whiteboard tools
Use a Pen from the Pen tray to write. Convert handwriting to text by selecting it and choosing the Recognise option from the dropdown menu.

 Pen tray

 Select tool

 Highlighter pen

 Shapes tool

 On-screen Keyboard

 Delete button

Starter
Establish the learning objective on page 1 of the 'Adjectives' Notebook file. Go to page 2 and ask the children to describe the two animals on display. Annotate their suggestions on the page.

Whole-class shared work
● Look at the collected words together. Ask the children if they are all the same type of words. Through questioning, lead them to understand that some words are nouns (such as *animal* or *mammal*) but others are adjectives. Highlight the adjectives.
● Discuss the term *adjective*. What is it? What is it used for? Annotate the children's responses on page 3. An adjective is a word used to describe somebody or something. Adjectives can be used to describe nouns.
● Ask the children to write a sentence on their whiteboards that uses at least one of the adjectives from page 2. For example: *The elephant is a big and strong animal.* Invite the children to read out loud or show their sentences.
● Go to page 4 and read the sentence out loud. Ask the children how they could change it using adjectives. Write some suggested adjectives around the sentence. Delete the bone at the bottom to reveal one example of the extended sentence.
● Discuss the benefits of adding adjectives to the text. (The reader learns more.) Ask the children for some more examples of sentences with and without adjectives.
● Play a speaking and listening game. Give each group of children a collection of objects. In turn, a child thinks of an object from the collection and has to describe it, using adjectives, to the rest of the group. The others have to correctly identify the object.

Independent work
● The next activity on page 5 emphasises the value of accurate adjectives. Challenge the children to compose short notices for the *Missing!* board.
● Explain that there is no room for a missing item's photograph, so the children will have to think of a detailed description. For example: *It is furry, yellow and old.* (Teddy.) Remind them of the importance of using accurate adjectives as they have just done in the game (see Whole-class shared work).
● The children may think of a personal item or use a classroom object if they need visual support.
● As an extra challenge, ask the children to produce computer-written versions of their final work.

Plenary
● Listen to and add some of the examples to page 5 of the Notebook file. Use the Shapes tool to add a box in which to write the notices.
● Identify all the adjectives that have been used.
● Ask the children to think of a notice for the missing dog on page 6. Drag the picture of the dog to one side to reveal the notice.
● On page 7, summarise what the children have learned. Take a vote on the top five most interesting adjectives that have been used in this lesson.

PNS: Text structure and organisation

Learning objective
PNS: Text structure and organisation
● Signal sequence, place and time to give coherence.

Resources
'Storyboard' Notebook file; individual whiteboards and pens.

Links to other subjects
Speaking and listening
Objective 29: To choose and prepare poems for performance, identifying appropriate expression, tone, volume and use of voices and other sounds.
● Explain that fables originated in an oral form of storytelling. Give the children opportunities to tell stories rather than read them. Ask the children to identify the differences between telling and reading.

Whiteboard tools
Use the Fill Colour tool to reveal each of the elements of a fable. Use the Area Capture tool to take a snapshot of the completed sequencing activity, which can be kept for later reference. Upload scanned storyboards by selecting Insert, the Picture File, and browsing to where you have saved the image.

 Pen tray

 Select tool

 Area Capture tool

 Fill Colour tool

Story planning (2)

Starter
Show page 2 of the Notebook file and discuss how you might make a story out of the content. How would you continue the story? Annotate the screen with some of the ideas and opinions. Question the children about the type of story likely to result. What genre is it likely to be? Go to page 3 and discuss and make a note of the features of a *fable*.

Whole-class shared work
● Move to page 4. Press the image to open *The Hare and the Tortoise* sequencing activity. Ask the children to look at the pictures and discuss them with a partner.
● Discuss what the children think is happening in the pictures. Which events are important? Is there a main character? Exchange views.
● Ask the children what is wrong with the pictures. (They are in the wrong order.) Allow thinking time as the children decide and note on their individual whiteboards what the picture order should be.
● Share answers. Question possibilities, debating and experimenting with different orders. Emphasise the need for a correct sequence to be logical.
● Agree on final selections and drag the pictures into the correct sequence. Are there any surprises? Compare the correct sequence with the children's predictions. Were there any points they had not thought about?
● Point out that a correctly sequenced set of pictures forms a storyboard: it is an effective method of planning a story. Ask: *What genre could the story be?* (A fable.)
● Remind the children of your Starter text and your discussion on genre. Discuss the essential elements of a fable. (If you have not worked on fables, try focusing on myths or legends.)
● Use page 5 to agree on the essential elements of a fable:
  ● a complete story
  ● most characters are animals
  ● the animals behave like people
  ● a fable teaches a lesson or a moral
  ● the moral is advice to people about how to live
  ● the moral links with what has happened in the story.
● Reveal each of the elements when they are correctly identified.
● Read a short fable to the children, identifying these points.

Independent work
● Ask the children to use a picture storyboard to plan a fable of their own. Suggest the animals or moral involved if necessary.
● Stress the importance of the correct sequence for the pictures.
● Encourage the children to ask themselves: *Could someone else follow this plan correctly?*
● Support less confident learners by providing the animal characters and the moral for the children's fable.
● Extend the task by asking the children to move on to a story they have written and create a picture storyboard for it.

Plenary
● Scan in some completed storyboards and display them on page 6 of the Notebook file. Could other children write a story, with the plot in the correct order, from these story plans?
● Discuss ideas for one complete story.

Silent letters

Starter
Type the words *knife*, *wrapper* and *gnome* on the screen. Allow a minute's thinking time as the children try to work out what the words have in common. Highlight the first letter of one of the words. Ask the children to think about its sound in the word. Do the same with the other words. The children should recognise that all the words begin with a silent letter. Highlight the silent letters.

Whole-class shared work
● Add additional words to the screen: *kneel, gnash, half, chemist, sword, lamb*.
● Explain that each word has a silent letter. Focusing on each word in turn, ask the children to write the silent letter on their individual whiteboards. Show the correct answers by highlighting the appropriate letters.
● Discuss the children's success. Was it easy to identify the silent letters? Were some so silent they forgot they were there? Agree that silent letters within or at the end of words are less obvious than first letters; these letters often lead to spelling mistakes.
● Put your spelling theory to the test by playing the two games below:
  ● Give each child two cards: *gn* and *kn*. As you call out a word, the children must hold up the letters they think are needed. Write the correct version on your screen. Ask the children to keep track of how many they get right.
  ● Give pairs of children *A* and *B* cards. Display pairs of words on a Notebook page, one word labelled *A*, the other *B*. When you say the word, partners decide the correct spelling, holding up the appropriate card. Highlight the correct one. Pairs could include: *ryme, rhyme; calm, carm; wirl, whirl*.
● Ask the children to compare their results from the two games. Which was the trickiest silent letter?

Independent work
● Give out the 'Silent letters' photocopiable sheets. Explain that the silent letter(s) are missing from these words.
● Ask the children to place the letters in the words before writing the words in the columns.
● Support less confident learners by presenting them with just two or three silent letters at a time.
● As an extra challenge, ask the children to add more words of their own to the columns.

Plenary
● Go to a new Notebook page. Organise the page into six columns using the Lines tool ⬐. Add the column headings: *k; g; w; h; b; l*.
● Take answers from the children as you complete the chart on the whiteboard.
● Can the children identify any patterns in the placing of the silent letters?
  ● *k* and *g* before *n*
  ● *w* often before *r*
  ● *l* after the vowels *a, o*, and *ou*.
● Can the children think of words where *p* is silent? For example, *receipt* or *pneumonia*.

Essential words

Starter
Display page 2 of the 'Healthy teeth' Notebook file. Read the sentence out to the children: *Quietly and miserably, the unhappy girl with no key shivered in her thin coat in the front garden.*

Suggest that you have been writing a story, but are short of space. Ask the children to help you to shorten this sentence. Experiment with the children's suggestions on the whiteboard. Which words are essential? Which words are not so important? Highlight the important and less important words in different colours. Stress that the passage must make sense and retain its core meaning.

Whole-class shared work
● Go to page 3. Ask the children to read the text and tell you what it is about.
● Point out that the children's oral summaries were quite short. Press the hyperlinked button to open an editable version of the text. Complete a word count of the written text (using the Word count facility in Microsoft Word). Explain that you need to reduce this text to no more than 75 words without losing the sense of the text.
● Work through the text, sentence by sentence. Ask the children to identify and highlight key words in sentences using Microsoft Word's Highlighter function (in View/Toolbars/Formatting).
● Repeat the investigation, identifying words that are unnecessary (such as *precious, strict, sensible*). Highlight these in a different colour.
● Discuss if further reductions could be made. Which words are also not essential?
● Now delete some of the highlighted non-essential words in the second version of the text. Keep checking that the text makes sense and undo any mistakes. Agree on a final version.
● Compare the edited text with the original text. Point out how some of the original details were useful (as long as the writer had room for them), but some were unnecessary because they repeated obvious information.
● Which version of the text do the children prefer? Why?

Independent work
● Ask the children to complete photocopiable page 49 'Essential words'. They need to rewrite sentences using fewer words.
● Support less confident learners by suggesting they work with a partner, underlining adjectives and unnecessary detail. Check their progress before they start to rewrite the sentences.
● As an extra challenge, ask the children to look at a recent piece of writing. Are there places where shorter sentences would have been better? Can they identify unnecessary words?

Plenary
● Compare results. Type the shortest versions on page 4 of the Notebook file. Have the children noticed which type of word is often unnecessary? (Adjectives.) Which classes of word are usually essential? (Nouns and verbs.)

Writing instructions

Learning objectives

PNS: Understanding and interpreting texts
● Identify how different texts are organised, on paper and on screen.
● Explore how different texts appeal to readers using varied sentence structures and descriptive language.

PNS: Creating and shaping texts
● Use layout, format, graphics and illustrations for different purposes.

Resources

'Healthy teeth' Notebook file (from previous lesson); access to a computer suite (optional); paper and pens. (Microsoft Word is required to view the embedded text document in the Notebook file.)

Links to other subjects

Science
QCA Unit 3A 'Teeth and eating'
● Link the independent task to the science unit on teeth and eating.

ICT
QCA Unit 3A 'Combining text and graphics'
● Ask children to use various text effects on the prepared text, for example, font type, size, or use of bullets to produce an information leaflet on 'Healthy teeth'.

Whiteboard tools

Add a new page to the 'Healthy teeth' text file. Use arrow tools, bullet points and a range of text effects (bold, italics) to produce an information leaflet on healthy teeth. Close or minimise the window opened by the link to return to Notebook.

 Pen tray

 Select tool

 Floating tools

 On-screen Keyboard

Starter

Open the 'Healthy teeth' Notebook file and press the button next to Lesson 17 to go to page 5. Revise sentence beginnings and endings. Remind the children that sentences begin with a capital letter and end with a full stop. Write a few sentences on the page, some of them statements, some of them questions (but without the question marks). Read them aloud. Can the children spot the problem? (Some need a question mark instead of a full stop.) Explain that statements and questions are two sentence types.

Whole-class shared work

● Go to page 6. Allow time for the children to read the text.
● Discuss the text. Ask: *Is it part of a story? Is it fiction or non-fiction?* Agree that the text is non-fiction, and probably taken from a science or healthcare book.
● Talk about the way in which the text is written. How does the writer communicate with the reader? Does the writer ask questions or make statements?
● Explain that the text is made up of a series of *instructions*.
● Discuss how the layout of the text could be improved. Ask for the children's ideas (such as: *bullet points, diagrams with arrows, lists* and *numbered points*). Make a list of these ideas on page 7 of the Notebook file, explaining and giving examples each time.
● Open the editable version of the text. Experiment with the text and use some of the suggested devices. Point out where a diagram would be useful and discuss what the diagram would look like.
● Investigate the wording of the text. Delete words, so that each instruction is a short line of writing (see Lesson 16).
● Remind the children of your Starter work. What type of sentences are these? (Command sentences.)
● Ask the children to identify the verbs in some of the sentences. Point out the verbs at the start of the sentences. Explain that these verb forms are called *imperative verbs*, and they give commands. Instructions should contain sentences using imperative verbs. The imperative verb is usually the first word in the sentence.

Independent work

● Provide paper and pens and ask the children to write a set of instructions about feeding a pet. Remind the children to use the organisational devices you have listed.
● Support less confident learners by encouraging use of illustrations and diagrams.
● Challenge the children to test their instructions on a friend. Ask: *Are they clear and easy to follow?* Invite them to appraise each other's work.

Plenary

● Scan the independent work and read some of the children's instructions.
● Annotate any of the features of instructional texts listed above. Do the children find these types of instructions clear and easy to follow?
● Press the image on page 8 to see an example of how text could be presented.

Singular and plural

Learning objective
PNS: Word structure and spelling

Resources
'Singular and plural' Notebook file; a copy of photocopiable page 50 'Singular and plural' for every child; individual whiteboards and pens.

Links to other subjects
Citizenship
QCA Unit 11 'In the media – what's the news?'
● Provide small groups of children with newspaper articles on the same topical issue. Ask the children to do a word search, listing all the plural nouns and grouping them. Ask them to distinguish between fact and opinion in the article.

Starter
Show page 2 of the Notebook file, on which a number of words are given. Ask for suggestions as to how the words can be separated into two groups? Share ideas. Write and explain the terms *singular* and *plural*. Use these as labels and sort the words into two sets.

Whole-class shared work
● Read the text on page 3. Work with the children, identifying and highlighting plural nouns ending in *-s*.
● Can the children tell you the total number of plurals in the text. (There are 19.) Pull down the Screen Shade to reveal the highlighted plurals.
● Explain that the addition of *-s* is the usual way for a noun to change from singular to plural.
● Go to page 4. Agree and write singular forms of the words in the table.
● Next, ask a child to read aloud a singular form and invite another child to say its plural. Ask: *How many syllables did you hear?* Note that the addition of *-s* does not add another syllable.
● Now examine some other plural forms. Write the words: *church*, *bench* and *witch* (which all end in a shushing sound) on page 5. Invite individuals to read one and say its plural. Establish that a new syllable is always added to these words. Write the plurals on the board and explain that *-es* created the new syllable.
● Go back to page 3 and activate the Spotlight tool . Set the shape of the spotlight to Rectangular (using the dropdown menu) and focus on the word *cherries*. Discuss the spelling change between the singular and plural forms of the word. Repeat this for the word *knives*.
● Display page 6 and discuss the spelling patterns for words that end in *-y*.
● Test examples such as *Play* and *Penny* and annotate the plural endings.
● Add some of the children's examples onto page 5.
● Talk about the difficulty with singular words containing *f*: most become *-ves*, but some plurals are *-fs*. A few are either! For example, *roof* can become *roofs* or *rooves*.

Independent work
● Using the 'Singular and plural' photocopiable sheet, ask the children in groups to make five plurals.
● Support less confident learners by concentrating on one or two plural groups.
● As an extra challenge, ask the children to add their own words to the groups.

Plenary
● Go to page 7 of the Notebook file. Discuss the singular nouns and ask individuals to say the plural forms.
● Check the answers by moving each word across the black bar in the centre of the screen; the plural version of the word will appear on the other side of the bar.
● As you reveal the plurals, emphasise the spelling patterns. Discuss any misconceptions that may have arisen.

Whiteboard tools
Convert handwritten words to text by selecting them and choosing the Recognise option from the dropdown menu. Use the Spotlight tool to identify irregular plurals.

 Pen tray

 Select tool

 Highlighter pen

 Screen Shade

 On-screen Keyboard

 Spotlight tool

Compound words

Learning objective
PNS: Word structure and spelling
● Spell unfamiliar words using known conventions including morphological rules.

Resources
'Compound words' Notebook file; individual whiteboards and pens; print the activity on page 6 of the Notebook file and give one copy to each pair (optional).

Links to other subjects
History
QCA Unit 6A 'Why have people invaded and settled in Britain in the past? A Roman case study'
● Demonstrate Roman influence on the English language with compound words which have Latin prefixes and suffixes (*cruciform; porcupine; porcelain; portfolio*).

Starter
On page 2 of the Notebook file show the words: *drawbridge, broomstick* and *earthquake*. What do the words have in common? Use the Eraser to reveal that they are *compound words*. Pull out the definition at the bottom of the page: compound words occur when words are joined to form a new word. Separate the words on the board to show how and where each one is joined.

Whole-class shared work
● Explain that the meanings of the different parts of a compound word add together to form the meaning of the new word. Pages 3 to 5 provide a visual explanation on the whiteboard with the word *lifeguard*. Press the hyperlinked arrow to reveal each stage, demonstrating that *life + guard = someone who guards life*.
● Demonstrate how the three compound words from the Starter can be broken down in the same way. Separate them and write an addition sign between each pair of words.
● Explain the activity on page 6: the compound words must be assembled and matched to the correct definitions. Press the image to start the activity.
● Work on one definition at a time. Invite the children to drag and drop the words to create the appropriate compound words. Press the *Am I correct?* button to see if the words have been placed correctly.
● Move on to page 7. Ask the children to look around the room to spot some compound words. Delete the boxes to reveal some possible examples: *classroom, whiteboard, blackboard, cupboard*. Add other compound words that the children identify.
● Separate the compound words. Point out that the word *board* is used in more than one of the compound words.
● Link your investigations to text-level work on character descriptions. Read a piece of narrative with interesting details about a fictional character. Make sure that the text contains some compound words.
● Ask the children to write, on individual whiteboards, the compound words they hear. Compare and write the results on the whiteboard. Demonstrate how the words can be split into two by addition signs.

Independent work
● Explain that some words appear frequently in compound words. Provide ten base words for the children to work with (for the beginning or end of the compound words): *day; no; any; some; time; every; eye; sand; out; play*.
● Challenge the children to find at least two or three answers for each word.
● Support less confident learners by using pictures, with arrows pointing to relevant objects.
● Challenge the children to investigate two pages of a class text, searching for further examples. Add the words to a *Compound words bank* (see below).

Whiteboard tools
Use the Eraser from the Pen tray to reveal the focus of the lesson. If a microphone is available, use Windows® Sound Recorder (accessed through Start - Programs - Accessories - Entertainment) to record compound words identified by the children.

 Pen tray

 Select tool

 On-screen Keyboard

 Delete button

Plenary
● Share and display results on page 8. Use Windows® Sound Recorder to record their compound words (if a microphone is available).
● Save the page to add compound words in later sessions, and encourage the children to keep collecting words.

Alphabetical texts

Learning objective
PNS: Word structure and spelling

Resources
'Alphabetical texts' Notebook file; internet access; website containing lists of books such as **www.scholastic.co.uk**; individual whiteboards and pens; a dictionary or thesaurus for each group. (Microsoft Word is required to view the embedded text document in the Notebook file.)

Links to other subjects
Art and design
QCA Unit 9 'Visiting a museum, gallery, or site'
● Give the children opportunities to explore the children's/teachers' sections of a museum or art gallery's website. Ask them to find out how much use is made of alphabetical order.

Whiteboard tools
Use the On-screen Keyboard to type synonyms into the embedded table. Fix text to the table by selecting Insert Drawing as Text from the SMART Aware toolbar in the top-left corner. Use Microsoft Word's Thesaurus (in Tools/ Language/Thesaurus) to check the validity of the children's synonyms. Upload scanned lists by selecting Insert, then Picture File, and browsing to where you have saved them.

 Pen tray

 Select tool

 On-screen Keyboard

 Area Capture tool

 Insert Drawing as Text

Starter
Organise the children into groups of three. Give each group a thesaurus. Display page 2 of the Notebook file and allocate one adjective to each group. Allow two minutes for the group to find a synonym for it. Open the text document which presents the synonyms in a table format. Collect and type the results. For example: *humorous* = funny; *contented* = happy and so on. Use Microsoft Word's Thesaurus to check the validity of each synonym.

Whole-class shared work
● Use your computer's web browser to view a bookshop website, such as **www.scholastic.co.uk** (press the link to the Scholastic *Teachers' Shop*).
● Ask the children for suggestions as to how you would search for a particular title. You could, for example, browse the shop by subject or by key stage.
● Lead them to see that books can be listed in alphabetical order. Discuss the benefits of using alphabetical order.
● Exit the internet and return to the Notebook file. On page 3, prompt the children to think of some uses for alphabetical order in classroom organisation. Press the button in the lower right of the page for some suggestions.
● Open the *Alphabetical texts* activity on page 4. Explain the scenario: the library books are not in order. How can the librarians help themselves and their users? (Use alphabetical order.)
● With the children's help, drag and drop the books onto the shelves in alphabetical order. Encourage the children to use the on-screen alphabet as a guide.
● Discuss difficulties: for example, two books may begin with the same word so later words need to be considered. Finally, press the *Am I correct?* button to see if the books are correctly placed.
● If you would like to keep the correct sequence for reference, use the Area Capture tool to take a snapshot which you can add to the current Notebook page.
● Explain that you have some new (short) titles to add. Call out a title at a time and ask the children to write, on individual whiteboards, which book it should follow.
● Check and discuss the answers.

Independent work
● Ask the children to look around the classroom and write a list (in alphabetical order) for a *Classroom guide to important resources*.
● Support less confident learners by suggesting items for the list.
● As an extra challenge, ask children to provide a further section of the classroom guide (such as a code of conduct) in alphabetical order.

Plenary
● Scan or type the children's lists onto page 5.
● Point out places where alphabetical order was tricky (perhaps two words beginning with the same letter).

Conjunctions

Learning objective
PNS: Creating and shaping texts
PNS: Sentence structure and punctuation
● Show relationships of time, reason and cause through subordination and connectives.

Resources
'Conjunctions' Notebook file; photocopiable page 51 'Conjunctions' for every child; individual whiteboards and pens.

Links to other subjects
Citizenship
QCA Unit 6 'Developing our school grounds'
● Link the independent writing to ideas for developing your school grounds.

Starter
Show page 2 of the Notebook file, which includes the words *and; but; or.* What type of words are these? Use the Eraser to reveal that they are conjunctions (joining words). Explain that conjunctions are useful for joining one short sentence to another. Pull the tab to reveal the definition.

Remind the children about the use of conjunctions and point out that *and, but,* and *or* are useful examples, but that we tend to use them too much and forget about other possibilities.

Move on to page 3 and ask the children, using individual whiteboards, to identify different conjunctions that could be added to the examples.

Check the children's answers; then move each sentence, in turn, through the container to reveal the completed sentence.

Whole-class shared work
● Point to some short sentences on notices around the classroom. Ask: *Which pairs of sentences could be joined? What conjunction would you use?* Discourage the use of *and* unless it is the most appropriate choice.
● Use page 4 to create a *Conjunctions word bank* that you can keep adding to. Clone some examples from the earlier activities and add them in here if necessary.
● You can save this page into the Gallery to use the words in future lessons. Follow the instructions in the *What to do* section on page 4.
● Read the narrative text on page 5. Work through the text, one sentence at a time, allowing thinking time as the children search for a conjunction.
● Explain that conjunctions are not always in the middle of the new, longer sentence; sometimes they join at the beginning. Identify examples of this in the text with the children. Check that they can identify all of the conjunctions before pulling down the Screen Shade to check.

Independent work
● Introduce the photocopiable sheet 'Conjunctions'. Explain that the sheet includes ideas about the school grounds which can be joined together using conjunctions. Show the examples on page 6 which demonstrate the idea. Focus on each stage of the activity in turn.
● Invite the children to create eight sentences using a conjunction in each sentence. Some helpful conjunctions are presented on the sheet.
● As an extra challenge, ask the children to redo the exercise, using an alternative conjunction each time. Ask them to decide if one choice is more appropriate than the other.

Whiteboard tools
Clone words by selecting Clone from the dropdown menu. They can then be moved onto another page by dragging them onto the thumbnail of you destination page in the Page Sorter.

 Pen tray

 Select tool

 Highlighter pen

 On-screen Keyboard

 Page Sorter

 Screen Shade

Plenary
● Compare answers. Point out that there are many alternatives because more than one conjunction may be appropriate. Write notes on page 7 if required.
● Write the preferred sentences on the whiteboard, highlighting the conjunctions. Add these conjunctions to the *Conjunctions word bank* on page 4, adding new pages as required.

Speech and narrative

Learning objective
PNS: Sentence structure and punctuation
● Clarify meaning through the use of speech marks.

Resources
'The mystery grows' Notebook file; photocopiable page 52 'The mystery grows' for every child.

Links to other subjects
History
QCA Unit 6A 'Why have people invaded and settled in Britain in the past?'
● Ask the children to write about a situation in which a Roman is talking to a Celt about life in Ancient Rome.

Starter
Improvise a drama. Ask another adult to leave the room and then return looking unwell. Read out the following extract:

> It was 11 o'clock in Class 3. The literacy lesson had already started. Mr Singh suddenly went out of the room. Then he returned looking miserable.
>
> "You must whisper," groaned Mr Singh when he came back. "My head is aching."
>
> "If you're ill," replied Mrs Bloggs, looking at him, "you can go home."
>
> "That's very kind of you," said Mr Singh as he packed his bag, "and I'll try to be back tomorrow."
>
> Mrs Bloggs got on with teaching the class.

Ask the children to recall what was said. Repeat the scene if necessary and write it on page 2 of the Notebook file. Use the Recognise option to convert it into typed text. Compare it to the completed version on page 3.

Whole-class shared work
● Read the text on page 3 with the children.
● Count and write on the board the number of paragraphs (five). Point out instances of new paragraphs (when someone speaks; different paragraphs for different speakers).
● Examine sentences containing narrative and dialogue. Ask the children to work in pairs to look for other punctuation conventions. Compare findings. Stress that the first word spoken always starts with a capital letter and that a punctuation mark (often a comma) separates narrative and speech.
● Write all of these identified features on the right-hand side of page 3.
● Highlight examples of commas separating speech from narrative.
● Focus on the second paragraph. Let someone be Mr Singh and say his words. Highlight his words and explain that they are interrupted by narrative. Highlight the narrative words in a different colour and call them a *reporting clause*.
● Repeat the process for the next paragraph, identifying *replied Mrs Bloggs, looking at him* as the reporting clause (be consistent in colour highlighting).
● Draw the children's attention to the use of either full stops or commas after a reporting clause (depending on whether the sentence is finished or not).

Independent work
● Explain that photocopiable page 52 'The mystery grows' is the second chapter in the story. The children must fill in the gaps to complete the chapter.
● Support less confident learners by directing them towards the picture for each gap.
● Challenge more confident learners to write Chapter 3, using a similar mixture of speech and narrative.

Plenary
● Go to page 4 and review the children's versions of Chapter 2. Add some of their suggestions to the board. Identify reporting clauses and highlight the accurate use of speech marks and punctuation.

Whiteboard tools
Customise the Highlighter pen to include new colours. Convert handwritten words to text by selecting them and choosing the Recognise option from the dropdown menu.

 Pen tray

 Highlighter pen

Story planning (3)

Learning objectives
PNS: Creating and shaping texts
● Use beginning, middle and end to write narratives in which events are sequenced logically.
PNS: Text structure and organisation
● Signal sequence, place and time to give coherence.

Resources
'Story planning' Notebook file; photocopiable page 53 'Story planner' for each child.

Links to other subjects
Speaking and listening
Objective 25: To explain a process or present information, ensuring items are clearly sequenced, relevant details are included and accounts ended effectively.
● Provide opportunities for the children to present their plans to one another.

Starter
Remind the children of the story from Lesson 22. Show page 2 of the 'Story planning' Notebook file, which includes a series of incidents from the story, positioned out of sequence around the board. Point out that the story will not work without a plan. Ask the children to think about grouping the information into four chapters and adding to it if time is available. Move the notes around the board until the information is sequenced to the children's satisfaction.

Whole-class shared work
● Move to page 3 and explain that this is an author's plan for a mystery story. Pull the tab to reveal details of the first chapter. Talk about the incidents mentioned in the first box. Stress their logical sequence.
● Move to the Chapter 2 box. Discuss how events are building up. Are the children reminded of a familiar story?
● Invite the children to suggest probable ideas for the third chapter. Compare the class's ideas with what is revealed.
● Discuss what the author must plan to do in the final chapter (resolve the mystery and bring the story to a conclusion). Share some ideas for the author's plan. Compare the children's ideas with what is revealed.
● Ask what the children would call the story and each chapter. Use the Eraser to reveal the suggested titles.
● Discuss the completed plan. Point out that a plan is written before the real story. Do the children think they would find it easy to come back to this plan a few days later and write the story?
● Emphasise the helpful elements of this plan:
  ● the shape of the plan (the story hill plan reminds the author to build up details before coming down the other side of the hill with the ending)
  ● a title
  ● sequence of chapters
  ● chapter headings
  ● notes of incidents to occur in each chapter
  ● clear notes, without too much confusing detail.

Independent work
● Ask the children to plan their own mystery story using on photocopiable page 53 'Story planner', with a title, four chapters (with chapter titles) and incidents for each chapter. Stress the use of clear notes rather than whole sentences.
● Suggest that the children base their mystery story on a familiar story (such as using *Little Red Riding Hood* for *The Mystery of the Gruff Granny*).
● Support less confident learners by asking them to create a pictorial plan first.
● As an extra challenge, ask children to write their first chapter.

Plenary
● Scan and view some of the plans. Invite individuals to talk about their plans. Suggest that they use the Spotlight tool to bring important points to the class's attention.
● Alternatively, ask the children for their chapter headings and key incidents and write these onto page 4.

Whiteboard tools
Use the Eraser from the Pen tray to reveal each chapter heading on the Notebook file. Upload scanned images by selecting Insert, then Picture File, and browsing to where you have saved the image.

 Pen tray

 Select tool

 Text tool

 On-screen Keyboard

 Spotlight tool

Learning objective
PNS: Creating and shaping texts
● Make decisions about form and purpose.
PNS: Sentence structure and punctuation

Resources
'Apostrophes' Notebook file; individual whiteboards and pens; exercise books.

Links to other subjects
Geography
QCA Unit 6 'Investigating our local area'
● Ask for two reports on the features of the local village or town: one in formal language, the other in informal language.

Apostrophes (contractions)

Starter
Read each of the following phrases from page 2 of the Notebook file in turn: *the pencil of the boy; the bags of the children; the car of the teacher.*

Ask the children to work with partners and use them in spoken sentences. Ask: *Is that the way you usually speak?* Discuss how we normally express possession more economically with an *s*, and how in writing, we use an apostrophe. Agree on the short form for each phrase and reveal them.

Whole-class shared work
● Show the phrases on page 3. Continue partner conversations, using these phrases in quick conversations. Encourage natural speech. Record some conversations if a microphone is available.
● Invite individuals to write exactly what a partner has said and link it to the complete phrase on the whiteboard.
● Discuss how the speaker has run words together. Introduce and define the term *contraction*. Pull the definition tab.
● Emphasise that the missing letter in a contraction needs to be marked by an apostrophe. The Starter activity used an apostrophe for possession; a contraction is another use of an apostrophe.
● Demonstrate and analyse contractions of the other phrases on the board.
● Move to page 4 and remind the children of the story of Cinderella used in earlier lessons. Highlight the apostrophes in the text.
● Prove that the apostrophes are all being used for contractions by asking the children to read a character's words to a partner. Can the children speak the words more formally? Discuss and agree on the full versions. Pull the panel across to check answers.
● Copy and paste or type a list of more difficult contractions onto the table on page 5. Challenge the children to provide the full versions of the words on their individual whiteboards. Continue over page 6 if necessary.

Independent work
● Describe the scenario outlined on page 7: A robbery has occurred. Two people are being asked for a report: the policeman (trained in making formal reports) and the victim, who speaks and writes more naturally.
● Two sentences are modelled on page 7. Discuss the differences between the two styles.
● Ask the children to write a report for each character (one formal, one using contractions).
● Give support by providing phrases for the first report which will be contracted in the second report.
● As an extra challenge, ask the children to search a reading book for examples of contractions not mentioned in the lesson.

Plenary
● Scan the reports onto page 8 and view, highlighting the contractions. Are apostrophes used correctly? Are there more places where contractions could be used?
● Add any new contractions to your list on page 6. Create a *Contractions word bank* for use in future lessons. Add new pages if required.

Whiteboard tools
Use the Spotlight tool to focus attention on phrases and contractions. If a microphone is available use Windows® Sound Recorder (accessed through Start - Programs - Accessories - Entertainment) to record the children's conversations (to hear how phrases are contracted in natural speech.

 Pen tray

 Select tool

 Highlighter pen

 On-screen Keyboard

 Blank Page button

 Spotlight tool

Pronouns

Learning objective
PNS: Sentence structure and punctuation

Resources
Photocopiable page 54 'Placing pronouns' for each child; individual whiteboards and pens.

Links to other subjects
Speaking and listening
Objective 26: To follow up others' points and show whether they agree or disagree in a whole-class discussion.
● Use the Plenary session to encourage class discussion.

Starter
Play a game in which you are not allowed to use people's names. Begin by saying something about yourself, such as: *I like chocolate cake!* Then point to others making statements such as: *They seem puzzled!*

Challenge the children to join in the game, always pointing at themselves, you, or others before saying something. If they accidentally use a name, someone else has a go. Take over occasionally to introduce new words, for example *you* instead of *he* or *she*. Do not explain what you are doing, just model it.

Whole-class shared work
● Discuss the Starter activity. Ask the children to think about the words they used instead of names.
● Open a new Notebook page. Use and define the term *pronoun*: a word that can replace a noun. Point out that it is a way of writing and speaking economically; it avoids unnecessary repetition of a name.
● Ask the children if they noticed any possible problem with using pronouns during the Starter. (You had to look to see where someone was pointing.) Emphasise that speakers or writers should only use pronouns when it is going to be clear which names they stand in place of.
● Type or write the following nouns on the whiteboard:
   1. Jasmine
   2. Luke
   3. Mr and Mrs Kumar
   4. football.
● At the bottom of the board, type these pronouns: *they, he, it, she.* Let the children guide you in matching a pronoun to a number.
● Next, add these pronouns to the whiteboard: *her, them, him.* Again follow the children's directions until they identify the correct match. If necessary, put words into sentences, for example: *Luke loves football. ___ plays___ all the time.* (*He; it*)
● Delete the names, but keep the list of pronouns on the whiteboard. Tell the children a story, missing out necessary pronouns. Ask them to write your missing pronouns on individual whiteboards. For example: *My car is a mess! My daughter has promised to clean (it).* Check that the children are holding up the correct pronoun before you move on.

Independent work
● Explain that the 'Placing pronouns' story (photocopiable page 54) has too much repetition. There are many places where nouns are repeated which could be replaced by pronouns.
● Ask the children to identify and highlight ten of those places, and then choose a substitute pronoun from the box.
● Support children by helping them to identify appropriate nouns.
● As an extra challenge, ask the children to write an extension of the story, using at least ten pronouns.

Plenary
● View a copy of the story on the screen. Read the story aloud, highlighting where you suggest a pronoun could be used. Encourage views from the children. Write the replacements.

Whiteboard tools
Use the Lines tool to match pronouns to nouns.

 Pen tray

 Highlighter pen

 On-screen Keyboard

⬚ Lines tool

Learning objectives
PNS: Creating and shaping texts
PNS: Engaging with, and responding to, texts
● Empathise with characters.

Resources 💿 🅿
'The mystery grows' Notebook file (with page 4 text completed); completed photocopiable page 52 'The mystery grows' (from 'Speech and narrative' lesson). (A word processing program, such as Microsoft Word, will be required to edit text on screen.)

Links to other subjects
History
QCA Unit 7 'Why did Henry VIII marry six times?'
● Ask the children to write a first person report of one of Henry VIII's divorces, writing as if they are Henry or his wife.

Whiteboard tools
Copy the text from pages 3 and 4 of the 'Speech and narrative' lesson and paste into a text document (press on the padlock and select unlock, if necessary, then select Copy from the dropdown menu, and paste it into your document.) Use the word-processing program's Find and Replace function to change words. Annotate the document with the Floating tools, and fix annotations to the document by selecting Insert Drawing as Text from the SMART Aware toolbar in the top-left corner.

 Pen tray

 Floating tools

 On-screen Keyboard

 Insert Drawing as Text

Perspective and character

Starter
Tell the children a brief story about your day. Make a point of using *I* as much as possible and include your feelings as well as your behaviour in the story. Invite the children to ask you questions. Next, ask a child to tell the story of her day. Make sure that *I* is used throughout.

Whole-class shared work
● Copy and paste, into a text document, your saved text about Mr Singh and Mrs Bloggs from pages 3 and 4 of the Notebook file, 'The mystery grows'.
● Discuss what happens in the story, perhaps adding new details. Talk about the characters. *What is Mr Singh like? What sort of person is Mrs Bloggs? What do you think about each character's behaviour?* Refer to the text to support views.
● Explain that the story is written in the third person (the characters are seen through the eyes of the author).
● Highlight a place where Mr Singh is referred to as *he*. Identify it as a third person pronoun. Remind the children of the first person pronoun (*I*). Replace the highlighted word with *I*. Use the word-processing program's Find and Replace function to change all of the pronouns to *I*.
● Read the changed text aloud. Discuss the effect of the new words (confusion). Emphasise that writers must use pronouns consistently, or readers will be unsure whose name a pronoun refers to.
● Talk about writing a story in the first person. What are the advantages? (A character speaks for himself and the reader may learn more about the character's thoughts.)
● Model narrative writing in the first person (as Mrs Bloggs), for example:
    I was explaining pronouns to Class 3 when a noise distracted me. I felt cross because this was an important lesson. I noticed...
● Highlight these as first person pronouns. The story has become a first person narrative account. Is this an interesting and informative way to tell the story?

Independent work
● Ask the children to retell this story, writing a first person account. They must decide which character to be, Mr Singh or Mrs Bloggs.
● Suggest that they do not have to keep to your story; they may add or change incidents.
● Encourage the children to keep checking that they are staying in the first person. Support less confident learners by providing some sentences beginning with *I*.
● As an extra challenge, ask the children to choose the other character and write another account in the first person.

Plenary
● Ask the children to read their narratives to the class. Does the writer stay in the first person? Ask listeners to be alert for slips in pronoun consistency.

Homonyms

Learning objective
PNS: Word structure and spelling

Resources
'Homonyms' Notebook file; writing materials.

Links to other subjects
Art and design
PoS (5a) Exploring a range of starting points for practical work.
● Use homonyms as a starting point for class art work. Work in small groups, collaborating on class visual images of the differences in meaning of homonyms.

Starter
Display the sentences on page 2 of the Notebook file. Let the children study these sentence pairs. What do they notice? (Each pair has one word the same.) Highlight these words. What is strange about these words? (They change meaning.) Use the Eraser to reveal that they are called *homonyms*. Ask for synonyms (words of the same meaning) for some of them. Write them at the end of each sentence.

Pull out and discuss the term *homonym*: words that have the same spelling, but different meaning or origin. Identify the Starter words as examples. Can the children think of other everyday examples? (*Dear, light, table* and so on.)

Whole-class shared work
● Explain that some homonyms have a different sound and a different meaning.
● Investigate the homonyms on page 2. Differentiate homonyms with the same pronunciation (*fit; rose*) from those that change pronunciation (*wound; bow*). Use two highlighter colours to group the homonyms.
● Go to page 3 and open the *Homonym impostors* activity. Explain the game: all except one word are homonyms in each group. After thinking time, a child or small group should choose a homonym impostor.
● You can use the Area Capture tool ▦ to take a snapshot of the final pages that list the words that are and are not homonyms.

Independent work
● Use the homonyms listed from the game (shown on page 4). Ask the children to write a pair of sentences for each homonym (each pair of sentences must use the homonym with two different meanings).
● Support less confident learners by suggesting that they work with a partner. Alternatively, use illustrations to show different meanings and then write sentences.
● As an extra challenge, ask the children to think of synonyms for the words and invite them to plan a humorous word-play poem or joke using homonyms.

Plenary
● Share answers. Invite the children to write their sentences on page 5 of the Notebook file. Supply some appropriate illustrations from the Gallery to highlight the differences.
● To extend the lesson, or for homework, introduce work on the draft of a class poem using the homonyms and guidance on page 6.

Whiteboard tools
Use the Eraser to reveal the main focus of the lesson. Find contrasting pictures for different homonyms in the Gallery.

 Pen tray

 Highlighter pen

 Area Capture tool

 Select tool

 Gallery

IT publishing

Learning objectives

PNS: Understanding and interpreting texts
● Identify how different texts are organised, on paper and on screen.
PNS: Creating and shaping texts
● Use layout, format and graphics for different purposes.
PNS: Presentation
● Develop accuracy and speed when using keyboard skills to type, edit and re-draft.

Resources

'All sorts' Notebook file; computer access for all children (or planned use in future lesson); poetry books. (Microsoft Word is required to view the embedded text document in the Notebook file.)

Links to other subjects

ICT
QCA Unit 3A 'Combining text and graphics'
● The children alter the look of a text to create an effect.

Whiteboard tools

Use the Floating tools to annotate the embedded text document. Fix annotations to the page by selecting Insert Drawing as Image from the SMART Aware toolbar at the top-left.

 Pen tray

 Select tool

 Highlighter pen

 Area Capture tool

 Floating tools

 On-screen Keyboard

 Insert Drawing as Image

Starter

Ask the children to look around at the notices in the room. Which two are they most likely to read? Share views and discuss reasons for their choices. Consider the importance of text presentation, not just content. Ask: *How might some of my notices be improved?* (Size of text? Font?)

Show the two different presentation types on page 2 of the Notebook file to prompt further discussion.

Whole-class shared work

● Go to page 3 and ask the children to read the text.
● Work together, analysing the text. Ask: *Does the text make sense? What is it about? Is it punctuated correctly?* Agree on some conclusions. Press the red box to reveal some ideas.
● Investigate the language. Emphasise and highlight any alliteration. Point out the use of hyphenated words, explaining that these words have been put together by the writer.
● Consider the classification of the text. Conclude that the random punctuation, lack of sentences, and made-up hyphenated words make the text a poem.
● Ask the children for their comments on the presentation of the text. Ask: *Does this text appeal to the audience? Do you feel like reading it?*
● Move to page 4. In one column of the grid, list criticisms.
● Discuss ideas for improvement and list them in the other column (such as: *set out in lines; words in appealing font; word shapes to match meanings* and so on).
● Use poetry books to remind the children of possible layouts. Point out the common use of a capital letter to start each line. Emphasise that there is no correct way to set out a poem; the aim is *audience appeal.*
● Demonstrate on the whiteboard how to achieve different effects, using sample words of your own, not the words of the poem.

Independent work

● Say that you are an editor and that you need to improve the presentation of this poem before publication. Ask the children to plan, making notes about how to present this poem. Print copies of the poem from the editable Microsoft Word document for them to annotate (press on the link at the top of page 3.)
● Challenge the children to present the poem on a computer, using a range of text-editing features.
● Support children by placing them in mixed-ability pairs.
● Challenge the children to plan one of their own poems for publication.

Plenary

● Let children explain and demonstrate some of their plans, focusing on the features of the presentation and the text-editing tools that were used.
● Use the Capture tool 📷 to take snapshots of their presentations.
● Go to page 5 to open a version of the poem which has been created using the WordArt options in the Microsoft Word program. Discuss its improved audience appeal. Point out:
  ● line layout
  ● the appealing symmetry of most the verses
  ● the match between word meaning and font layout.

Words within words

Learning objective
PNS: Word structure and spelling
● Spell unfamiliar words using known conventions including morphological rules.

Resources
'Words within words' Notebook file; photocopiable page 55 'Words within words' for every child; individual whiteboards and pens.

Links to other subjects
Mathematics
Understanding shape: Read and record the vocabulary of position, direction and movement.
● Make and describe shapes, such as quadrilaterals. Challenge the children to find *inside words* in the words that they use to describe shapes.

Starter
Show page 2 of the Notebook file. Explain that the words shown have something in common. Can the children identify what it is? Provide more clues if necessary to help the children to recognise that all the words contain the word *in*. Highlight this in each example. Pull the tab to reveal the answer.

Whole-class shared work
● Explain that many words in English have other words within them. A word within a word must have all its letters next to one another, and in the correct order.
● Show the children the different names on pages 3 to 6. Ask them to think about each name in turn and to write (and then hold up) one *inside word* for each name on their individual whiteboards. Once everyone is agreed, double-press on the name, highlight those letters, and drag the *inside* word to the space provided.
● Repeat until the children cannot find any more *inside* words. Finally, press the green box and use the Fill Colour tool to fill it with white and reveal the words. Repeat for pages 4 to 6.
● Give the children time to investigate their own names. Compare results.
● If there is time, try the words on page 7.
● Let the children come to the whiteboard to write their words. Ask the other children: *Are the letters next to one another? Are they in the correct order?*
● After a child has recorded a word within a word, give someone else the chance to identify and record a different word. Convert handwritten words to text by selecting them and selecting the Recognise option from the dropdown menu.
● Check the answers by pressing on the red box.

Independent work
● Provide photocopiable page 55 for each child and ask the children to list the words they can find. Remind them that the letters must be next to each other. Encourage them to use a dictionary when needed.
● Support less confident learners by providing some initial letters.
● Challenge the children to create a new vocabulary list linked to numeracy or science. Each word on the list must contain at least two other words within it.

Plenary
● Share the results using page 9 of the Notebook file. Check that a word's letters are all in the correct order on the whiteboard. Make use of the Highlighter pen to identify unusual answers. Regularly point out that remembering the hidden words helps with remembering the spelling of the longer word.
● Press the red box to reveal the answers.

Whiteboard tools
Use the Fill Colour tool to reveal answers for the main activity. Let children scribe words in different colours with the Pen tool.

 Pen tray

 Select tool

 Highlighter pen

 Fill Colour tool

 Pen tool

Time signals

Learning objectives
PNS: Text structure and organisation
● Signal sequence, place and time to give coherence.
PNS: Sentence structure and punctuation
● Show relationships of time, reason and cause through subordination and connectives.

Resources
'Direct speech' Notebook file; individual whiteboards and pens.

Links to other subjects
Speaking and listening
Objective 34: To identify key sections of an informative broadcast, noting how the language used signals changes or transitions in focus.
● Listen to the language in an information video, listening for phrases and words such as *now, then, next.*

Starter
Play *All change!* Set an event for children to recount to a partner. After one minute, call *All change!* where speakers and listeners swap roles. At the next *All change!* announce a new topic.

Listen to conversations, sometimes providing contributions. Finish with a recount of your morning, overusing *and then, and then.* For example:

> I came into the building. Then I went to the staffroom for a coffee and then I came to the classroom. I put up a poster and then I put some writing around it. Then I marked the numeracy books and then the literacy books. Then I did some work on the computer and then I went to fetch my class.

Ask the children to write, on individual whiteboards, any criticism they have of the words you used.

Whole-class shared work
● Did the children notice your repetitions? Write the repeated words on a new Notebook page. Discuss the use of those words: to make incidents follow on from one another in a time sequence.
● Discuss how recounts need chronological sequences. Ask the children to think about their earlier recounts. Did they or their partner link parts of an event in sequence? Did they overuse any words?
● Repeat your recount from the Starter, this time using a variety of words and phrases to signal time sequence. Ask the children to jot down on individual whiteboards the time words they identify.
● Share results, listing words and phrases on the whiteboard.
● Open page 4 of the 'Direct speech' Notebook file. Point out that this is a narrative text, but that the time sequence helps the audience's understanding. Work with the children, identifying words and phrases which signal time sequences.
● Give thinking time, directing the children to search in a particular paragraph. Highlight the answers: *now, after, next, meanwhile*
● On a new Notebook page, write the following phrases: *later, afterwards, eventually, suddenly, straightaway, just, immediately, at once, from now on.* Point out that these phrases can also be used to show time when telling a story. Discuss what each phrase means.
● Choose a recent school event and discuss important incidents within the event. Note six to eight incidents on a new page of the whiteboard, but not in time order.

Independent work
● Ask the children to write a recount (in the past tense) of the event, using a variety of words and phrases to signal time sequence.
● Link this to other text work, such as a letter to a friend or relation. Support less confident learners by ordering the incidents.
● As an extra challenge, ask the children to review a piece of their recent writing, adding or substituting time words and phrases.

Plenary
● As children read their recounts, ask listeners to identify any words which signal time sequences.
● Play a final game of *All Change!* with the children monitoring each other's language. Has their use of time words improved?

Whiteboard tools
Add a new page with the Blank Page button.

 Pen tray

 Highlighter pen

 On-screen Keyboard

 Blank Page button

A mixed menagerie

What a noisy crowd!

The parrot squawks
The monkey chatters

The _____

_____

_____

What a din of noise!

What an active bunch!

The lion leaps
The snake slides

The _____

_____

_____

What a bustle of movement!

What a greedy gang!

The cat lapped

The _____

_____

_____

What a feast of food!

What a _____

_____

_____

_____

_____

What a _____

High frequency words

■ Highlight 20 high frequency words. Put a number next to each one.

■ Copy the list into your books or on the back of this sheet, putting a synonym beside each word. Make sure that all the synonyms are different.

Wizard Wilbur had only been at Wizardry Academy a little time. Although he was little, he knew a big amount of magic. Wilbur had a big sense of humour, so he thought all his tricks were funny. Some of his spells were great. He could make a great flash like lightning. He could make a big roar come out of an empty cupboard. He could make the Professor too big to squeeze through the narrow doorway. He could make the Assistant so big her head banged on the ceiling.

Obviously, Wilbur was good at magic, but he was not good to the other wizards. Some of his tricks were awful. He had played some nasty tricks. He locked an infant wizard in a classroom by making him too little to reach the door handle. He thought it nice to turn a Year 1 wizard's nice lunch of spaghetti into great worms. He gave a homesick wizard's breakfast a nasty smell. Wilbur was becoming a great nuisance.

Illustrations © Andy Keylock / Beehive Illustration

Story planning in paragraphs

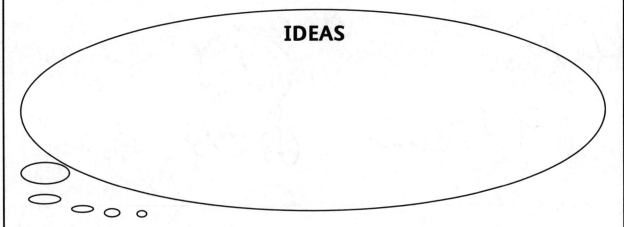

IDEAS

Where? settings: house; seaside; park; swimming pool; supermarket

Who? characters: boy; girl; footballer; lifeguard; checkout cashier

What? objects: ball; bike; lifebelt; pile of tinned food; inflatable boat

PARAGRAPH PLAN

1 _____

2 _____

3 _____

STORY TITLE

_____

OPENING WORDS OF STORY

_____

_____

_____

_____

Direct speech

Cinderella

Ugly sister

_____   _____

_____   _____

Fairy godmother

A cat

_____   _____

_____   _____

Ugly sister

The Prince

_____   _____

_____   _____

SCHOLASTIC
www.scholastic.co.uk

Prefixes

■ Add a prefix to each word in the box below to make its antonym. Then write the new word under the correct prefix heading. You should find five answers for each prefix.

un____

_____

_____

_____

_____

in____

_____

_____

_____

_____

dis____

_____

_____

_____

im____

_____

_____

_____

mis____

_____

_____

_____

_____

WORDS

kind, please, correct, able, possible, agree, place, convenient, lucky, behave, action, polite, obey, do, sensitive, spell, perfect, honest, zip, qualify, understand, probable, formal, mature, lead

Website review sheet

Website

Good features

- _____
- _____
- _____
- _____

Suggested improvements

- _____
- _____
- _____
- _____

Other comments _____

_____

_____

Would you recommend this website?   Yes ☐   No ☐

Why/why not? _____

_____

Website

My summary

Signed _____

Website Reviewer

Using commas

■ Complete the sentences in your writing books, using a list in each one.

1. The magician wore a _____

_____ .

2. He carried a _____

_____ .

3. Out of his pocket came _____

_____ .

4. Mice ran _____

_____ .

5. Children cheered _____

_____ .

6. The manager screamed _____

_____ .

7. The magician packed up _____

_____ .

Silent letters

k	g	w	h	b	l

ans_er	hi_h	sa_mon	_not
tom_	plum_	_nee	w_irl
_nat	w_ale	_rapper	crum_
_retch	ca_m	cha_k	ca_f
thum_	_rite	r_ino	w_en
_now	_nome	_night	_naw

■ Now enter the words in these rows:

k				
g				
w				
h				
b				
l				

Essential words

■ Re-write these sentences, shortening them to the number of words suggested in the brackets.

Different teeth have lots of different jobs. (4–5)

_____

The clever incisors cut all the food. (3–4)

_____

The long and sharp canines tear pieces of food. (3–4)

_____

The big molars crush the food very well. (3–5)

_____

The incisors are placed very obviously at the front. (5–7)

_____

The dagger-like canines come next in the mouth. (3–4)

_____

The strong molars sit at the very back. (5–6)

_____

Each and every tooth has strong enamel. (4–5)

_____

The tough enamel protects the tooth well. (4)

_____

The enamel is often weakened by its enemy called plaque. (5–6)

_____

Singular and plural

■ Write the plural forms of these words and place them in the correct groups. Each group needs five words.

Word Bank

puppy	shoe	daisy	watch	book
school	thief	donkey	glass	sheaf
fox	match	scarf	tick	key
city	party	shelf	berry	sandwich
day	monkey	bean	toy	wolf

+s	+es	y̸ ies	ys	f̸ ves

Conjunctions

■ Choose a conjunction to join each pair of sentences. Remember to use only one capital letter and one full stop.

while	so	because	but	if
so	although	until	since	though
before	after	when	that	as

Everyone can enjoy school grounds.
There is plenty to do.

_____

_____

Quiet areas are set aside.
Children can talk quietly.

_____

_____

The grounds are developed.
They have been planned.

_____

_____

Some children play ball.
Others chat to friends.

_____

_____

Climbing equipment is fun.
It can lead to accidents.

_____

_____

There must be benches.
People can rest.

_____

_____

A climbing trail should be on grass.
No one gets hurt.

_____

_____

Cricket balls must be banned.
They are too hard.

_____

_____

The mystery grows

The next day Mrs Bloggs arrived at her normal time. She hoped Mr Singh would be waiting for her. Unusually, he arrived very late.

"_____ ," moaned Mr Singh, as he staggered into the room. "Let _____ _____."

"You _____ ," replied Mrs Bloggs, looking closely at him, "but _____ _____."

"My _____ ," mumbled Mr Singh, clutching his face. "It _____."

Mrs Bloggs left the room, and Mr Singh stayed moaning in a chair. A few minutes went by.

"Here you are," announced Mrs Bloggs, when she returned carrying _____. "This is _____."

◼ Use this space to complete the chapter.

_____

_____

_____

_____

_____

_____

Story planner

Story title:

Chapter 1:

Chapter 2:

Chapter 3:

Chapter 4:

Placing pronouns

■ Find 10 places where you could replace words in the story below with a pronoun from the box.

I	you	he	she
it	we	they	me
him	her	them	

Joshua was playing an amazing computer game. The game was made up of different zones. There were ten of the zones. Whenever Joshua entered the zones, Joshua felt really inside the zones.

Joshua had sort of borrowed the computer game from his sister, but without permission. His sister loved computer games. In fact, his sister was obsessed with playing computer games!

"You'd better give the game back to your sister when your sister gets home," warned Mum and Dad when Mum and Dad saw him.

"You know the game belongs to your sister. It does not belong to Joshua."

Name _____

Words within words

◼ Find the hidden words.

investigate	shallowest

greatest	prediction

different	underneath

altogether	clockwise

operation	quadrilateral

Mathematics

This chapter provides 30 lessons based on the objectives taken from the Primary National Strategy's *Primary Framework for mathematics*, covering all seven strands and a range of objectives. The curriculum grids below are also provided, in editable format, on the accompanying CD-ROM.

The interactive whiteboard can enhance all three parts of the lesson, allowing you to demonstrate concepts and model strategies. Children will become actively involved by highlighting, writing and dragging the particular elements of each lesson. Mathematical resources such an interactive 100-square and a random number generator can appear on screen from a Gallery; a bar chart can take minutes to draw (allowing time to interpret and discuss); picture images will allow the children to take the mathematics outside the classroom and link it to real-life scenarios or objects.

On the CD-ROM you will also find links to relevant DfES *Interactive Teaching Programs* (ITPs). The whiteboard is an ideal medium for making the most of these exciting and interactive resources.

Lesson title	PNS objectives	NLS objectives	Expected prior knowledge	Cross-curricular links
Lesson 1: Ordering numbers	**Counting and understanding number** • Read, write and order whole numbers to at least 1000 and position them on a number line.	• To order whole numbers to at least 1000.	• Order whole numbers to 100. • Read, write and count numbers to 1000.	**Science** PoS Sc1 (2f) To make systematic measurements.
Lesson 2: Hundreds, tens and units	**Counting and understanding number** • Read, write and order whole numbers to at least 1000. • Partition three-digit numbers into multiples of 100, 10 and 1 in different ways.	• To read, write and order whole numbers to at least 1000. • To know what each digit represents in terms of place value.	• Read and write numbers to 100. • Understand place value for tens and ones (units).	There are no specific links for this lesson.
Lesson 3: Add and subtract nine	**Calculating** • Add or subtract mentally combinations of one-digit and two-digit numbers.	• To add and subtract mentally a *near multiple of* ten to or from a two-digit number.	• How to add and subtract ten.	There are no specific links for this lesson.
Lesson 4: Shopping	**Using and applying mathematics** • Represent information using £.p notation.	• To understand and use £ and p notation.	• Understand p notation. • Recognise coins.	**Speaking and listening** Objective 27: To use talk to organise roles and actions.
Lesson 5: Venn diagrams	**Handling data** • Use Venn diagrams or Carroll diagrams to sort data and objects using more than one criterion.	• To solve a given problem by organising and interpreting numerical data in simple lists, tables and graphs.	• Can count a set of objects. • Can select criteria to sort.	**Science** PoS Sc3 (1a) To compare the properties of everyday materials and objects. **History** PoS (1a) To place events, people and changes into correct periods of time. **Geography** PoS (4a) To recognise and explain patterns made by individual physical and human features in the environment.
Lesson 6: Collecting and recording data	**Handling data** • Answer a question by collecting, organising and interpreting data; use tally charts to represent results and illustrate observations.	• To solve a given problem by organising and interpreting numerical data in simple lists, tables and graphs.	• Can count a set of objects when moving quickly. • Discuss outcomes and respond to posed questions.	**Geography** QCA Unit 6 'Investigating our local area' **Speaking and listening** Objective 25: To explain a process or present information. **Speaking and listening** Objective 26: To show whether they agree or disagree in a whole-class discussion.

Mathematics Chapter 2

Lesson title	PNS objectives	NLS objectives	Expected prior knowledge	Cross-curricular links
Lesson 7: What do I use to measure...?	**Measuring** • Know the relationships between kilometres and metres, metres and centimetres, kilograms and grams, litres and millilitres; choose and use appropriate units to estimate, measure and record measurements.	• To suggest suitable units and measuring equipment to estimate or measure length, mass or capacity.	• Understand that liquid, mass and length can be measured.	**Science** QCA Unit 3B 'Helping plants grow well'
Lesson 8: Lines	**Measuring** • Read to the nearest division and half-division, scales that are numbered or partially numbered; use the information to measure and draw to a suitable degree of accuracy.	• To measure and compare using standard units, including using a ruler to draw and measure lines to the nearest half centimetre.	• Can use a ruler.	**Geography** PoS (2c) To use maps and plans at a range of scales.
Lesson 9: Quadrilaterals	**Understanding shape** • Relate 2D shapes to drawings of them; describe, visualise, classify, draw and make the shapes.	• To classify and describe 2D shapes, including the quadrilateral.	• Classify and describe simple regular 3D and 2D shapes.	**Art and design** QCA Unit 3B 'Investigating pattern'
Lesson 10: Base-10 numbers	**Counting and understanding number** • Read, write and order whole numbers to at least 1000. • Partition three-digit numbers into multiples of 100, 10 and 1 in different ways.	• To read, write and order whole numbers to at least 1000. • To know what each digit represents.	• Read and write numbers to 100. • Understand place value for tens and ones.	There are no specific links for this lesson.
Lesson 11: Bead sets	**Knowing and using number facts** • Derive and recall all addition and subtraction facts for each number to 20.	• To know by heart all addition and subtraction facts for each number to 20.	• Know by heart all addition and subtraction facts for each number to ten.	There are no specific links for this lesson.
Lesson 12: Number bars	**Knowing and using number facts** • Derive and recall all addition and subtraction facts for each number to 20.	• To know by heart all addition and subtraction facts for each number to 20.	• Know by heart all addition and subtraction facts for each number to ten.	**Art and design** QCA Unit 3B 'Investigating pattern'
Lesson 13: 2s, 5s and 10s	**Knowing and using number facts** • Derive and recall multiplication facts for the 2-, 5- and 10-times tables.	• To know by heart facts for the 2, 5 and 10 multiplication tables.	• Count up and back in multiples of two, then five, then ten.	There are no specific links for this lesson.
Lesson 14: Repeated subtraction groups	**Calculating** • Understand that division is the inverse of multiplication and vice versa; use this to derive and record related multiplication and division number sentences.	• To understand division as grouping and recognise that division is the inverse of multiplication.	• Can subtract a repeating number.	There are no specific links for this lesson.
Lesson 15: Sharing and grouping	**Calculating** • Understand that division is the inverse of multiplication and vice versa.	• To understand division as repeated subtraction and recognise that division is the inverse of multiplication.	• Can divide by physically sharing a number of objects.	There are no specific links for this lesson.
Lesson 16: How many squares?	**Using and applying mathematics** • Identify patterns and relationships involving numbers or shapes, and use these to solve problems.	• To solve mathematical problems or puzzles and to explain methods and reasoning.	• Can explain methods orally. • Has a level of perseverance to carry out an investigation.	**Speaking and listening** Objective 33: To sustain conversation, explaining or giving reasons for their views or choices. **Art and design** QCA Unit 3B 'Investigating pattern'
Lesson 17: What time is it?	**Measuring** • Read the time on a 12-hour digital clock and to the nearest five minutes on an analogue clock.	• To use units of time and know the relationships between them.	• Can read an analogue and digital clock on the hour, half and quarter.	**Science** QCA Unit 3F 'Light and shadows'
Lesson 18: Birthdays	**Measuring**	• To use units of time and know the relationships between them.	• Recognise the relationship between days, months and years.	**History** PoS (1b) To use dates and vocabulary relating to the passing of time.

Lesson title	PNS objectives	NLS objectives	Expected prior knowledge	Cross-curricular links
Lesson 19: Shapes and patterns	**Understanding shape** • Relate 2D shapes to drawings of them; describe, visualise, classify, draw and make the shapes.	• To make and describe shapes and patterns.	• Can identify 2D shapes. • Can identify and continue simple repeating patterns.	**Art** QCA Unit 3B 'Investigating pattern'
Lesson 20: Spot the right angle	**Understanding shape** • Identify right angles in 2D shapes; compare angles with a right angle.	• To recognise and identify different types of angles: right, acute, and obtuse.	• Know that two strips of paper can turn about a point. • Can recognise that the corner of a square is a right angle.	**PE** QCA Unit 1 'Dance activities'; QCA Unit 14 'Gymnastic activities' **Art and design** QCA Unit 3B 'Investigating pattern'
Lesson 21: Sorting right angles	**Understanding shape** • Identify right angles in 2D shapes; compare angles with a right angle.	• To recognise right angles and to sort shapes according to the number of right angles they have.	• Know that two strips of paper can turn about a point. • Can recognise that the corner of a square is a right angle.	**PE** QCA Unit 19 'Outdoor and adventurous activities'
Lesson 22: Counting	**Counting and understanding number** • Count on from and back to zero in multiples of 10.	• To count on or back in tens or hundreds from any two- or three-digit number.	• Count on in tens up to 100.	There are no specific links for this lesson.
Lesson 23: Fractions	**Counting and understanding number** • Read and write proper fractions, interpreting the denominator as the parts of a whole and the numerator as the number of parts; identify and estimate fractions of shapes.	• To recognise unit fractions such as $1/2$, $1/3$, $1/4$, $1/5$, $1/10$ and use them to find fractions of shapes.	• Understand the link to division. • Recognise and use ½.	There are no specific links for this lesson.
Lesson 24: Half a number	**Counting and understanding number** • Read and write proper fractions, interpreting the denominator as the parts of a whole and the numerator as the number of parts; identify and estimate fractions of shapes; use diagrams to compare fractions.	• To recognise unit fractions such as $1/2$, $1/3$, $1/4$, $1/5$, $1/10$ and use them to find fractions of shapes and numbers.	• Understand the link to division. • Recognise and use ½.	There are no specific links for this lesson.
Lesson 25: Word problems	**Using and applying mathematics** • Solve one- and two- step problems involving numbers, choosing and carrying out appropriate calculations.	• To choose and use appropriate operations to solve word problems.	• Use known multiplication and division facts.	**Speaking and listening** Objective 25: To explain a process or present information clearly.
Lesson 26: Animals pictogram	**Handling data** • Answer a question by collecting, organising and interpreting data; use pictograms to represent results.	• To solve a given problem by organising and interpreting numerical data in simple lists, tables and graphs.	• Can read a scale. • Can extract data from a table.	**Science** QCA Unit 3A 'Teeth and eating'
Lesson 27: Colours bar chart	**Handling data** • Answer a question by collecting, organising and interpreting data; use frequency tables and bar charts to represent results.	• To solve a given problem by organising and interpreting numerical data in simple lists, tables and graphs.	• Can read a scale. • Can extract data from a table.	Cross-curricular use of bar charts.
Lesson 28: Reflections	**Understanding shape** • Draw and complete shapes with reflective symmetry; draw the reflection of a shape in a mirror line along one side.	• To identify lines of symmetry in simple shapes and recognise shapes with no lines of symmetry.	• Understand the language of fold, reflection, mirror line.	**Art and design** QCA Unit 3B 'Investigating pattern' **PE** QCA Unit 14 'Gymnastic activities'
Lesson 29: Lines of symmetry	**Understanding shape** • Draw and complete shapes with reflective symmetry; draw the reflection of a shape in a mirror line along one side.	• To identify lines of symmetry in simple shapes and recognise shapes with no lines of symmetry.	• Understand the language of fold, reflection, mirror line.	**Art and design** QCA Unit 3B 'Investigating pattern' **PE** QCA Unit 14 'Gymnastic activities'
Lesson 30: Compass points	**Understanding shape** • Read and record the vocabulary of position, direction and movement, using the four compass directions to describe movement about a grid.	• To recognise and use the four compass directions relating to NSEW.	• Give instructions to move a robot right, left, forward and back.	**Geography** PoS (2c) To use maps and plans at a range of scales. **PE** QCA Unit 19 'Outdoor and adventurous activities'

Ordering numbers

Learning objective
PNS: Counting and understanding number
● Read, write and order whole numbers to at least 1000 and position them on a number line.

Resources
'Ordering numbers' Notebook file; number lines; individual whiteboards and pens; sets of ten numbers; paper and glue.

Links to other subjects
Science
PoS Sc1 (2f) To make systematic measurements.
● Ensure that the children can read measurements accurately by asking them to weigh/measure a series of items and to order them from smallest to biggest.

Starter
Load the *Number Line* Interactive Teaching Program on page 2 of the 'Ordering numbers' Notebook file. Ask the children to identify the position of numbers along a number line up to 100 and later extend this to 500. Ask questions such as: *If this is 200 and this is 250, by how much are the lines increasing?* Hide the boundary numbers and ask the children to identify different marks along the line.

Whole-class shared work
● Read the numbers on page 3 out loud. Ask the children if they notice anything about the numbers. Lead them to understand that there are ten consecutive numbers but they are not in the correct order.
● Ask one child to come to the board to select the highest number in the set and drag it to the corresponding position on the line.
● Repeat this with another child, selecting the smallest number, middle numbers and so on.
● Go to page 4. On this page are ten more consecutive numbers that bridge a hundreds number (300). However, they are not in order.
● With the children, position the numbers in order on the number line.
● If the children struggle with placing these numbers (from their non-sequential positions), support them in identifying the smallest number and help them to count up from that number.
● On page 5 there are ten numbers between 150 and 210. Ask the pupils to order these numbers along an empty number line.
● On individual boards or paper, ask the children to suggest a number that could be added to this set of numbers.
● Challenge more confident learners to record all the numbers in order, to make this a complete sequential set.

Independent work
● Give each child a number line and a set of ten number cards (consecutively bridging a tens number for less confident learners, and non-consecutively bridging a hundreds number for more confident learners).
● Ask them to position or glue the numbers onto a blank number line. Alternatively, let them record the completed number line in their books.
● The children should then fill in the missing numbers to complete the non-consecutive lines and read the numbers to a partner.

Plenary
● Go to page 6. Use the Random Number Generator on page 6 generate ten random three-digit numbers. Write the numbers in the space provided.
● Ask the children to order them from largest to smallest and record them on their individual whiteboards. Encourage them to show their whiteboards, or invite a child to order the numbers on the board.
● Count around the class, starting at 470 then over and back from 500. Continue the exercise starting at 854 and bridging 900. Discuss any misconceptions if there are any incorrect answers.

Whiteboard tools
Add text to the Notebook file with the On-screen Keyboard. Alternatively, use the Pen from the Pen tray to write.

 Pen tray

 Select tool

 On-screen Keyboard

 Text tool

Learning objectives
PNS: Counting and understanding number
● Read, write and order whole numbers to at least 1000.
● Partition three-digit numbers into multiples of 100, 10 and 1 in different ways.

Resources
'Hundreds, tens and units' Notebook file; photocopiable page 89 'Hundreds, tens and units'; writing materials.

Links to other subjects
There are no specific links for this lesson.

Hundreds, tens and units

Starter
Display the number grid on page 2 of the 'Hundreds, tens and units' Notebook file. One row and one column have been hidden. Ask the children to work out the missing numbers.

When they suggest a missing number, press on the relevant rectangle and delete the coloured block to reveal the number. Ask the children how they worked out the missing number. Did they count on or back in ones or in tens?

Extend the Starter, by pressing on the *Starter extension* button, to a hidden 5 × 5 square of numbers, bridging tens numbers and 100, to encourage the children to count on in fives.

Whole-class shared work
● Look at the number grid on page 2 or 3. Ask the children to generate facts they know about the grid. For example: as the numbers go down a column, the numbers increase by ten, so the tens number changes, but the ones (or units) number stays the same.
● Display the hundreds, tens and units table on page 4. Write a tens number and a units number in the appropriate columns and ask a volunteer to write a two-digit whole number (the integer) on the board and read it out.
● Say some two and three-digit numbers to the children and ask them to write down the hundreds, tens and units numbers. Invite volunteers to write their answers in the table on the whiteboard.

Independent work
● Using a copy of photocopiable page 89 'Hundreds, tens and units', ask the children to lightly colour in one hundreds, one tens and one ones (or units) number.
● They should then swap sheets with their partner, who must write out the hundreds, tens and unit numbers, and the completed three-digit number in their book. Repeat a few times, ensuring that the children understand the place value of each of the digits.
● For less confident learners, limit this activity to two-digit numbers. Show them how to cut out the cards and place them over each other to find the completed number.

Plenary
● Discuss any numbers that the children found difficult to represent using place value cards (such as 406).
● Go to page 5 and open the *Place Value* Interactive Teaching Program. Drag the bottom-right corner to resize the pop-up window.
● Press the furthest left of the three arrows until 400 appears in the window; then press 400; a number card for 400 will appear on screen. Repeat this process with 6 in the third window. Discuss what needs to be pressed to reveal the tens number. (The middle window.)
● Once the number is displayed on screen, drag each part of the number apart to show 400 and 0 and 6. The arrow at the bottom of the place value numbers shows the number represented by red beads.

Whiteboard tools
Convert handwritten words to text by selecting them and choosing the Recognise option from the dropdown menu.

 Pen tray

 Select tool

 Delete button

Add and subtract nine

Learning objective
PNS: Calculating
● Add or subtract mentally combinations of one-digit and two-digit numbers.

Resources 💿
'Build your own' file; blank dice marked with +9, +19 -19 and -9; writing materials.

Links to other subjects
There are no specific links for this lesson.

Starter
Open the 'Build your own' file, which contains a blank Notebook page and a selection of Gallery images. Display the interactive 100-square from the Mathematics folder under My Content 🔲 Use the Pen tool to select a two-digit number and ask the class to count on in ones. Say *Stop* at any number and ask the children to count on in tens. What is the easiest strategy for the children? Do the children identify that the ones (or units) number stays the same (when counting in tens) or recognise that they count down the grid?

Choose another two-digit number, count on in ones, then say *Stop*. This time, ask the class to count back in tens. Ask the children what is the same for all the numbers being counted back.

Whole-class shared work
● Repeat the Starter activity, but when *Stop* is said, ask the children to subtract nine. (Some children will not automatically link counting back in tens to counting back in nines.)
● Draw the children's attention to what they did in the Starter (above). *How can this help us when subtracting nine?*
● Insert the blank number line from the Mathematics folder in the Gallery.
● Demonstrate how the empty number line can be used to subtract ten and show this will be a jump backwards (add the numbers to the line using the Pen tool). Stress that you have subtracted too many; only nine should have been subtracted. Ask the children what they should do now.
● The next step is to count on one. Demonstrate this on the whiteboard.

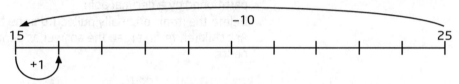

● Ask the children to use this to work out a quick way for subtracting 19 from a two-digit number. Insert another number line and demonstrate subtracting 20 and adding one, or subtracting ten twice and adding one.

Independent work
● Give the children a dice marked with +9, +19, -9, and -19. Ask them to pick a number from a 100-square, roll the dice and follow the instruction, so that they will have to add or subtract 9 or 19 from their chosen number.
● Ask the children to write these calculations in their exercise books. They can use an empty number line to help them.
● Challenge more confident learners by asking them to subtract 9 or 19 from three-digit numbers.

Whiteboard tools
Use the Pen tool to select different colours for values on the interactive 100-square.

 Pen tray

 Pen tool

 Select tool

🔲 Gallery

Plenary
● On a new Notebook page, write 86 - 39 = ? Ask the children to reflect on what they have learned that could help with this subtraction.
● Model suggested strategies on the board. For example, show an empty number line with 86 at one end. Jump back 40 and add one, or repeatedly subtract ten and add one.
● Discuss which is the most efficient method of working out the answer.
● On a new page write 86 - 28 = ? Ask whether the children can see a link between the last calculation and this one. Model suggested strategies on the board to work out the answer.

Shopping

Starter
Page 2 of the 'Shopping' Notebook file shows a ten pence coin that has been partially hidden. Move the purple window around the coin and ask the children to guess what is being shown. Write down their suggestions around the box. How could they tell that it was a ten pence coin? Ask them how much they would have if they had ten of these coins. Consolidate the children's knowledge that one hundred pence equals one pound.

Repeat with a two-pound coin on page 3. Ask the children to record this amount. Point out that there are two ways it can be recorded: 200p and £2.00. Ask what the *.00* means.

Whole-class shared work
● Look at the £ sign on the screen on page 4. What does the symbol stand for? Ask them to practise writing this symbol on their individual whiteboards and on the interactive whiteboard.
● Page 5 offers a shopping exercise. Drag two or three items out of the shopping basket and ask the children to calculate the total cost of these items (using mental or informal strategies). Ask volunteers to present their answers on the whiteboard. Write the total again on page 6 and invite the children to decide which coins they need to pay for the items.
● Check the answers using the number line on page 5.
● Ask the children to read the answer in pence only, for example, *one hundred and fourteen pence.* Is there another way to say this? Demonstrate that the 100p is the same as £1. Stress that the 14p is 14p. When the £ symbol is used, the *p* is not, and the pounds and pence are partitioned by a decimal point.
● Delete the items originally pulled from the box and repeat the activity. Ask children to first read the answer as pence and then as pounds and pence.

Independent work
● Give each group a selection of objects with price labels on them.
● Invite them to estimate which items, when added together, will come to 50p or more. Let them check their answers on a number line, carefully entering the amount.
● Encourage the children to take turns reading the answer, first as pounds and pence, and then just pence.
● Ask the children to find other items that total over 50p when added together.
● Ensure that the children record their items and calculations, using the *receipt pad* template as shown on page 7 of the Notebook file.
● Challenge the children to make four different amounts over £1 and £2. Simplify the activity by reducing the amount of money.

Plenary
● Ask pairs to complete the receipt pad on page 7 for specified prices. Invite them to demonstrate the strategies they used.
● Ask different children to use the number line to check the answers.
● Ask the whole class to read the final total as pence only and then as pounds and pence.
● Erase all the annotations and repeat if required.

Learning objective
PNS: Handling data
● Use Venn diagrams or Carroll diagrams to sort data and objects using more than one criterion.

Resources
'Venn diagrams' Notebook file; set of classroom objects/shapes to sort; sorting rings; labels.

Links to other subjects
Science
PoS Sc3 (1a) To compare the properties of everyday materials and objects.
● Sort materials and objects by their characteristics.
History
PoS (1a) To place events, people and changes into correct periods of time.
● Sort artefacts or people into time periods.
Geography
PoS (4a) To recognise and explain patterns made by individual physical and human features in the environment.
● Sort physical and natural features.

Venn diagrams

Starter
Open the 'Venn diagrams' Notebook file and go to page 2. Look at the aliens that have been placed around the page. Ask the children to discuss, in pairs, how they would sort this group using one criterion (such as colour, number of legs, and so on). Select one of the children's suggestions. Write the criterion in the *sorting label* then drag the relevant aliens into the sorting ring. State that the aliens outside the ring do not fit the data set, but they too could be labelled. Create a label for these aliens.

Whole-class shared work
● Go to page 3. This shows the same objects, but this time there are two sorting rings.
● Ask the children how they could sort the objects into the two rings. Choose different criteria to that used in the Starter activity. Decide on the two criteria together. Label the rings by double-pressing *Set 1* and changing the text to your new sorting label. Do the same for *Set 2*.
● Ask whether all the objects can be sorted into these two rings and if there are objects that match both criteria. One example where one alien will meet both criteria is *Green aliens* and *Two eyes*.
● Discuss how to present objects if both criteria are met. Demonstrate how the rings can overlap. Introduce this sorting format as a Venn diagram.
● Invite the children to the board to sort the objects into the rings. Pose questions such as: *How has this object been sorted? Why has it been placed there?*
● Use the Undo button until the page is reset and experiment with different criteria to explore the ways in which the aliens can be sorted. For example, *Yellow aliens* and *Aliens with four legs*, or *Green aliens* and *Yellow aliens*.

Independent work
● Invite the children to classify and then sort a series of objects (pencils, shapes and so on) according to one criterion. Write a label on the sorting ring and against the non-matching objects.
● Repeat the activity for two criteria, challenging the children to present the sorted objects in a Venn diagram.
● Groups of children can take turns to sort the aliens on page 3 of the Notebook file. Allow the children to add their own labels to the sorting rings. They can either convert handwritten words to text by pressing the Right Mouse button and selecting the Recognise option or they can add text using the On-screen Keyboard.

Plenary
● Go to page 4 of the Notebook file to assess whether the children understand how to sort using a Venn diagram.
● Ask groups of children to think about how the objects have been sorted and what the ring labels could be. Annotate their suggestions. For example, one label could be *Aliens with three eyes* and the other *Aliens with two mouths*.

Whiteboard tools
Use a Pen from the Pen tray or the On-screen Keyboard to add labels to sorting rings.

 Pen tray

 Select tool

 On-screen Keyboard

 Undo button

Collecting and recording data

Learning objective
PNS: Handling data
● Answer a question by collecting, organising and interpreting data; use tally charts to represent results and illustrate observations.

Resources
Digital video camera; clipboards and pens. A prepared Notebook file: create a table using the Lines tool on a blank Notebook page. Place it on one side of the screen so a video clip can be played on the other side.

Links to other subjects
Geography
QCA Unit 6 'Investigating our local area'
● Record a wide range of collected information in a tally and/or in a table, for example, local traffic, types of houses in the local area, or the number of shops and houses in a set area.
Speaking and listening
Objective 25: To explain a process or present information.
Objective 26: To show whether they agree or disagree in a whole-class discussion.
● Use the findings from the collated information as the basis for a debate. For example, ask: *What are the disadvantages/advantages of the buses travelling along the school road?*

Starter
Prior to the actual data-handling lesson, decide upon a *How many?* question that relates to a current topic (such as: *How many cars and buses pass our school entrance during playtime?*) or ask the groups for suggested investigations (such as: *How many children wear the school jumper?*) Take a class vote to decide the investigation.

Whole-class shared work
● Record the data before this lesson using a digital video camera. One effective and efficient method is to use a video camera set in a fixed position such as on a school wall. Remember to obtain permission from parents before taking photographs or video footage of children.
● Review the investigation question with the children. Ask groups to discuss the exact data they will collect. For example, if they are investigating how many children wear the school jumper, do they count jumpers that are in the school colour, or only ones with the school logo? What about cardigans? It is important to define the data that they want to collect; they may choose to count tops with and without the logo, for example.
● Open the Notebook page containing your prepared table (see Resources). Ask pupils to suggest and agree upon a title for the table and a heading for each column.
● Ask the children how they can record data quickly using clipboards and pens. Demonstrate that the tally method is a quick and easy way to record data. Remind them that they need to cross every group of four tally marks to make a total of five.
● Open SMART Video player from the SMART Board tools menu. Select File, then Open, and browse to where you have saved the video file. Drag the new window onto the page beside your table.
● Play it once for the children to watch and then again for them to collect their data. Pause the video regularly taking screen shots with the Image Capture tool on the SMART Video player toolbar.
● Play the video one more time, this time demonstrating the method of tallying by completing the table on screen.
● If a video camera is not available, supply the groups with printouts of the table and encourage them to collect the data through field observation, with appropriate adult supervision.

Independent work
● Ask each member of the group to collate, compare and contrast their collected data.
● Ask each group to organise and present their data. Discuss whether the tally or numbers should be recorded in the table. Generally, the tally collects the data effectively but numbers are a *neater* representation.

Plenary
● Write each group's data in the table. *Are any results different?* Agree upon a class consensus figure for each column. *Does the data answer the investigation question?* Ask the groups to record the answer in a sentence.
● Write out other questions that this question may have raised on a new Notebook page. Save this Notebook file for future data-handling lessons.

Whiteboard tools
To embed a video, open SMART Video player, select File, the Open, and browse to the video file. Drag the new window onto the required page.

 Pen tray

Lines tool

 SMART Video player

Image Capture tool

Learning objective
PNS: Measuring
● Know the relationships between kilometres and metres, metres and centimetres, kilograms and grams, litres and millilitres; choose and use appropriate units to estimate, measure and record measurements.

Resources
'Measurements' Notebook file; set of measuring equipment, one per table (ruler, metre stick, tape measure, measuring jugs and weights/scales); photocopiable page 90 'Measurements'.

Links to other subjects
Science
QCA Unit 3B 'Helping plants grow well'
● Find out what a plant needs to grow well. Measure and monitor its growth in height and the amount of water that it needs.

What do I use to measure...?

Starter
Discuss the objective for this lesson as shown on page 1 of the 'Measurements' Notebook file. Recap what the abbreviations for measurements mean. Discuss which is larger or smaller: km, m, cm, or mm?

Ask the children which measurement would be used for each of the questions shown on page 2. Drag the correct abbreviation to answer each question.

Discuss the range of responses, as well as the reasons why some measurements have not been chosen.

Whole-class shared work
● Reiterate what is actually being measured when you are talking about length (how long/tall something is); mass (how heavy something is); and capacity (how much liquid something will contain).
● Look at the images of different measuring equipment on page 3 and provide each table with a set of measuring equipment. Select and drag the correct labels for each piece of equipment (bearing in mind what each item measures and the units it measures in).
● Prompt the children with questions such as: *What equipment would you use to measure the height of a tree/the amount of juice left/the mass of a car?* Let the children discuss the answer as a group, then invite one child from each table to come to the board to draw a circle around the correct image.
● Often the understanding of a kilometre is difficult for the children to grasp. Use opportunities such as walking to the swimming pool or library to discuss what walking a kilometre actually feels like.

Independent work
● In order to estimate, the children need to have knowledge of the maximum measurement displayed on the equipment. Ask them to look at the equipment on their table and to record the maximum measurement from the scales.
● Hand out copies of photocopiable page 90 'Measurements' to each group. Ask the group to identify suitable units of measurement (in the *What are we measuring?* column) and to estimate measurements for objects within the school or classroom. For example, the height of the door, the distance around the playground, the amount a paint pot holds and so on.
● The group need to record their estimates in the table on the photocopiable sheet.

Plenary
● Ask each group to present their estimates. Use the range of answers as a teaching point to look at how to find out which estimate is nearest.
● Establish that the estimate for the classroom door is over one metre. Discuss how to measure the length of a door if you only had a one metre stick. Ask: *What strategies could you use?* Demonstrate how to use a metre stick to measure the door.
● Complete the table on page 4 of the Notebook file with the children using the results from their independent work.

Whiteboard tools
Use the Recognise option to convert handwriting to text.

　Pen tray

　Select tool

　On-screen Keyboard

Lines

Starter
Look at the measuring equipment on page 3 of the 'Measurements' Notebook file. Ask the children to decide which unit of measurement each piece of equipment uses, and to record what each abbreviation stands for on their individual whiteboards. Drag the correct abbreviation to the boxes under each piece of equipment. Ask the children to consider what the equipment measures (for example, scales measure how heavy something is, and a ruler measures how long something is). Encourage them to relate this to the terms: capacity, mass or length. Drag these terms to the relevant piece of equipment. Ask them when you would use these pieces of equipment.

Whole-class shared work
● Open the 'Build your own' file, which contains a blank Notebook page and a selection of objects from the Gallery 🖼. Use the Lines tool ✏ to draw a straight line of approximately 10cm. Choose an appropriate thickness so that the line is bold and clear. Use the ruler in the Mathematics folder under My Content in the Gallery to measure it.
● Ask the children to think about how they would measure this line and what type of equipment would allow them to do this. Provide a selection of rulers and metre sticks on their tables.
● Select the ruler and drag and rotate it until it lies alongside the line. Illustrate how the ruler is read from the 0 and not from the actual end of the ruler.
● Ask the children to think why it would be a problem to measure from the end. For example, it may be difficult to read a ruler that has blunt edges.
● Demonstrate how the length of the line is measured and read. Use language such as, *The line is __ cm/mm/m long.*
● Repeat with another line which measures 7.5cm. Repeat the above, drawing the children's attention to the fact that the measurement is not 7 or 8cm. Illustrate how a half-centimetre is read off.

Independent work
● In pairs, each child draws ten lines of different lengths to both half and complete centimetres. To simplify the task, ask some pairs to draw only to whole numbers, and to use rulers where the 0 falls on the end of the ruler. For children with fine motor skill difficulties, use rulers with handle grips.
● The pairs then swap their drawn lines with the task of accurately measuring and recording the lengths.
● As an extension, use large paper to draw lines up to one metre in length.

Plenary
● Draw a wavy or curved line. Ask the children how they would measure this line.
● Ask pairs what equipment they would use to measure the line. If a pair suggests string, ask them to come to the board to measure the line using string and highlight the difficulties (the string needs to be held or taped to the line). Repeat with another pair if a tape measure is suggested.

Quadrilaterals

Learning objective
PNS: Understanding shape
● Relate 2D shapes to drawings of them; describe, visualise, classify, draw and make the shapes.

Resources
'Build your own' file; pin boards and elastic bands. Open the 'Build your own' file and prepare a simple picture constructed from 2D shapes, drawn with the Shapes tool. Enable the Screen Shade, so that the children cannot see the shapes when the lesson begins.

Links to other subjects
Art and design
QCA Unit 3B 'Investigating pattern'
● Investigate the patterns that can be made using different quadrilaterals.

Starter
Put the children into pairs and label them *A* and *B*. The *B*s must close their eyes or turn around while the *A*s are shown the picture (see Resources). Select the interactive timer from the Mathematics folder under My Content in the Gallery and set the countdown for 30 seconds to one minute. Start the timer and, as soon as time is up, activate the Screen Shade.

The *B*s can now open their eyes and be given a piece of paper and pencil. The *A*s must describe the picture using mathematical language and correct 2D shape names, while the *B*s draw it according to these instructions.

Reveal the picture after about five minutes. Allow the pairs to discuss the difficulties they had in describing and drawing this picture, and to finish off the picture.

Whole-class shared work
● Insert ten different shapes with straight sides at the top of a blank page. Press on the shapes and select Properties from the dropdown menu to add colour.
● State that, in this lesson, the class will be investigating quadrilaterals. Type or write the term *quadrilateral* on the page and establish that it refers to any four-sided shape.
● Use the Lines tool to create a two-column table (a rectangle with an outline and lines to mark the rows and columns) underneath the shapes and label the columns *Quadrilaterals* and *Not quadrilaterals*.
● Ask the children to select a shape and drag it to the table in the corresponding column. Can they tell you how many of the shapes are quadrilaterals?
● Ask the class to list the properties of a quadrilateral. Write their suggestions next to the *Quadrilaterals* column.
● Display this throughout the lesson so that the children can refer to it when working on the independent activity.

Independent work
● Using a pin board and an elastic band, ask the children to investigate the different quadrilaterals that can be made. Extend the investigation by asking them to find the total number of quadrilaterals made on the pin board.
● Invite the children to record the shapes in their exercise books. By recording, the children can check for repetitions.
● Ask the children to record the names of any familiar quadrilaterals.

Plenary
● Reflect on the investigation and invite the children to the whiteboard, one at a time, to draw a quadrilateral they have found. Invite each child to draw a quadrilateral, working through the whole class; the difficulty will be in not repeating one already found.
● Discuss whether a large square is the same as a small square or a square rotated to look like a diamond. Ask: *Do you count these as one or two quadrilaterals?*

Whiteboard tools
Use the Screen Shade to hide the screen in advance. Use the Lines tools to create a table. Use the interactive timer from the Gallery images supplied in the 'Build your own' file (under My Content) to add a timed element to an activity.

 Pen tray

 Shapes tool

 Screen Shade

 Lines tool

 Gallery

Base-10 numbers

Starter
Display page 2 of the 'Place value' Notebook file. Ask the class to count, in turn, the hundreds numbers, the tens and the ones (or units). Highlight a tens number and a ones number. Invite a child to write the two-digit number that it produces on screen and read it out.

Press the Undo button until the page has been reset and repeat for a three-digit number.

Go to page 3 and use the Fill Colour tool to fill one of the yellow boxes to reveal a number. Ask the children to make the given number using the hundreds, tens and units on the page.

Whole-class shared work
● Go to page 4. Point out the numeral 1 and ask the children how it could be shown with base-10 blocks. Reveal the base-10 block by deleting the red panel.
● Ask the children what the blocks under the 10 will look like. Again, delete the rectangle to reveal the shape beneath it.
● Repeat with 100 and 1000. Point out that 100 is shown by ten blocks across and ten blocks down (10 × 10 = 100), and 1000 by ten layers of 100 squares (10 × 100 = 1000).
● Write a three-digit number in the box on page 5. Ask the children to read the number out loud. Prompt them to consider place value, with questions such as: *How many hundreds are in the number? Which digit represents the tens number?*
● Ask the children to drag the correct number of base-10 cubes to the centre of the page to represent this number. Ask the rest of the class to check whether they are correct.
● Reset the page by using the Undo button and repeat with other numbers such as 999 or 600.

Independent work
● In pairs, the children should take turns to write a two- or three-digit number on their whiteboard, while the other represents it using base-10 cubes.
● Reverse the activity; one child selects a number of hundreds, tens and ones blocks and the other has to write down the number represented.
● This activity can be extended to include base-10 cubes to 1000 or simplified to numbers less than 100.

Plenary
● Ask children to demonstrate the numbers they have made, especially if anyone made numbers over 1000.
● Using a child's example of a three-digit number, ask the class what they would need to do to add 10. For example, 188 would be represented by one 100-square, eight 10-sticks, and eight 1-cubes. Add a 10-stick to the eight 10-sticks and discuss why the hundreds and tens numbers remain the same. Challenge the class to think about the effects of adding another 10. *What would change? Could the number be represented differently using the base-10 blocks?* This can be modelled on page 5.
● Repeat with subtracting 1, 10 or 100.

Learning objective
PNS: Knowing and using number facts
● Derive and recall all addition and subtraction facts for each number to 20.

Resources
'Number beads' Notebook file; set of bead strings per pair; 0-20 number cards; individual whiteboards and pens.

Links to other subjects
There are no specific links for this lesson.

Bead sets

Starter
Open the *Number facts* ITP on page 2 of the 'Number beads' Notebook file. Select the hiding jar option (press on the *plus* (+) symbol to activate a minus calculation) and switch off the number sentence function. Start by showing the ten purple beads. Ask the children what subtraction fact is shown if nine beads are dropped into the hiding jar. (The number sentence should be hidden.)

Question how this subtraction fact could be recorded. Ask the children to write this on their individual whiteboards before revealing it on screen. Repeat with a different number bond to 10. The purple spots will change to yellow as they are added to the jar; encourage the children to watch the changes to the number sentence.

Whole-class shared work
● Go to page 3. On the page are two sets of 20-bead strings. Each set of ten is represented by a different colour to aid adding and subtracting numbers larger than ten.
● Discuss what the two colours represent and establish that there are ten beads of each colour. Drag across ten beads of one colour and one bead of the other colour. Ask the children to consolidate their understanding of place value and work out what is being represented.
● Record this as an addition sentence (10 + 1 = 11). Repeat with other addition bonds up to 20.
● Start at 20 beads and pull 18 back towards the left. Write it as a number sentence (20 - 18 = 2).
● Ask the children to discuss similarities and differences with the previous addition sentences. By taking away beads, you are showing a subtraction fact.
● Use the Undo button to reset the page and repeat this process with other subtraction facts from 20.

Independent work
● Working in pairs, one child turns over a number card and makes this number on a string of beads. Their partner records this number and works out the corresponding bond to 20. For example, with a number card for 12, one child drags across 12 beads, and the other works out that 12 + 8 = 20. They then swap roles.
● This activity can be extended or simplified using higher or lower number bonds and sets of number cards.
● After recording 10 bonds, the pairs then work through a different pile of cards using subtraction facts. For example if 11 is on the cards, 11 beads are pulled away from 20. The subtraction sentence will be 20 - 11 = 9.

Plenary
● Ask some children to demonstrate different addition or subtraction facts. This can be done using the whiteboard bead string or their own bead string on the table.
● Write their examples of number sentences on page 4.

Whiteboard tools

 Pen tray

 Select tool

 Undo button

Number bars

Starter
Consolidate the children's rapid recall of addition and subtraction facts to 10.
Prepare a series of blank Notebook pages with an enlarged number from 0–
10 written on each page in a random order.

Allow thinking time for the class to say the corresponding number bond to
10 before forwarding to the next number. Alternatively, ask them to respond
using a number fan.

Use a variety of questions to encourage mental subtraction and addition
such as: *10 subtract 6 leaves what? 5 and what number bond makes 10?*

Whole-class shared work
● On the whiteboard, display a set of Cuisenaire rods representing all the
numbers from 1 to 10. Invite individuals to the board to drag images for
number bonds to 10 from the Gallery 🖼 (such as 2 and 8). Record the
addition sentence next to it.
● Ask the children to think how the rods can be used to represent 12 and 8
for number bonds to 20. Referring back to the place value of 12,
demonstrate how 12 can be made from 10 and 2. Ask how other numbers
from 11 to 19 could be made.
● Invite the children to think about the subtraction facts. Probe their
understanding by showing 20 as 10 and 10 and ask what would be left if
7 were taken away. Demonstrate replacing the 10 rod for a 7 and a 3, then
removing the 7 rod.
● Record the subtraction sentence next to the rods and repeat with other
subtraction facts.

Independent work
● Ask pairs of more confident learners to use a set of Cuisenaire rods to
represent addition and subtraction facts to 20. Let them record the work
in their exercise books.
● While the children are doing this, ask the remainder of the class to work
towards producing a class display for number bonds to 20, which will show
the bond represented by Cuisenaire rods, with the addition and
subtraction number sentences below. For classes of up to 30 children,
extend the activity to number bonds to 30.
● Ensure that all the children use the same length and colour of paper to
represent different numbers, or use photocopiable page 91 as a template
and colour the rods. Prepare strips for children with fine motor skills
difficulties.

Plenary
● Consolidate the children's rapid recall of addition and subtraction facts to
20. Prepare a series of blank Notebook pages with an enlarged number
from 0–20 written on each page.
● Allow thinking time for the class to say the corresponding number bond to
20 before forwarding to the next number.
● Alternate questions where the answer requires a mental subtraction and a
mental addition. For example: *20 subtract 16 leaves?* or *15 and what
number bond makes 20?*

2s, 5s and 10s

Learning objective
PNS: Knowing and using number facts
● Derive and recall multiplication facts for the 2-, 5- and 10-times tables.

Resources
'2s, 5s and 10s' Notebook file; photocopiable page 92 '2s, 5s and 10s'; sorting rings or pens and large paper.

Links to other subjects
There are no specific links for this lesson.

Starter
Open the '2s, 5s and 10s' Notebook file and go to page 2. Count up and back to 100 in multiples of 10, then 5. Count up and back in twos starting from any two-digit number.

Delete the square covering the interactive 100-square. Ask the children to repeat the counting, and change the multiples of 2 in yellow as they do so. Repeat with red for multiples of 5 and blue for multiples of 10. Ask the children to discuss why some yellow squares change to red and then to blue.

Talk about the created pattern and how that pattern would look on a 200-square grid.

Whole-class shared work
● Establish the definition of a multiple on page 3.
● Ask the children to discuss with a partner how they recognise whether a number is a multiple of 5, 2 or 10. Write these ideas on the board.
● On page 4, there are various two- and three-digit multiples of 2, 5 and 10. Point to a multiple of 2 and ask questions such as: *How can we tell __ is a multiple of 2?*
● Highlight a number ending in zero. Ask questions such as: *Is this a multiple of 2? How do we know? Is it a multiple of another times table? How do you know?*
● Go to page 5, which shows some numbers around a sorting ring. Invite the children to drag and re-position a multiple of 2 into the ring.
● Press the Undo button until the numbers return to their unsorted position. Clone the sorting ring and position it to overlap with the existing ring to form a Venn diagram.
● Sort the numbers according to multiples of 2 and 5 and discuss where to place those numbers ending in zero (multiples of both 2 and 5).

Independent work
● In small groups, sort a set of two- and three-digit numbers using photocopiable page 92, '2s, 5s and 10s'.
● Sort the given numbers into a Venn diagram with three rings and label the rings.
● There may be confusion over those numbers that are not a multiple of either 2, 5 or 10 and children can discuss whether they are multiples of other times tables. These numbers are placed outside the rings.
● Encourage the children to state that they know that *y is a multiple of x because...*

Plenary
● Load the *Number dial* ITP on page 6; the number *2* should be the default number in the centre. Ask the children to complete the dial with the corresponding multiplication fact. Press the empty boxes to reveal the answers.
● Hide both inner and outer numbers by pressing on them. Ask questions such as: *If the answer is 18, what is the question?*
● If there is time, repeat with either the five- or ten-times table. Discuss any misconceptions.

Whiteboard tools
Use the Pen tool to select different colours for values on the interactive 100-square. Press on an object and select Clone from the dropdown menu to duplicate it.

 Pen tray

 Select tool

 Pen tool

 Highlighter pen

 Delete button

 On-screen Keyboard

 Undo button

Learning objective
PNS: Calculating
● Understand that division is the inverse of multiplication and vice versa; use this to derive and record related multiplication and division number sentences.

Resources
Number Line ITP from 'Ordering numbers' Notebook file, dry-wipe number lines and pens.

Links to other subjects
There are no specific links for this lesson.

Repeated subtraction groups

Starter
Recap the language used for division, such as *shared by, grouped, divided into, divided by* and so on.

Use the Shapes tool 🔲 to insert an equilateral triangle on a blank page. Display two numbers at the base and their product at the top as illustrate below.

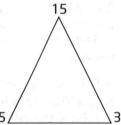

Ask the children to use these numbers to record three multiplication or division sentences. For example: 5 × 3 = 15; 3 × 5 = 15; 15 ÷ 3 = 5; 15 ÷ 5 = 3. Emphasise that division is the inverse of multiplication.

Repeat with another trio of numbers.

Whole-class shared work
● Load the *Number Line* ITP on page 2 of the 'Ordering numbers' Notebook file. Display a number line to 30. Draw arrows jumping back in equal steps of ten, demonstrating that there are three equal steps.

● Stress that one way to say this is that ten can be repeatedly subtracted from 30, three times. Ask the children if there is another way we could say this calculation. For example: *30 divided by 10 is 3.*

● Show that multiplication is an inverse of division: check the calculation by counting up in steps of ten from zero to 30. If we know that three tens are 30, we also know from the Starter that 30 ÷ 10 is 3.

● Repeat and check with other calculations such as 30 ÷ 5; 30 ÷ 2; 28 ÷ 4 on a new Notebook page. Check using the inverse operation.

● Emphasise that the repeated subtraction steps must be equal, so 28 ÷ 4 means that the children have to subtract groups of four.

● Show a division calculation on the number line with an uneven backwards jump. Ask children to spot the mistake and invite a volunteer to come to the board to correct it.

Independent work
● Using empty number lines, invite the children to work through a series of division calculations displayed on the board. For example, 20 ÷ 4; 36 ÷ 6; 10 ÷ 2, and so on.

● Ensure they mark equal numbers of repeated subtraction jumps on the line and record how many jumps/multiples are subtracted, before recording the calculation in their mathematics books. For example, 20 ÷ 4 takes five jumps to get back to zero, so 20 ÷ 4 = 5.

● Choose end-numbers and calculations that suit the children's abilities.

Plenary
● Present an empty number line, which shows four jumps backwards. Write 8 at the far end and 0 at the beginning.

● Ask the children to write a division calculation for this image. (8 ÷ 2 = 4.)

● Emphasise the relationship between division and multiplication by jumping forward in steps of two, so four jumps of two will result in eight. Ask the children how they would write this as a calculation. (4 × 2 = 8.)

Whiteboard tools
Use the Shapes tool to draw a triangle.

 Pen tray

 Shapes tool

 Highlighter pen

Sharing and grouping

Learning objective
PNS: Calculating
● Understand that division is the inverse of multiplication and vice versa.

Resources
Number bars or Cuisenaire rods; exercise books.

Links to other subjects
There are no specific links for this lesson.

Starter
As a whole class, count up and back in multiples of 2 from any given two-digit number. Ask children to distinguish a multiple of two from its end digit.
Repeat with multiples of 10 and then 5.
Type the four calculation symbols on a new Notebook page and ask for their meanings.
Ask the children to compare and contrast the calculations 10 ÷ 2 and 2 ÷ 10.

Whole-class shared work
● Go to a new Notebook page. Demonstrate two different ways to divide 16 by 2. Use eight *2*-rods from the Gallery to make 16 (eight sets of 2 makes 16); match two identical rods to find out which ones add up to 16 (two 8-rods will make 16).
● Drag two *10*-rods and a *5*-rod onto the page. Rotate the rods to form a vertical tower and write the calculation 25 ÷ 5 = at the top of the page. Match the height of the tower with rods of 5. How many *5*-rods are needed to be equivalent to the 25-rod?
● Subtract one *5*-rod at a time from the tower of 25 (made by five lots of 5). Stress that 25 divided by 5 is 5.
● Ask the children how this answer can be checked, and emphasise the relationships between division and multiplication: 5 × 5 = 25.
● Repeat with other calculations such as 24 ÷ 3 or 50 ÷ 10, using multiplication to check the answers.

Independent work
● Give each group a set of number bars or Cuisenaire rods.
● Set a series of calculations for the class or each group on the whiteboard. The children should work through the calculations, first building the dividend with the number bars, and then equally subtracting the divisor. Let the children record the calculations in their exercise books.
● Once finished, the children make up five of their own calculations, write them down and swap them with a partner.

Plenary
● Reflect on the lesson, stressing the fact that division is the inverse of multiplication.
● Ask the children to list the multiplication and division facts they know about ten, five and two. Challenge them to write these facts in number sentences.
● Using this information, ask the children to respond to *empty box* type questions such as 10÷__ = 5 or __ ÷ 5 = 2.
● Challenge the children to invent *empty box* type questions for 30, 6 and 5.

Whiteboard tools
Select Cuisenaire rods from the Gallery.

 Pen tray

 Select tool

 On-screen Keyboard

 Gallery

How many squares?

Learning objective
PNS: Using and applying mathematics
● Identify patterns and relationships involving numbers or shapes, and use these to solve problems.

Resources
Photocopiable page 93 'Squares'.

Links to other subjects
Art and design
QCA Unit 3B 'Investigating pattern'
● Investigating different patterns and spotting different 2D shapes.
Speaking and listening
Objective 33: To sustain conversation, explaining or giving reasons for their views or choices.
● Ask the children to explain and justify their answers.

Starter
Ask the children to explain to a partner their definition of a *square*. Use the Shapes tool to insert a square on a blank Notebook page. Ask a volunteer to describe how this can be changed so that it is no longer a square.

Select the square and then press and drag the bottom right-hand corner until it clearly becomes a rectangle. Ask the children to explain the definition of a rectangle. Write some of their suggestions on the board.

Whole-class shared work
● Prepare a five-square grid on the next page (using an outlined white square and lines). Ask the children to state how many squares they see.
● To promote the objective of explaining and reasoning, carry out paired work first (see below) before returning to whole-class work.
● Allow the children to experiment on their copies of the photocopiable page and, if necessary, hint that a square may also contain four squares. Demonstrate this by highlighting a 2 × 2 square in a bright colour.
● Ask how many of these they can find by working it out on their sheets.
● Prompt the children to think about how big the squares could be (they should suggest that you can have 3 × 3 and 4 × 4 squares).
● Push the children to explain to their partners what they are thinking and doing. Encourage them to work systematically.
● Help the children to think of ways to indicate the number of different types of squares.

Independent work
● Give each child a copy of photocopiable page 93 'Squares', and tell them that they have to investigate how many squares they can see.
● Ask the children to work individually for a few minutes then ask them to discuss their initial responses with partners. Initially they may only count the obvious 25 individual squares.

Plenary
● Ask the children to explain how they reached their final number of squares.
● Invite one child to the whiteboard to demonstrate orally and to indicate how they found the total number, using a Highlighter pen. Repeat with another child. Emphasise that they need to give a clear reason for their answer.
● Finish the lesson by demonstrating that 55 total squares are in the grid. It is made up of 25 single squares; sixteen 2 × 2 squares, nine 3 × 3 squares, four 4 × 4 squares and one 5 × 5 square. Use different colours to highlight the different-sized squares.
● Demonstrate your reasoning by working through the different-sized squares systematically, keeping track of the number using a tally, and then adding up the totals.

Whiteboard tools
Create a 5 × 5 table using an outlined square, from the Shapes tool, crossed with lines from the Lines tool.

 Pen tray

 Select tool

 Lines tool

 Shapes tool

 Highlighter pen

What time is it?

Learning objective
PNS: Measuring
● Read the time on a 12-hour digital clock and to the nearest five minutes on an analogue clock.

Resources
'What time is it?' Notebook file; photocopiable page 94 'What time is it?'; individual whiteboards and pens; paper; pencils; scissors; glue.

Links to other subjects
Science
QCA Unit 3F 'Light and shadows'
● Use units of time for measuring experiments, for example, the growth of plants in terms of days or weeks and sundials in terms of hours.

Starter
Open the 'What time is it?' Notebook file and establish the learning objective with the children: they will be learning about telling the time with analogue and digital clocks. Go to page 2. Ask the children to say and then record the time on their individual whiteboards. Establish that the time is 4 o'clock.

Draw attention to the digital clock next to the analogue clock. Again, ask the children to say and then record the time on a whiteboard. Establish that the two clocks show the same time. Ask the children to compare and contrast how the times appear.

Repeat with the times on pages 3 and 4. Page 3 shows the times to the half hour and quarter past on both the analogue and the digital clocks, and page 4 shows the time at quarter to the hour and at five minutes to the hour.

Whole-class shared work
● Ask the children to discuss, in pairs, what time they do certain things such as getting up, eating breakfast, leaving for school and arriving at school.
● Go to page 5 and open the *What time is it?* activity. This sequencing program shows different images of morning routines. Ask the pairs to order the images according to their experiences. There may be discussions about whether the face should be washed before the teeth are cleaned or vice versa.
● Drag the agreed first image into the first space (top left), then continue to sequence the other pictures according to the opinions of the majority of the class. (Although there is an *Am I correct?* button that takes one particular sequence as correct, the children's own routines may vary.)
● Once the sequence is agreed, ask the children what time is displayed on the analogue clock in the first image of the sequencing activity. *How would this be written on the digital clock?*
● Drag the digital clock template from the right to the first image and write the correct time onto it.
● Repeat with another picture (using the digital and analogue clock templates) until all six images have a time written in both formats.

Independent work
● Hand out copies of photocopiable page 94 'What time is it?'. Ask the children to cut out and sequence night-time routines, according to their own experiences.
● Once the pictures have been cut out and glued into the correct order, ask the children to record an approximate time for each events in both analogue and digital formats.
● Simplify the activity by asking the children to sort the pictures to given times on the hour and half-hour, from 5 to 7pm and/or use the analogue clock only.

Plenary
● Ask the children to share their sequenced pictures. *Do you go to bed at different times or about the same time? Who has tea at half-past five?*
● Invite the children to think about important times in their school day.
● Make a list of all of these times on page 6. Recognise which activities happen in the morning or afternoon and whether they use *am* or *pm*.

Whiteboard tools
Use a Pen from the Pen tray to write the time on digital clock faces. Use the Select tool to add and position the hands on the analogue clocks. Rotate the hands by moving the arrows around.

 Pen tray

 Select tool

Learning objective
PNS: Measuring

Resources
'Birthdays' Notebook file; a calendar for each table; the months of the year written on cards. (Microsoft Excel is required to view the embedded spreadsheet in the Notebook file.)

Links to other subjects
History
PoS (1b) To use dates and vocabulary relating to the passing of time.
● Recognise significant dates in a year in history and work out how much time is in between each date.

Birthdays

Starter
Read out the following rhyme from page 2 of the 'Birthdays' Notebook file:
> *30 days hath September, April, June and November*
> *All the rest have 31 except for February alone*
> *Which hath but 28 days clear and 29 in each leap year.*

Ask the class to say it in unison. Ask questions such as: *How many days does July have? Which months have 30 days?*

Give 12 children a card with a month written on it and repeat the rhyme. When the month is said the child with the correct card should raise it. Repeat the rhyme, but faster!

Whole-class shared work
● On page 3, establish the correct order of the months of the year with the children. Drag and drop the months into the numbered boxes.
● Press the hyperlinked button to open a calendar in a spreadsheet format. Display the correct year by selecting the appropriate worksheet at the bottom of the page. Ask three children at a time to come to the whiteboard and identify the month and date they were born.
● Highlight the dates by filling the cells with a colour. Record the children's birthdays by selecting the appropriate cell, using the Pen tool from the Floating tools to write, and pressing Insert Drawing as Text.
● When all the children's birthdays been have highlighted on the board, assess the information. Do any of them share a birthday? How many birthdays are in January? Which is the least popular birthday month? Many of these questions could form the basis of future data-handling investigations.
● Highlight what is meant by a leap year. Discuss whether the current year is a leap year. Ask how the children could find out.
● Choose two different birthdays and ask the class how they would work out how many months and days are between them.
● Model counting on from the first birthday in days to the end of the month, and then counting the whole months and the subsequent individual days to the second birthday. Present the answer as x months and x days.
● Establish which child will have the next birthday and count the number of months and days to it.

Independent work
● Let the children use the correct year diary to count on the number of whole months and days from the current day to other significant dates such as the end of term or the teacher's birthday!
● Ask the children to find out significant dates in the lives of their family and investigate how many months/days there are between birthdays, whose birthday is next and by how long, and so on.

Plenary
● Go to page 4. Choose one child's birthday. State that the class are going to investigate that child's age to the nearest day. Check the exact number of days the child has been alive by counting on whole years from their birth date, then whole months and finally days.
● Children know their age in years but will be less familiar with the year they were born. Consequently, start counting back in years to establish the year of birth.

Whiteboard tools
Use the Floating tools to annotate the embedded spreadsheet in the Notebook file. Fix annotations to the page by selecting Insert Drawing as Text/Image from the SMART Aware toolbar.

 Pen tray

 Select tool

 Floating tools

 Insert Drawing as Text

 Insert Drawing as Image

Learning objective
PNS: Understanding shape
● Relate 2D shapes to drawings of them; describe, visualise, classify, draw and make the shapes.

Resources
'Shapes and patterns' Notebook file; a selection of 2D shapes (or copy photocopiable page 95 'Shapes and patterns' onto card and cut out the shapes); paper; pencils; individual whiteboards and pens.

Links to other subjects
Art and design
QCA Unit 3B 'Investigating pattern'
● Create a repeating pattern using colours and shapes and/or printed images.

Shapes and patterns

Starter
Look at the sequence of shapes on page 2 of the 'Shapes and patterns' Notebook file. Ask the children to predict what the next shape in the sequence might be. Discuss why this is difficult to predict at this stage. Move the box to reveal the shape. Uncover a smaller version of the sequence at the bottom of the page, then ask the children to describe verbally the sequence for the next four places. (There is an infinite number of these shapes on the page, so they can be dragged from behind each other to continue the sequence, if required.)

In pairs, using individual whiteboards, ask one person to choose two shapes and start a pattern. After the fifth shape in the pattern, their partner predicts what the next one will be and draws the pattern for the next five places.

Whole-class shared work
● Go to page 3 of the Notebook file. Tell the children that a shape is hidden in the dark. Move the torch around to see it. Ask the children to guess what the shape is.
● Move slowly around the edges of the shape and encourage the children to count the sides.
● Ask those who predicted correctly to say how they could tell it was an octagon. Write the octagon's properties around the shape.
● Go to page 4 and build up a pattern around the hexagon. Insert a square using the Shapes tool and position it against a flat edge of the hexagon using the rotate function. The square may need to be resized to fit.
● Repeat with seven further squares. Establish the properties of a square. Are the squares positioned at an angle still squares?
● Ask the children to identify the shape that would fit the gaps between the squares. This could be a triangle, rhombus or parallelogram. Add one of these shapes and resize, rotate and drag them to fit between the squares.
● Decide whether to tessellate the image (discuss the definition) or create a pattern containing gaps.

Independent work
● Ask the children to build up a vertical or horizontal pattern using three different shapes from an assortment of 2D shapes.
● Ask the children to record the pattern on paper. They may use a different colour for specific shapes. Some may be able to develop this by filling a whole page. Less confident learners may find it easier to use one or two shapes.

Plenary
● Look at the images on page 5. Focus on one of the images and using a Highlighter pen, trace around the shape that is repeated. Ask the children to list the properties of that shape and to decide whether this shape can tessellate. Annotate the image with their suggestions. Repeat this with the rest of the images.
● Finish the lesson by creating an example of a repeating pattern using the Shapes tool on page 6 and agreeing on a definition of the term *tessellation* on page 7.

Whiteboard tools
Use the Shapes tool to add shapes to the Notebook page.

 Pen tray

 Select tool

 Highlighter pen

 Shapes tool

 Delete button

Spot the right angle

Starter

Ask pairs of children to use two geostrips with a pivot or two strips of paper with a split-pin to discuss and make right angles. Ask questions to reinforce the definition of a right angle (being the point at which the vertical and horizontal lines meet). State that we use the term *acute* and *obtuse* for angles smaller or larger, respectively, than a right angle. Look at and discuss the different angles on page 2 of the 'Right angles' Notebook file.

If the children find it difficult to make a right angle, suggest that they fold a piece of paper and use the fold as a right-angle template. Secure the paper or geostrips into position and use them for the main part of the lesson.

Whole-class shared work

● Look at page 3 of the Notebook file. Ask the pairs to identify three right angles in the picture, using their right-angle templates to justify their findings.
● Use the right-angle shape, which has already been placed on the page, to confirm the children's answers, rotating the shape by pressing it and dragging the green dot, if necessary.
● Select a red Pen to draw over the right angles. The children may mistake obtuse and acute angles as right angles. Discuss the differences between obtuse (more than 90°) and acute angles (less than 90°) and highlight the obtuse angles in yellow and acute in blue.
● On angles that require further clarification, use the Area Capture tool to take a snapshot of the relevant section of the image, paste this onto a blank page, and then enlarge it to look at the image in more detail.
● Repeat this process for the images on pages 4 to 7.

Independent work

● Using the right-angle template, identify right angles from a printed or magazine picture.
● Challenge the children to find five right, five obtuse and five acute angles. Encourage them to record their findings by: drawing over the angle with the colours used during the whole-class teaching; cutting out the image and positioning it in a table with headings for the three different types of angles; or drawing the objects, and highlighting and labelling the angles.
● To extend more confident learners, discuss that angles are measured in degrees, and allow pupils to investigate what a protractor might be used for.

Plenary

● A number of angles are hidden behind circles on page 8. Reduce the size of a circle to gradually reveal a small section and ask pupils to state whether the angle is right, acute or obtuse. Ask whether they have enough information or whether they need more to be revealed.
● Reveal the whole angle by reducing or deleting the circle. What kind of angle is it?
● Drag the black box over the angle to reveal whether it is an obtuse, acute or right angle.
● Repeat this, if necessary, with more of the hidden angles.
● Re-establish the definition of a right angle on page 8.

Sorting right angles

Learning objective
PNS: Understanding shape
● Identify right angles in 2D shapes; compare angles with a right angle.

Resources [P]
Photocopiable page 96 'Sorting right angles'; scissors; glue; large paper; sorting hoops.

Links to other subjects
PE
QCA Unit 19 'Outdoor and adventurous activities'
● Challenge the children to devise a route that involves right angles and ask them to work out how many right angles were on their route.

Starter
Ask the children to hold one arm out straight and then to bend the elbow so that their fingertips are pointing directly to the ceiling. Tell them that their arm is now in a right-angled position. Ask them to move their arm into a right-angled position that points to the floor, and then one that points forwards.

Whole-class shared work
● Ask the children to fold a square or rectangular piece of paper in half. The corner will act as a right-angled template for this lesson.
● Insert a square onto a blank Notebook page using the Shapes tool . Ask a child to come to the whiteboard to confirm, with the use of their template, that the square has four right angles.
● Select a rectangle and ask another child to confirm whether this shape has right angles, and if so, how many. Highlight each of the right angles.
● On the next page, create a Venn diagram with two sorting rings. Create the circles with the Shapes tool.
● Place five different shapes around it. At least one shape should have: no right angles; one right angle; only right angles. Children may not know the names of all these shapes, but should be asked to identify which shapes have no right angles at all.
● Label one hoop *all right angles*, the other *one or more right angles* and the outer area *no right angles*.
● Invite one child at a time to drag a shape to the appropriate area of the Venn diagram.
● After all five shapes have been sorted, discuss whether any were difficult to place.

Independent work
● Hand out a copy of photocopiable page 96 'Sorting right angles', scissors and a large piece of paper to each child.
● Ask them to sort the set of assorted shapes into groups with: *all right angles*; *one or more right angles* and *no right angles*.
● Invite them to copy the Venn diagram circles and labels onto their piece of paper. Challenge them to sort and glue their shapes into the correct areas of the Venn diagram.

Plenary
● Delete the shapes from the Venn diagram on your Notebook page and drag and drop a variety of 20 different shapes to the side of the page. Create irregular shape outlines with the Lines tool . Marquee select your shape and choose Group from the dropdown menu to convert the lines into one object.
● Invite individuals to identify a shape and to drag it to the correct part of the Venn diagram.
● If the class do not agree where a shape has been placed, use this as a teaching point to consolidate the definition of a right angle and to allow the child to check whether the shape has right angles, using the folded template.

Whiteboard tools
Add labels to your Venn diagram with the On-screen Keyboard. Use the Lines tool to create irregular shapes.

 Pen tray

 Select tool

 Shapes tool

 On-screen Keyboard

 Lines tool

 Delete button

Learning objective
PNS: Counting and understanding number
● Count on from and back to zero in multiples of 10.

Resources
'Build your own' file; number lines; 100/200 grids (you will need to copy the 200-square grid from the 'Hundreds, tens and ones' Notebook file); photocopiable page 97 'Counting'.

Links to other subjects
There are no specific links for this lesson.

Counting

Starter
Display the interactive 100-square grid from Mathematics folder under My Content 📷. Highlight a row and ask the children what is common to each number along the row. Identify the place value of the digits.

Choose one number in the row and count up and/or back in tens. Establish what is common to these counted numbers. Repeat with another number.

Display the 200-square grid (see Resources) on a new Notebook page. Locate a digit below 100 and count on by 10, ten times. Point out that the children have just counted on by 100 because 10 × 10 = 100. Ask: *How have the start and end numbers changed?*

Whole-class shared work
● Display a number line to 100. Starting at zero, mark the jumps forward in tens as the class count aloud.
● On reaching 100, extend the line to 200, and continue counting on in tens and marking the jumps. Some children may struggle bridging the 100, so draw the similarities between the 0–100 line and the 100–200 line.
● On reaching 200, count back in tens past 100.
● Erase the jump marks and return to a clear number line. Choose a three-digit number between 150 and 200 and mark it clearly on the whiteboard, for example, 186.
● Ask the children to count back from this number by 100. Discuss strategies for working this out. These may include mentally subtracting 10, ten times or using place value to quickly subtract the 100 from 186, to leave 80 and 6. Mark the jump of 100.
● From 86 count back in tens to 36. Ask how many tens have been counted back. Ask the children to describe what is happening when counting back in tens, and mark the jumps on the line.
● From 36 count up in tens, questioning the strategies children use.

Independent work
● Give a copy of photocopiable page 97 'Counting' to each child. Ask them to count on or back in tens or hundreds from the start number to the end of the line. Suggest that they record the numbers on the marks along the line.
● Display the 200-square grid and/or the number line to support the children.

Plenary
● Open the PDF of the photocopiable page 'Counting' on the CD-ROM. Work through the page together, using the Floating tools 🔲 to complete the number lines on the board.
● Write a series of cloze-style questions that require adding or subtracting 10 or 100 on the board, and ask the children to fill in the blanks. For example: *350 - __ = 250* or *__ + 65 = 75.*
● Ask the class to count from zero to 100 in tens, and then from 100 to 1000 in hundreds. Finally count back in hundreds and then tens until they get back to zero.

Whiteboard tools
Select number lines and 100-square grids from the Gallery images supplied under My Content.

 Pen tray

 Gallery

 Floating tools

Half a shape

Starter
Establish what $\frac{1}{2}$ or $\frac{1}{10}$ means when applied to a shape. Ask how a quarter or a fifth is written. Ask what the 4 in $\frac{1}{4}$ means and what the difference is between the 1 and the 3 in $\frac{1}{3}$.

Ask pairs to investigate how many ways a rectangle can be divided in half. Invite different children to come to the board and record their solutions on separate rectangles. Establish that if a shape is divided in half, then both halves should be equal.

Challenge the children to consider whether there would be more ways to divide a square in half than a rectangle.

Whole-class shared work
● Use the Shapes tool to produce an unfamiliar shape on a blank page such as a cross made from five squares.
● Write the following fractions: $\frac{1}{2}$, $\frac{1}{5}$ and $\frac{1}{10}$. Ask into which fractions the shape can be easily divided. Investigate whether there is only one way to show half this shape.
● Invite individuals to the whiteboard to show how they would divide the shape in half using the Pen tool on a thin setting. To clarify the $\frac{1}{2}$, use the Pen tool on a thick setting to colour in half the shape.
● Repeat the process, finding how many ways $\frac{1}{5}$ can be shown.
● Challenge the children to investigate how $\frac{1}{10}$ could be shown when the shape is made from only five squares.

Independent work
● Give the children different pre-cut shapes such as the cross or an L shape, a rectangle or circle.
● List $\frac{1}{2}$, $\frac{1}{3}$, $\frac{1}{4}$, $\frac{1}{5}$ and $\frac{1}{10}$ on the board and ask the children to choose one to be used to divide the shape. Challenge more confident learners by choosing $\frac{1}{5}$ or $\frac{1}{10}$ or simplify by asking the children to find a half or a quarter of regular shapes.
● The children may fold and colour the shapes, but will need many of the same shapes to investigate different solutions.

Plenary
● Invite each child to take 10, 20 or 30 cubes depending on their ability. Encourage the children to make a model with the cubes, showing half of the number of cubes in red and a tenth in yellow.
● Challenge the children to show $\frac{1}{3}$, $\frac{1}{4}$ or $\frac{1}{5}$ in other colours.
● Break up the models and draw a shape made up of 10, 20 or 30 squares. Repeat the above by colouring in the correct number of squares and producing a colour-coded key to the side.

Fractions

Learning objective
PNS: Counting and understanding number
● Read and write proper fractions, interpreting the denominator as the parts of a whole and the numerator as the number of parts; identify and estimate fractions of shapes; use diagrams to compare fractions.

Resources 🅿
Number bars, such as Cuisenaire rods; a variety of objects, counters or cubes; photocopiable page 98 'Fractions of shapes'. Prepare a six-column by five-row table in a text document ready to import into a new Notebook page during the Plenary (see below).

Links to other subjects
There are no specific links for this lesson.

Starter
Ask the children for rapid recall of halving facts of even numbers to 50. Ask pairs to share strategies and record some of these on the whiteboard. For example, half of 40 then half of 10.

To clarify any misunderstandings, drag Cuisenaire rods from the Gallery 🖼 and demonstrate dividing these into two equal amounts.

Discuss what you need to divide a number by to find half of the number. What would the number be divided by to find $\frac{1}{5}$ or $\frac{1}{10}$? Reiterate that fractions are linked to division.

Whole-class shared work
● Insert an object from the Gallery in a blank Notebook page and duplicate it until there are 20.
● Ask the children how they would find half of the 20. Model suggested grouping or sharing strategies. Establish that half of 20 is 10 and record this sentence on the board. Ask the children to think of another way of writing this, such as: *20 ÷ 2 = 10*.
● Ask the children to rewrite the sentence using a multiplication fact. Establish a link to the multiples: 10 × 2 = 20.
● Repeat this process to find $\frac{1}{5}$. Show that $\frac{1}{5}$ of 20 is 4 while $\frac{4}{5}$ is 16 because it is the same as 4 × 4.
● Use this technique to find $\frac{1}{3}$. Some children will attempt to do this, so model any strategies they have used. Lead the children to conclude that $\frac{1}{3}$ of 20 cannot be found (unless there is a remainder).
● Write 20 on a new Notebook page and ask the children to work out $\frac{1}{4}$ and $\frac{1}{10}$.

Independent work
● Give each group a copy of photocopiable page 98 'Fractions of shapes' and ask the children to divide them to find $\frac{1}{2}$, $\frac{1}{3}$, $\frac{1}{4}$, $\frac{1}{5}$, and $\frac{1}{10}$ of that number. Invite the children to record these fractions in a number sentence in their books, such as 12 ÷ 4 = 3.

Plenary
● On a new page, use the Lines tool ◥ to create a table with six columns and five rows. In the top row, leave the first cell blank and then enter the following as headings: $\frac{1}{2}$, $\frac{1}{3}$, $\frac{1}{4}$, $\frac{1}{5}$, and $\frac{1}{10}$. Write in a variety of two-digit numbers in the left-hand column (See diagram below).

	$\frac{1}{2}$	$\frac{1}{3}$	$\frac{1}{4}$	$\frac{1}{5}$	$\frac{1}{10}$
30	15	10		6	3
44	22		11		
27		9			

● Ask the class to work out $\frac{1}{2}$, $\frac{1}{3}$, $\frac{1}{4}$, $\frac{1}{5}$, or $\frac{1}{10}$ of the numbers, filling in the cells where possible. Blank cells would mean that fractions can't be found for certain numbers, without a remainder.
● Discuss any remaining numbers and establish that these cannot be divided by these fractions because they are not multiples of 2, 3, 4, 5 or 10.

Whiteboard tools
Select number bars or Cuisenaire rods from the Gallery. Press on an object and select Clone from the dropdown menu to create multiple copies.

 Pen tray

 Select tool

 Gallery

 Blank Page button

 Lines tool

Word problems

Learning objective
PNS: Using and applying mathematics
● Solve one- and two- step problems involving numbers, choosing and carrying out appropriate calculations.

Resources
'Word problem' Notebook file; counters or interlocking cubes; digital camera or scanning equipment.

Links to other subjects
Speaking and listening
Objective 25: To explain a process or present information clearly.
● Encourage the children to explain how they worked out the problem by role playing the situation.

Starter
Ask a group of children to demonstrate how to role play a real life scenario, but represent the problem in writing. For example: *There are three swings in the playground, and 18 children in our class. How many need to line up behind each swing so an equal number of children use each swing?* Write the problem on page 2 of the 'Word problem' Notebook file.

The group need to represent the swings with, for example, a chair, and divide the children one at a time to stand behind it. Ask: *How many children are lined up?*

Return the children to their seats and ask them how they would write the answer to the word problem in a sentence. Emphasise that the problem was carried out using a division/sharing method.

Whole-class shared work
● Read the text on page 3 of the Notebook file and look at the picture of the tractor and trailer. Children are generally more motivated by a word problem if it is illustrated.
● Ask the children to imagine the context. Have they ever visited a farm or gone on a tractor ride? If so, can they remember how many children travelled on the trailer?

Independent work
● Ask the children to work in pairs on an initial response. The emphasis here is not on recognising key words, but on understanding the context, and with it imagining the scenario. They will be using their own experience to answer the question.
● The children may not recognise the type of calculation needed immediately. They may use role play, illustrations, jottings or representations using equipment such as counters for children.
● Use page 4 with less confident learners to help them to visualise the problem. Demonstrate with a smaller number of children if necessary. (50 figures are provided on screen but delete the number as appropriate.)
● Move four children into the trailer. Drag the tractor and trailer around the farm to the finish line and then move the children out of the trailer.
● Stop the class after ten minutes and share initial responses.

Plenary
● During the course of the lesson, scan in or photograph with a digital camera different initial responses, and display them on screen.
● Ask the pairs who made the responses to share how they thought about the problem.
● Conclude with the reasoning behind the answer. Demonstrate on page 5, using repeated subtraction along a number line, that 50 divided by four equals 12 with a remainder of two. Discuss what this remainder means. Ask: *Will the two children miss a tractor ride?* Discuss what would happen and conclude that the tractor would have to make an extra trip around the farm (a total of 13).
● Write this answer in a sentence underneath the initial question on page 3 of the Notebook file.

Whiteboard tools
Use the Select tool to move the children and trailer around the screen.

 Pen tray

 Select tool

Animals pictogram

Learning objective
PNS: Handling data
● Answer a question by collecting, organising and interpreting data; use pictograms to represent results.

Resources
'Animals pictogram' Notebook file; photocopiable page 99 'Animals'; plain or squared sheets of paper; pencils.

Links to other subjects
Science
QCA Unit 3A 'Teeth and eating'
● Pictograms can be used in many contexts to record a wide range of collected information. Devise a pictogram to record the different foods that the children like to eat.

Starter
Open the 'Animals pictogram' Notebook file and start the pictogram activity on page 2. Point out the animals at the side of the pictogram. Ask general questions about the animals, such as: *Is your favourite animal here? Do you have one of these animals as a pet?*

Ask children why this data might have been collected (for example, to see which animals the children like).

Tell the children that for this lesson, they will be using the pictogram to look at which animals the children like the most. Ask the children what the title should be and where you should write it.

Whole-class shared work
● Encourage suggestions as to what the title of this pictogram could be. Type the agreed title in the box provided, using the On-screen Keyboard.
● Tell the children that when the pictogram is completed, they can use the results to find out which animals the class like best and least.
● Demonstrate how to build up the pictogram by dragging and dropping a picture from the grid into a column. Each animal has its own column; you can't put one type of animal in a column of another. To remove a picture, simply drag it off the grid.
● Invite each child to come to the front to select their favourite animal.

Independent work
● Ask the children to devise their own animals pictogram. They can choose a different question, such as: *Which animal would you like to see in a zoo?*
● Show the children how to create their own pictogram chart on squared paper, reminding them to draw the two axes and to include a title.
● Ask the children to cut out the animals on photocopiable page 99 'Animals' and glue them onto the squares in the chart. Let the children make up their own results for others to interpret.
● Suggest that pairs swap completed pictograms and interpret the new pictogram, recording answers to a series of questions written on the board. For example:
  ● *What is this pictogram about?*
  ● *Which animal has the most pictures? How many?*
  ● *Which has the least? How many?*
  ● *Were some animals not used at all? Why do you think this is?*

Plenary
● Keep the pictogram on screen and press the *Start again* button to reset the pictogram.
● Ask a child to complete the pictogram on screen, using their own data.
● Take a snapshot of the completed pictogram using the Capture tool and drag it to page 3 via the Page Sorter . Alternatively, copy the snapshot, press the back button, and paste it onto page 3.
● Ask each group to propose a question about the pictogram to another group. For example *What was the most popular animal visited at a zoo?*
● Page 4 gives an example of how different pictograms can be created on a Notebook page.

Whiteboard tools
Use the On-screen Keyboard to type a title for the pictogram. Take snapshots of completed pictograms with the Capture tool.

Pen tray

 Select tool

Capture tool

 Page Sorter

 On-screen Keyboard

Colours bar chart

Learning objective

PNS: Handling data
● Answer a question by collecting, organising and interpreting data; use frequency tables and bar charts to represent results.

Resources

'Colours bar chart' Notebook file; a prepared file containing pictures of a completed pictogram and bar chart; paper; photocopiable page 100 'Bar chart'; mixed sets of coloured pens, pencils, paints or crayons.

Links to other subjects

Bar charts can be used to interpret a wide range of information for many uses across the curriculum. For example: to collate information about classroom resources; the different ways of travelling to school; favourite subjects; different foods preferred by particular animals and so on.

Starter

Show the completed bar chart and a completed pictogram on page 2 of the 'Colours bar chart' Notebook file. Ask the children to identify similarities and differences between the two charts, for example, both have numbers on the vertical axis. Explore more challenging questions such as the difference in sample size. List these on page 3.

Whole-class shared work

● Go to page 4. This shows a table with the column headings, *Coloured pencil supply* and *Number of pencils*. Tell the children that they will be transferring this information to a bar chart.
● Open the *Colours bar chart* activity. Discuss what the labels on the vertical and horizontal axes mean.
● All the columns are set to 1. Increase and reduce the number by dragging the top of the column up or down to line up with the numbers. Set the columns to 0.
● Ask the children to read the first colour and number from the table to you.
● Demonstrate how to represent this number in a bar chart. Repeat with the rest of the colours.
● Interpret the finished bar chart together. The children may conclude that one colour is popular because it has a large representation on the bar chart, or that the most popular is the one that has the least representation because it gets used up quickly!

Independent work

● Ask each group to sort a mixture of coloured pencils by colours. They should first record the number of each colour in a table and then transfer the information onto the bar chart on photocopiable page 100.
● Show them how to draw the table and fill in the bar chart. They should colour the bars using the correct colour.
● Pose questions on page 6 to encourage the children to interpret their data. For example: *How many red pens were there? What is the difference between the number of white and black pencils? Of which colour are there fewest?*

Plenary

● Ask each group to report back on their findings. Reset the bar chart by pressing the *Start again* button and use the children's figures to complete the bar chart on the board. If the number of pencils exceeds ten, annotate the top of the column with *+1* to signify 11, *+2* for 12 and so on. Pose the same questions as before and encourage the children to interpret this data.
● Use the Area Capture tool to take a picture of the completed bar chart and add it to page 6 via the Page Sorter.
● Ask the groups to discuss who in the school would find this information useful (such as the teacher that reorders art materials).
● Page 7 gives an example of how a bar chart can be created on a Notebook page if you opt to use different colours or wish to change the scale.

Whiteboard tools

Use the Area Capture tool to take pictures of a completed bar chart, and insert it onto another page via the Page Sorter.

 Pen tray

 Select tool

 On-screen Keyboard

 Text tool

 Area Capture tool

 Page Sorter

 85

Reflections

Starter
Load the 'Symmetry' Notebook file and display the learning objectives on page 1. Ask pairs of children to stand and face each other. One child should stand in a position that has a line of symmetry, for example, arms out straight to the front, touching at fingertips. The other child must copy that position and stand alongside their partner. Stress that the position should be mirrored in the same way as a real mirror.

Go to page 2 and discuss what the terms *mirror line* and *reflection* mean.

Whole-class shared work
● Page 3 shows an arrow with a mirror line on the y axis. Ask the children what this arrow would look like if it were reflected in a mirror that was placed along the vertical line.
● Clone the arrow and position the second arrow alongside the first. Ask the children if this is what they see in the mirror.
● If the children are unsure, place a large teaching mirror along the line on the board or ask them to sketch the arrow and use individual mirrors to work it out.
● Delete the incorrect reflection and invite a child to draw the correct position of the arrow.
● Press the Right Mouse button and set the background to a different colour to reveal the reflection.
● Repeat this on page 4 and ask what the single arrow would look like if it were reflected in a horizontal mirror line. Ask a child to draw the new reflection. Set the background to a different colour to reveal the correct reflection.

Independent work
● Ask the children to write their name in block capital letters on one side of a folded piece of coloured paper. Make sure that a strip is left along the fold line to hold the letters in place when cut.
● The children must cut out the letters, leaving the folded edge intact. When cut, unfold the paper to reveal the child's name reflected along one line of symmetry.
● Ask the children to work out how they could produce their name so that it is reflected in two lines of symmetry. Let them experiment with new paper. The easiest way is to place two sheets together and repeat the first step; when opened out, place the two sheets alongside each other.
● Support those children with fine motor skills difficulties by providing pre-cut letters reflected in one mirror line.

Plenary
● Ask the children to share their work by displaying it at the front of the class. Ask them if any letters look the same when reflected.
● Go to page 5. Ask the children to record what they think the first letter is and share answers. Reveal the letter and discuss how it could have been an F or E. Identify the line of symmetry.
● Ask the class to identify the second hidden letter (G). If there is time, consider which letters do or do not have lines of symmetry.

Lines of symmetry

Learning objective
PNS: Understanding shape
● Draw and complete shapes with reflective symmetry; draw the reflection of a shape in a mirror line along one side

Resources
'Symmetry' Notebook file; mirrors with straight edges; sets of everyday objects; rulers; paper; scissors. Draw the other half of an object and add its line of symmetry.

Links to other subjects
Art and design
QCA Unit 3B 'Investigating pattern'
● Make patterns with two lines of symmetry at right angles by folding and cutting paper.
PE
QCA Unit 14 'Gymnastic activities'
● Incorporate body symmetry in elements of dance or gymnastics.

Starter
Open the 'Symmetry' Notebook file and press the button next to Lesson 29 to go to page 6. Give each child a piece of paper and ask them to fold it in half. Ask them to cut a shape in the piece of paper, keeping the fold intact. When they fold out the paper, they will see that the shape on one side will be the mirror image of the other side. Use a mirror to test whether this is correct.

Ask them to fold a new sheet of paper in a different way, or to fold it twice. Tell them to cut out a different shape and open it out to show what they have reflected. Revisit what the terms: *mirror line* and *reflection* mean on page 2 of the Notebook file.

Whole-class shared work
● Go to page 7. Invite a child to draw the other half of the shield (its reflection).
● Move the box to reveal the hidden half of the shield. Establish that the shield is symmetrical. Demonstrate this by holding a mirror to the line where the image is exactly reflected, then draw that line in red along the mirror edge.
● Cover half of the shield and cut that shape out of a folded piece of paper. Unfold it and compare it to the shape on the board. Point out that the fold line is the line of symmetry.
● Ask the children to find the lines of symmetry in their cut-out shapes from the Starter (above).

Independent work
● Give each group a set of everyday objects. If the object is 3D, state that for the purposes of this activity they will need to choose one side of the object to look at.
● Using a mirror, ask the children to investigate whether the different objects have one or more lines of symmetry.
● They should then sketch the object and indicate the symmetry line using a ruler and a red pencil.
● If an object has no lines of symmetry, the children should draw it and write this fact underneath.
● In the meantime, small groups can take turns at the whiteboard. Using page 8, let the children draw the missing halves of the objects, deleting or moving the boxes to see if they are correct.
● Invite them to add the line of symmetry using the Pen tool and a real ruler laid on the whiteboard. Identify if there is more than one line of symmetry or even none.
● Press the Undo button until the page is reset and start the activity again for new groups.

Plenary
● Ask the children to share what they have learned about lines of symmetry in their investigation. Which objects have more than one or no lines of symmetry?
● Challenge the children to look for and make a list of examples of objects with one or more lines of symmetry on their way home.

Whiteboard tools
Use a Pen from the Pen tray with a real ruler to draw lines of symmetry.

 Pen tray

Select tool

 Undo button

Delete button

Compass points

Starter
Use a compass to find out the direction that faces north within the classroom. Ask the class to stand and face north. Invite them to turn clockwise or anti-clockwise and finish the turn to face west. Repeat to face east and south. Once the majority of the class agree the directions of the compass points, place *north, south, east* and *west* labels on the corresponding classroom walls.

Whole-class shared work
● To move an object in the direction of north, south, east or west, the object must be on a horizontal plane, such as the floor. Demonstrating on a vertical whiteboard can be confusing because north is usually placed at the top of the board but the direction upwards is not north. However, the board is excellent for showing something in 3D, for example, travelling north through a 3D plan of a house. This lesson offers an alternative method.
● Load the images from the playground onto the board (see Whiteboard tools, below). Bring each image up one at a time. Ask pupils to record what they see on paper.
● Go with the class to the playground and establish the direction of north. Ask groups to travel around and work out which images are found on the north side of the playground, the west side, and so on. Walk around and ask groups in which compass direction they are facing.
● Once all the children have identified the location of each of the images, return to the classroom. Show the pictures again, but ask whether the images were at the east, south, north or west side of the school.
● Scribe the appropriate direction over the image.
● Use the Lines tool ⟍ to draw a compass rose in the middle of the page, with north pointing upwards, and group the images according to their compass direction.

Independent work
● Give each child a copy of photocopiable page 101 'Compass points'. This worksheet shows a representation of a typical rectangular school playground.
● Establish and write in the four compass directions on the sheet. Write in two or three different things that could be seen if facing north, west, east and south in the playground.
● As an extension, work out and add a bird's eye or planned view of the school.

Plenary
● Ask one child to represent a robot. Position the robot facing the classroom door. Establish the compass direction in which the robot starts off facing. The robot cannot turn but can step left or right, forwards or backwards. Ask individual children to give one instruction to move the robot to various points across the classroom.
● Repeat with a different robot and starting point.

Hundreds, tens and units

100	200	300
400	500	600
700	800	900

| 10 | 20 | 30 | 40 |
| 50 | 60 | 70 | 80 |

| 90 | 1 | 2 | 3 | 4 | 5 |
| | 6 | 7 | 8 | 9 | |

Measurements

Object	What are we measuring?	What do we use to measure this?	What we think the measurement will be	The actual measurement

Name _____

Number bars

1	**2**	**3**	**4**	**5**	**6**	**7**	**8**	**9**	**10**

2s, 5s and 10s

▮ Some of these numbers are multiples of 2, 5 or 10.
Can you sort them?

345	72	380	990
546	14	7	44
523	999	87	85
26	18	25	74
675	300	340	388
102	395	546	1000

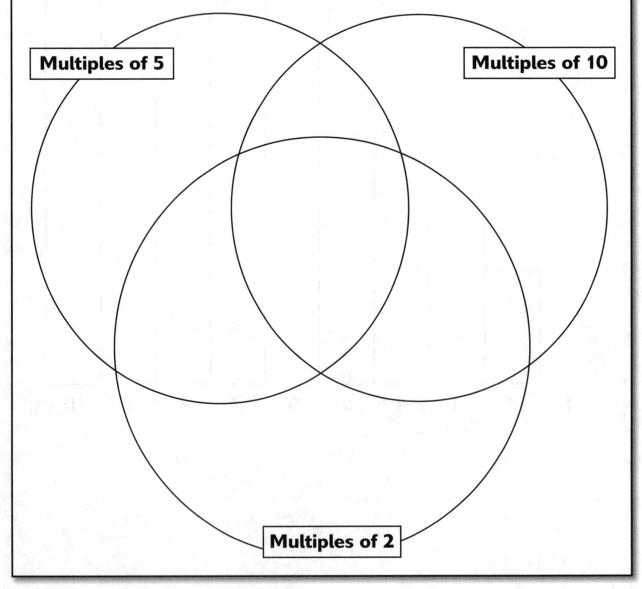

Multiples of 5   **Multiples of 10**

Multiples of 2

Squares

◼ How many squares can you see?
  The answer is not as easy as you think!

◼ Write your answer here: _____

What time is it?

Illustrations © Andy Keylock / Beehive Illustration

Shapes and patterns

■ Cut out these shapes. Use them to make a pattern.

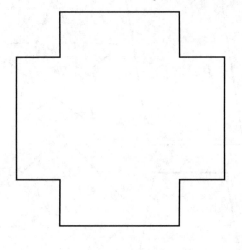

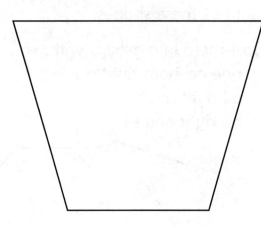

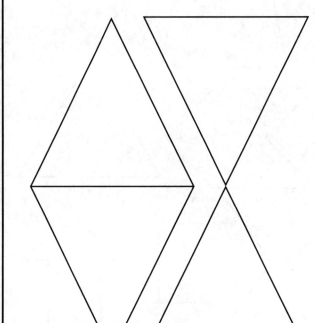

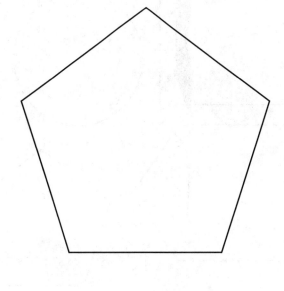

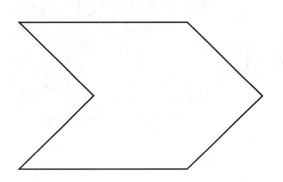

Sorting right angles

- ◼ Cut out these shapes.

- ◼ Sort them into groups with:
  one or more right angles;
  all right angles;
  no right angles.

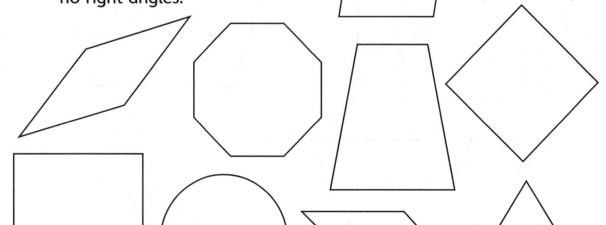

Counting

■ Count on, or back, in tens or hundreds from the start number to the end of the line.

Count up in 10s

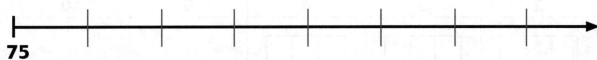

75

Count back in 10s

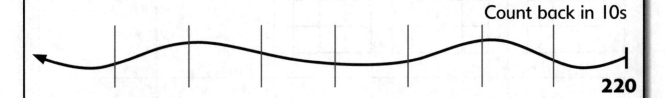

220

Count back in 100s

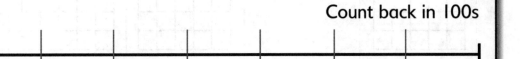

1000

Count up in 10s

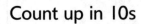

91

Count up in 100s

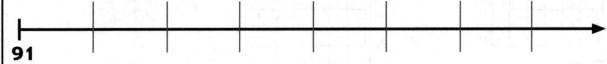

31

Count back in 100s

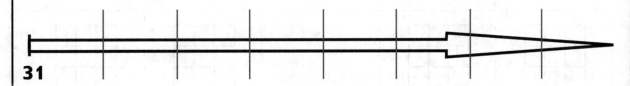

888

Name _____

Fractions of shapes

◼ Colour in different fractions of these shapes.

$\frac{1}{2}$	$\frac{1}{3}$	$\frac{1}{4}$	$\frac{1}{5}$	$\frac{1}{10}$

100 SMART Board™ LESSONS · YEAR 3

Animals

◼ Cut out these animals to create your own animals pictogram. If you want to, use the blank squares to draw a different animal.

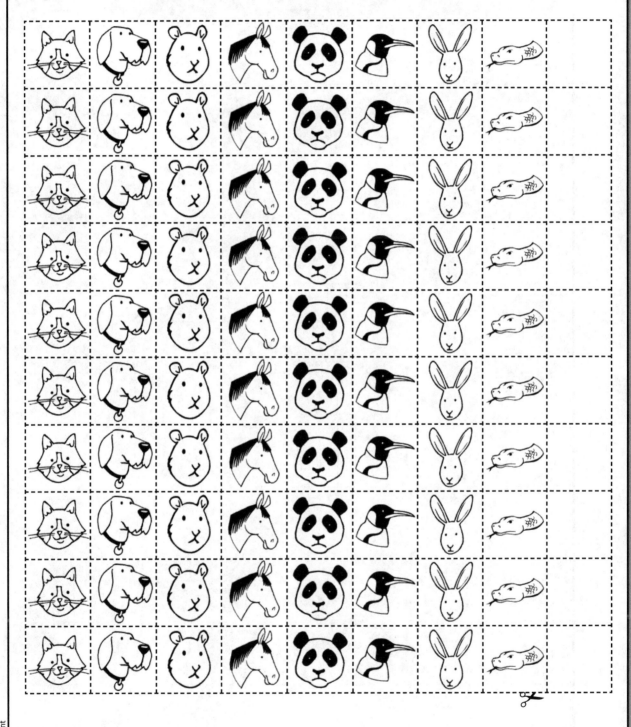

Illustrations by Ian Hunt

Bar chart

Name _____

Compass points

■ Record what you can see when you face north, south, east and west in your playground.

This direction is _____

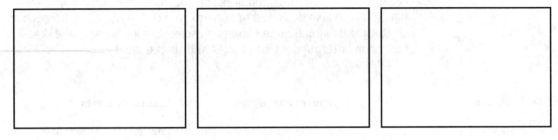

This direction is _____

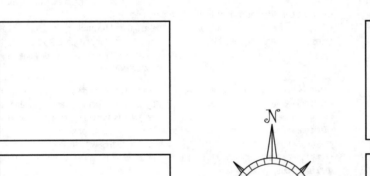

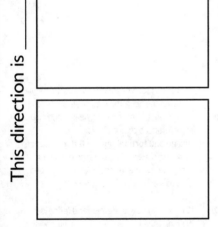

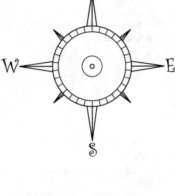

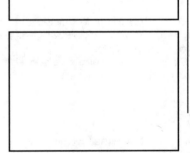

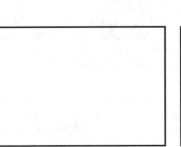

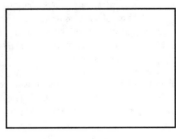

This direction is _____

Illustrations © Andy Keylock / Beehive Illustration

Science

This chapter provides 20 lessons based on the Year 3 units in the QCA Schemes of Work for science. A number of key objectives from each unit have been deliberately chosen where the use of an interactive whiteboard will particularly aid and enhance the teaching of those objectives.

The lessons and associated Notebook files are designed to encourage the whole class to discuss and demonstrate ideas, plan investigations effectively, record and evaluate results and make substantiated conclusions. In this way, many of the lessons will actively support you in teaching and evaluating key scientific enquiry skills (Sc1 National Curriculum). The flipcharts are also designed to enhance the children's ICT skills, such as creating and manipulating objects on screen, using writing and drawing tools, and entering data into tables and spreadsheets.

Lesson title	Objectives	Expected prior knowledge	Cross-curricular links
Lesson 1: Varied and balanced diets	QCA Unit 3A 'Teeth and eating' • To understand that an adequate and varied diet is needed to keep healthy.	• That we need to eat and drink to stay alive. • That we eat different kinds of food. • That sometimes we eat a lot of some foods and not very much of others.	PSHE PoS (3a) What makes a healthy lifestyle, including the benefits of exercise and healthy eating. Design and technology PoS (2d) To measure, mark out, cut and shape a range of materials, and assemble, join and combine components and materials accurately.
Lesson 2: Animal diets	QCA Unit 3A 'Teeth and eating' • To understand that different animals have different diets. • To raise questions about the diet of different pets. • To turn ideas about the diet of animals into a form that can be investigated. • To decide how many animals should be investigated and the range of foods to be considered. • To present evidence about the foods eaten by animals in a suitable bar chart or pictogram.	• That the term *animal* includes humans. • That animals reproduce and change as they grow older. • That babies and children need to be looked after while they are growing. • How to draw a conclusion and to say what they found out.	Mathematics Handling data: Answer a question by collecting, organising and interpreting data; use tally charts, frequency tables and bar charts to illustrate observations. ICT PoS (3a) How to share and exchange information in a variety of forms, including email.
Lesson 3: Healthy teeth and gums	QCA Unit 3A 'Teeth and eating' • To understand that healthy teeth need healthy gums. • To know that some foods can be damaging to our teeth.	• That humans have bodies with similar parts. • That humans need water and food to stay alive • That sometimes we eat a lot of some foods and not very much of others.	PSHE PoS (3a) What makes a healthy lifestyle, including the benefits of exercise and healthy eating, what affects mental health, and how to make informed choices. Design and technology PoS (2d) To measure, mark out, cut and shape a range of materials, and assemble, join and combine components and materials accurately.
Lesson 4: Growth investigation: Leaves	QCA Unit 3B 'Helping plants grow well' • To make careful observations and measurements of plants growing. • To use simple apparatus to measure the height of plants in standard measures. • To use results to draw conclusions. • To understand that plants need leaves in order to grow well.	• How to make and record observations and to make simple comparisons. • To recognise when a comparison is unfair. • How to use what happened to draw a conclusion and to say what they found out. • That plants grow. • That plants have leaves, stems and flowers.	ICT PoS (2a) How to develop and refine ideas by bringing together, organising and reorganising text, tables, images and sound as appropriate. Art and design PoS (2a) To investigate and combine visual and tactile qualities of materials and processes and to match these qualities to the purpose of the work.
Lesson 5: Growth investigation: Water	QCA Unit 3B 'Helping plants grow well' • To know that plants need water, but not unlimited water, for healthy growth. • To use simple apparatus to measure a volume of water correctly. • To use simple apparatus to measure the height of the plant.	• How to make and record observations and to make simple comparisons. • To recognise when a comparison is unfair. • That plants have roots. • That plants need water to grow.	Mathematics Measuring: Choose and use appropriate units to estimate, measure and record measurements; read to the nearest division scales that are numbered. ICT PoS (2a) How to develop and refine ideas by bringing together, organising and reorganising text, tables, images and sound as appropriate.

Lesson title	Objectives	Expected prior knowledge	Cross-curricular links
Lesson 6: Growth investigation: Light ⊙ 🅟	QCA Unit 3B 'Helping plants grow well' • To know that plants need light for healthy growth. • To ask questions about the growth of plants.	• How to make and record observations and to make simple comparisons. • To recognise when a comparison is unfair.	English Text structure and organisation ICT PoS (2a) How to develop and refine ideas by bringing together, organising and reorganising text, tables, images and sound as appropriate.
Lesson 7: Roots and stems ⊙ 🅟	QCA Unit 3B 'Helping plants grow well' • To know that water is taken in through the roots. • To understand that water is transported through the stem to other parts of the plant. • To make and explain observations and present these using drawings.	• How to make and record observations and to make simple comparisons. • To use what happened to draw a conclusion and to say what they found out. • That plants have roots. • That plants need water to grow.	ICT PoS (4b) To describe and talk about the effectiveness of their work with ICT, comparing it with other methods and considering the effect it has on others. Art and design PoS (1a) To record from experience and imagination, to select and record from first-hand observation and to explore ideas for different purposes.
Lesson 8: Common materials and their properties ⊙ 🅟	QCA Unit 3C 'Characteristics of materials' • To identify a range of common materials and know that the same material is used to make different objects. • To recognise properties such as hardness, strength and flexibility and compare materials in terms of these properties.	• That every material has many properties which can be recognised using our senses and described using appropriate vocabulary. • That different, everyday objects can be made from the same materials. • How to record observations of materials.	Design and technology PoS (4a) To know how the working characteristics of materials affect the ways they are used. English Creating and shaping texts
Lesson 9: Absorbency investigation ⊙	QCA Unit 3C 'Characteristics of materials' • To plan a test to compare the absorbency of different papers, deciding what evidence to collect, considering what to change, what to keep the same and what to measure. • To make comparisons and draw conclusions.	• How to make and record observations and to make simple comparisons. • To recognise when a comparison is unfair. • To suggest how to test an idea about whether a fabric or paper is suitable for a particular purpose. • That materials are chosen for specific purposes on the basis of their properties. • To use what happened to draw a conclusion and say what they found out.	English Understanding and interpreting texts Art and design PoS (2b) To apply their experience of materials and processes, including drawing, developing their control of tools and techniques.
Lesson 10: Stretching investigation ⊙ 🅟	QCA Unit 3C 'Characteristics of materials' • To plan how to find out which pair of tights is most stretchy, making a fair comparison. • To decide what to change, what to keep the same and what to measure. • To make careful measurements of length, to present measurements as a bar chart and to draw conclusions.	• To suggest how to test an idea about whether a fabric is suitable for a particular purpose. • To explore ways of answering the question. • To recognise when a comparison is unfair. • How to make and record observations and to make simple comparisons. • To use what happened to draw a conclusion and to say what they found out.	Science PoS Sc4 (2d) That when objects are pushed or pulled, an opposing pull or push can be felt. ICT PoS (3a) How to share and exchange information in a variety of forms, including email.
Lesson 11: Characteristics and purposes of rocks ⊙	QCA Unit 3D 'Rocks and soils' • To understand that rocks are used for a variety of purposes. • To understand that rocks are chosen for particular purposes because of their characteristics.	• That some naturally occurring materials are treated (shaped, polished) before they are used. • That materials are chosen for specific purposes on the basis of their properties.	Geography PoS (3e) To identify how and why places change. Art and design PoS (4b) To understand the materials and processes used in art, craft and design and how these can be matched to ideas and intentions.
Lesson 12: Soils ⊙	QCA Unit 3D 'Rocks and soils' • To understand that beneath all surfaces there is rock. • To understand that there are different kinds of soil depending on the rock from which they come.	• That some materials occur naturally and some do not. • The names of some naturally occurring materials. • That materials can be sorted in a variety of ways according to their properties.	Geography PoS (3e) To identify how and why places change. Art and design PoS (4b) To understand the materials and processes used in art, craft and design and how these can be matched to ideas and intentions.
Lesson 13: Water flow investigation ⊙ 🅟	QCA Unit 3D 'Rocks and soils' • To use simple apparatus to measure volumes of liquids and to measure time. • To recognise when a test is unfair. • To use results to make comparisons, and to draw and explain conclusions.	• How to make and record observations and to make simple comparisons. • To recognise when a comparison is unfair. • How to draw a conclusion from observations and to say what they found out.	Mathematics Measuring: Choose and use appropriate units to estimate, measure and record measurements. ICT PoS (3a) How to share and exchange information in a variety of forms, including email.

Lesson title	Objectives	Expected prior knowledge	Cross-curricular links
Lesson 14: Properties of magnets ⬤	**QCA Unit 3E** 'Magnets and springs' • To know that there are forces between magnets and that magnets can attract and repel each other. • To make and record careful observations of magnets. • To make generalisations about what happens when magnets are put together.	• That pushing or pulling things can make objects start or stop moving. • That it is not only ourselves that make things move by pushing. • To make and record observations and to make simple comparisons; • To draw a conclusion from observations and to say what they found out.	**Design and technology** PoS (2c) To explore the sensory qualities of materials and how to use materials and processes. **ICT** PoS (2c) To use simulations and explore models to investigate and evaluate the effect of changing values.
Lesson 15: Magnetic materials ⬤	**QCA Unit 3E** 'Magnets and springs' • To make and test predictions about whether materials are magnetic or not. • To make careful observations. • To know that magnets attract some metals but not others and that other materials are not attracted to magnets. • To use results to conclude whether predictions were accurate.	• That some materials are magnetic but most are not. • To make and record observations and to make simple comparisons. • To draw a conclusion from observations and to say what they found out.	**Design and technology** PoS (2c) To explore the sensory qualities of materials and how to use materials and processes. **ICT** PoS (2c) To use simulations and explore models to investigate and evaluate the effect of changing values.
Lesson 16: Elastic investigation ⬤ 🅿	**QCA Unit 3E** 'Magnets and springs' • To predict the effect of stretching elastic bands by different amounts. • To compare and identify patterns in results. • To draw conclusions and indicate whether the prediction was supported. • To explain the conclusions in terms of the size of the force.	• To explore ways of answering the question. • To make and record observations and to make simple comparisons. • To draw a conclusion from observations and to say what they found out.	**Design and technology** PoS (2c) To explore the sensory qualities of materials and how to use materials and processes. **ICT** PoS (2c) To use simulations and explore models to investigate and evaluate the effect of changing values.
Lesson 17: Shadow formation ⬤ 🅿	**QCA Unit 3F** 'Light and shadows' • To know that shadows are formed when light travelling from a source is blocked. • To make and record observations and to present information in drawing and writing.	• That light is essential for seeing things. • That there are many sources of light. • That objects cannot be seen in darkness. • That shiny objects are not light sources. • To make and try to explain observations.	**History** PoS (11b) A study of the impact of the Second World War. **Art and design** PoS (5a) Exploring a range of starting points for practical work.
Lesson 18: Shadow length investigation ⬤ 🅿	**QCA Unit 3F** 'Light and shadows' • To know that shadows change in length and position throughout the day. • To measure the length of a shadow in standard measures. • To make a table and line graph show how the length of shadows changes during the day.	• That the Sun is the source of light for the Earth. • That it is dangerous to look at the Sun because it is so bright. • To make observations and to try to explain these.	**Mathematics** Handling data: Answer a question by collecting, organising and interpreting data. **ICT** PoS (3a) How to share and exchange information in a variety of forms, including email.
Lesson 19: Shadow time-telling ⬤ 🅿	**QCA Unit 3F** 'Light and shadows' • To know that shadows can be used to tell the approximate time of day.	• That the Sun is the source of light for the Earth. • That it is dangerous to look at the Sun because it is so bright.	**Mathematics** Understanding shape: Identify right angles in 2D shapes. **Design and technology** PoS (2d) To measure, mark out, and cut materials, and assemble and combine components and materials accurately.
Lesson 20: Opacity and transparency investigation ⬤ 🅿	**QCA Unit 3F** 'Light and shadows' • To understand that opaque materials do not let light through and transparent materials let a lot of light through. • To predict and test which materials will form a shadow. • To compare the shadows formed by different materials and to draw conclusions from their results. • To decide whether the results support their predictions and to use knowledge about shadows to explain the conclusions.	• That shadows are formed when light travelling from a source is blocked. • To explore ways of answering the question. • To make and record observations and to make simple comparisons. • To use what happened to draw a conclusion and to say what they found out.	**Art and design** PoS (2c) To use a variety of methods and approaches to communicate observations, ideas and feeling, and to design and make images and artefacts.

Varied and balanced diets

Learning objective
QCA Unit 3A 'Teeth and eating'
● To understand that an adequate and varied diet is needed to keep healthy.

Resources
'Varied and balanced diets' Notebook file; photocopiable page 125 'A healthy meal' for each child.

Links to other subjects
Design and technology
PoS (2d) To measure, mark out, cut and shape a range of materials, and assemble, join and combine components and materials accurately.
● Use learning to design healthy-eating sandwiches and their containers.
PSHE
PoS (3a) What makes a healthy lifestyle, including the benefits of exercise and healthy eating.
● Use this lesson as part of work on developing a healthy, safer lifestyle.

Starter

Discuss the questions on page 2 of the 'Varied and balanced diets' Notebook file. Ask the children to tell you their definition of *diet*. Explain that, in scientific terms, a diet means the range of food a person eats, not a weight-loss regime.

Whole-class shared work

● Discuss why the plate on page 3 does not contain a healthy meal and consider what *healthy* means. What possible effects would such a diet have on a person's health?
● Repeat this for page 4, drawing out that both meals shown contain only fats, sugars and carbohydrates. Introduce the term *varied diet*.
● Complete and discuss the food pyramid on page 5. Emphasise that a daily diet should contain produce from each food group (varied), in different proportions (balanced). Press the food group labels to find out more information.
● Introduce page 6 and challenge the children to build a healthy meal on the plate from the produce available. Explain that the meal must include at least one item from each food group.
● Show the children how to select, drag and drop one item at a time on the plate. Ask a number of children to take turns to build up a meal on screen in this way by using the Undo button 🔁 to reset the page. Discuss any healthy-eating issues along the way.
● Discuss whether the completed meals are varied and balanced. Examine which food type the children choose to repeat in the sixth slot and why.

Independent work

● Hand out copies of photocopiable page 125 'A healthy meal'. Ask the children to draw and label a healthy meal on the plate by choosing six items from the list.
● Remind the children that their meals must include at least one item from each food group. Display page 5 of the Notebook file to help them.
● Encourage the children to make their sixth choice wisely according to the proportions on the food pyramid (so another choice from the cereal group is preferential to one from the sweet group).
● Let small groups use the whiteboard to explore the food items in the Gallery 🖼 to create a healthy meal on page 6.
● Support less confident learners in reading the choice of produce on the sheet and in identifying food types from the food pyramid.
● Extend the activity by asking the children to list six different items that a person could have for an evening meal later that day, ensuring that their diet remained varied and balanced.

Plenary

● Ask the children to share their work and discuss whether their own meals are varied and balanced.
● Emphasise that humans need a varied and balanced diet because our bodies need different food types for energy, growth and repair (for example, carbohydrates provide energy, and fats help nerves to function). Use page 7 to make notes.

Whiteboard tools
Press the Undo button repeatedly to reset the page and allow children to take turns building the meal on page 6. Investigate the Gallery to explore more food items.

 Pen tray

 Select tool

 Delete button

 Gallery

 Undo button

Animal diets

Starter
Load the 'Animal diets survey' Notebook file and go to page 2. Ask the children if they own a pet. Take a tally of the type of pets that the children own using the table on page 2. Create a pictogram or bar chart of the results on page 3. Discuss which pet is the most popular.

Whole-class shared work
● Ask the children about their pets and who has responsibility for caring for them, and especially for feeding them. Write their responses on page 4. Emphasise that *diet* means what an animal eats (not a weight-loss programme).
● Display page 5 and discuss what goldfish eat (don't forget to include naturally occurring pond weed).
● On page 6, ask the children to write the foods that a cat would eat on the page.
● Tell the children that they are going to carry out a survey to find out about the diet of an animal.
● Go to page 7. Decide upon a question to investigate (such as: *Do all dogs eat the same food?*) Write this at the top of the page.
● Discuss how many animals you are going to try to survey (pets at home, neighbour's pets and so on) and choose six sorts of food (such as: fish, chicken, rabbit, dried food and so on).
● Hand out copies of photocopiable page 126 'Animal diets' and ask the children to fill in the names of the six sorts of food in the first column.

Independent work
● Ask the children to complete the sheet for homework.
● Ask parents or guardians to supervise their children when asking neighbours for the information or when telephoning friends and relatives.
● Ensure that the children only tick the right column of the sheet if the animal in question has ever eaten that sort of food, not if the animal probably would.
● Extend the activity by asking the children to predict the overall outcome of the survey.

Plenary
● Ask a number of children to present the results of their own surveys.
● Inform the children that bar charts can be used to present results clearly so that comparisons can be made more easily.
● Go to page 8 and open the *Animal diets investigation* spreadsheet to input the children's results. Tally the results for each sort of food and use the On-screen Keyboard to enter the data into the spreadsheet cells on the worksheet.
● Examine and discuss the resultant bar chart. Ask the children what they can conclude (for example, half of the dogs eat beef).
● Consider how accurate the survey was. Discuss whether there is enough evidence to draw accurate conclusions (relatively few animals were surveyed and dogs might eat other sorts of food if they were given the opportunity). Write these points on page 8.

Healthy teeth and gums

Learning objectives
QCA Unit 3A 'Teeth and eating'
● To understand that healthy teeth need healthy gums.
● To know that some foods can be damaging to our teeth.

Resources
'Teeth and eating' Notebook file.

Links to other subjects
PSHE
PoS (3a) What makes a healthy lifestyle, including the benefits of exercise and healthy eating, what affects mental health, and how to make informed choices.
● Use this lesson to inform other work of healthy eating and lifestyles.
Design and technology
PoS (2d) To measure, mark out, cut and shape a range of materials, and assemble, join and combine components and materials accurately.
● Design healthy-eating snacks and their containers.

Starter
Display page 2 of the Notebook file 'Teeth and eating'. Ask the children about their playtime snacks and discuss how *healthy* they think the snacks are. Discuss the fact that what the children eat also directly affects the health of their teeth and gums. Ask the children how many times a day they brush their teeth and why they think it is important. Include the fact that brushing keeps the gums healthy. Survey how many children brush their teeth after sugary snacks and drinks.

Whole-class shared work
● Go to page 3 of the Notebook file. Drag the labels out of the box at the bottom of the page. Complete the diagram and review any prior work on the names and functions of the teeth. Fill the bottom of the boxes with white to check answers 🔳.
● Go to page 4 and tell the children that they will be looking at pictures of teeth.
● Display page 5 and discuss in detail the descriptions of healthy and unhealthy teeth and gums.
● Turn on the Spotlight tool 🔦 and practise moving it around. Resize the spotlight to increase/decrease difficulty.
● Go to page 6 and ask the children to take turns to move the spotlight to examine the first (healthy) set of teeth and gums. Ask the children to justify why they think the patient's teeth and gums are healthy or unhealthy.
● Repeat for the unhealthy set on page 7.
● Exit the Spotlight tool and examine both sets in full.
● Discuss what might have caused problems in the unhealthy set (such as not brushing regularly, certain foods or drinks). Do not, at this stage, mention sugar.
● Explain that some foods damage your teeth and gums and some foods protect and strengthen them.
● Display page 8 and ask the children to sort the food into two groups and discuss their reasons.
● Prompt the children to understand that the following foods (vegetables, cheese and milk) are good. Ask the children why these foods are good (for example, milk and cheese contain calcium).
● Discuss whether children think the other foods are bad for your teeth and what they have in common (high levels of sugar).
● Explain that sugar damages the teeth and gums, making sugary snacks at break time inappropriate, as children don't brush their teeth afterwards.

Independent work
● Ask the children to design a poster persuading other children in the school to have a snack at break time that is good for their teeth.
● Tell them that their posters must use pictures, slogans and other persuasive writing and must inform their audience about the dangers of sugary snacks.
● Encourage them to plan first and to use a simple, clear and bold design.

Plenary
● Ask the children to present their posters. Scan a selection of their work and display it on page 9.

Whiteboard tools
Use the Spotlight tool, accessed via the SMART Board tools menu, to highlight objects. Upload scanned posters by selecting Insert, then Picture File, and browsing to where you have saved the images.

 Pen tray

 Spotlight tool

🖱 Select tool

 Fill Colour tool

Growth investigation: Leaves

Learning objectives

QCA Unit 3B 'Helping plants grow well'
● To make careful observations and measurements of plants growing.
● To use simple apparatus to measure the height of plants in standard measures.
● To use results to draw conclusions.
● To understand that plants need leaves in order to grow well.

Resources

'Helping plants to grow' Notebook file; photocopiable page 127 'Plant investigations' for each child; two similar plants of the same species (for example, geranium); rulers; water; measuring cylinders.

Links to other subjects

Art and design

PoS (2a) To investigate and combine visual and tactile qualities of materials and processes and to match these qualities to the purpose of the work.
● Build sculptures of a variety of leaf shapes using a simple armature, papier mâché or Mod-Roc.

ICT

PoS (2a) How to develop and refine ideas by bringing together, organising and reorganising text, tables, images and sound as appropriate.
● Use a desktop publishing program to combine graphics and text about the parts of a flowering plant.

Whiteboard tools

Convert handwritten words to text by selecting them and choosing the Recognise option from the dropdown menu.

 Pen tray

 Select tool

Starter

Use page 2 of the Notebook file to recap any previous work on factors that affect the healthy growth of plants, such as water, temperature or light. Label the diagram together. Discuss the children's experiences of planting, growing and looking after plants at home. Show them the plants and identify the leaves, stem and flowers. Draw out their knowledge of the functions of these parts and those of any unseen parts, such as the roots.

Whole-class shared work

● Discuss how the children could find out whether plants need leaves in order to grow well. Help them to appreciate how removing the leaves from one plant, and then keeping both plants in the same place and watering them the same amount, would provide a fair comparison.
● On page 3 write down a suitable location for the plants, how much water they will be given and when, and what the children will need to measure and record.
● Invite the children to record this information on their copy of the photocopiable page 'Plant investigations'.
● Demonstrate how to measure the plant accurately from the top of the soil next to the stem, to the top of the plant.

Independent work

● Over a period of a few weeks, organise the children to water and measure the plants as planned.
● On page 4, write down the dates and measurements as the investigation progresses, remembering to save the Notebook file each time. Leave a printout of page 4 beside the plants to remind the children of the information that needs to be recorded.
● Monitor the investigation so that it remains fair, by ensuring that the children measure heights and volumes accurately.
● Support less confident learners by discussing how the fair testing will help produce more accurate results.
● Extend more confident learners by asking them to predict the outcome of the investigation and to explore their ideas about why leaves would affect growth.

Plenary

● Display the recorded measurements on page 4 and discuss what the results show.
● Establish that plants need leaves to grow well. Ask the children for their ideas about why this is so. Some children may have a basic awareness of the function of leaves and the oxygen/carbon dioxide transfer involved in photosynthesis.
● Write the conclusion at the bottom of page 4.
● As a precursor to other possible investigations, ask the children to suggest other factors that might influence growth, such as light, water and temperature.

Growth investigation: Water

Starter
Recap any previous work on factors that affect the healthy growth of plants, such as the number of leaves, temperature or light. Discuss children's experiences of watering plants at home. Many children will have experienced plants dying due to lack of water, but less so with over-watering. Look at some plant care labels to find out information about caring for them.

Whole-class shared work
● Display page 5 of the 'Helping plants to grow' Notebook file and discuss what will happen to the three plants. Ask the children whether the more water plants are given, the better they will grow. (Press the seedlings to see the results).
● Discuss how the children could find out how much water bean seedlings need in order to grow well. Elicit how to provide a fair comparison: by changing the amount each seedling is watered (whilst keeping other conditions the same) and regularly measuring the height of each plant.
● Decide how much each seedling will be watered (5ml, 20ml or 50ml per day). Establish that one seedling should not be watered at all to provide further comparison.
● On page 6 write down a suitable location for the plants; how much water each one will be given and when, and what the children will need to measure and record.
● Ask the children to record this information on their copy of photocopiable page 127 'Plant investigations'.
● Demonstrate how to measure the seedling accurately from the top of the soil to the top of the plant and how to fill the measuring equipment accurately with small quantities of water.

Independent work
● Organise the children to water and measure each plant as planned.
● On page 7, write down the dates and measurements as the investigation progresses, remembering to save the Notebook file each time. Leave a printout of page 7 by the plants to remind the children of what information needs to be recorded.
● Monitor the investigation to check that it remains fair by ensuring accurate measuring.
● Support less confident learners by discussing how fair testing will help to produce more accurate results.
● Extend more confident learners by asking them to predict the outcome of the investigation, and by exploring their ideas about how the amount of watering will affect growth.

Plenary
● Display the recorded measurements on page 7 and discuss what the results show. Establish that plants need water, but not unlimited water, for healthy growth. (Their root systems require air as well as water. An over-watered plant *drowns* because of lack of oxygen from the soil.)
● Write the conclusion on page 7.
● As a precursor to other possible investigations, ask the children to suggest other factors that might influence growth (such as number of leaves, light and temperature).

Growth investigation: Light

Learning objectives
QCA Unit 3B 'Helping plants grow well'
● To know that plants need light for healthy growth.
● To ask questions about the growth of plants.

Resources
'Helping plants to grow' Notebook file; photocopiable page 127 'Plant investigations' for each child; minimum of two containers of bean seedlings; rulers; water; measuring cylinders, syringes or medicine teaspoons (5ml) suitable for small quantities.

Links to other subjects
English
Text structure and organisation
● Invite the children to write instructions for how to care for a common house plant.
ICT
PoS (2a) How to develop and refine ideas by bringing together, organising and reorganising text, tables, images and sound as appropriate.
● Combine text and graphics to draw and label images of healthy and light-deprived plants.

Whiteboard tools
Convert handwritten words to text by selecting them and choosing the Recognise option from the dropdown menu.

📖 Pen tray

Starter
Recap any previous work on factors that affect the healthy growth of plants, such as the number of leaves, water or temperature.

Whole-class shared work
● Open the 'Helping plants to grow' Notebook file. Press the button next to Lesson 6, which takes you to page 8. Use this page to discuss what happens when a large object, such as a tent, is left on top of grass for a long time. (For example, it isn't as green as the surrounding grass). Discuss why this might happen: possible causes include lack of light.
● Discuss together how the children could find out how important light is to the healthy growth of plants (keeping two similar plants in separate light and dark locations, while watering them equally, would provide a fair comparison).
● Decide how much each seedling will be watered and what needs to be recorded (a physical description of the plant and its height) and how often.
● Record this information on page 9, along with suitable locations for the plants.
● Ask the children to record this information on their own copies of the 'Plant investigations' photocopiable sheet.
● Demonstrate how to accurately measure the seedling from the top of the soil to the top of the plant and how to precisely fill the measuring equipment with small quantities of water.

Independent work
● Every few days, organise the children to water and measure each plant as planned.
● On page 10 of the Notebook file, write down the dates and measurements as the investigation progresses, remembering to save the data file each time.
● Monitor that the investigation remains fair by ensuring that the children measure heights and volumes accurately.
● Support less confident learners by discussing how the fair testing will help to produce more accurate results.
● Extend more confident learners by asking them to predict the outcome of the investigation, and to explore their ideas about how the amount of light will affect growth.

Plenary
● Display and discuss what the recorded measurements on page 10 show.
● Establish that plants need light for healthy growth. Plants need energy from sunlight to photosynthesise (the conversion of carbon dioxide and water into glucose and oxygen). Write the conclusion at the bottom of page 10. (Without light, plants eventually become long, yellow and spindly.)
● Discuss why plants don't start dying at night. (Plants make enough energy from sunshine to last them through the night, and through lots of cloudy days.)
● Ask children to predict what would happen if the plant that has been kept in the dark was put back into the light for a few days.
● As a precursor to other possible investigations, ask children to suggest other factors that might influence growth, such as the number of leaves, water and temperature.

Roots and stems

Starter
Display the learning objective for Lesson 7 on page 1 of the 'Helping plants to grow' Notebook file. Show the children the roots of a pot-bound plant. Ask what has happened and what they would expect to see if the roots were in a larger pot (the roots would spread out). Encourage the children to recognise that roots spread out in order to take in water from the surrounding soil more easily. Use page 11 to emphasise this point.

Whole-class shared work
● Explain that the children will be investigating what happens to the water taken in by the roots.
● Show the children a whole head of celery and identify the stems, leaves and where the roots used to be.

Independent work
● Ask the children to examine the cut end of the stems closely with a magnifying glass, describing their observations.
● Hand out copies of photocopiable page 128, the 'Stem observation' sheet.
● Ask the children to place the stems upright, with the cut end down, in a shallow quantity of coloured liquid in a container.
● Invite them to draw the equipment in black and white, showing the position of the dyed water using a coloured pencil.
● After a few hours, ask the children to observe the stems closely and to redraw the equipment and the position of the dye.
● Repeat a final time a few hours later.
● Check the stems periodically until you can see evidence of colour in the veins of the celery leaves.
● Under supervision, ask the children to cut the stems several centimetres above the end to reveal a cross-section of the stem.
● Ask the children to observe the cut stem carefully and identify where the dye has travelled up it.
● Now ask them to cut the stems a few centimetres higher and repeat, following the path of the dye up the stem.
● Invite the children to examine the leaves with a magnifying glass to look for evidence of dye entering the veins of the leaves.
● Support less confident learners as they observe the experiment and provide help to accurately draw the equipment.
● Extend more confident learners by asking them to predict the outcome of the investigation.

Plenary
● Discuss the children's observations and recordings, drawing out evidence that water has travelled up the stem towards and into the leaves. Annotate their ideas on page 11.
● Use the *Roots and stems* interactive activity (page 12) to help the children to explain their observations by dragging the labels to their correct positions around the diagram.
● Explain that the water is transported to the leaves to aid the healthy growth of the plant. (It is required for photosynthesis.)
● Print out the correctly labelled diagram. Alternatively, use the Area Capture tool to take a snapshot of the completed activity and save the diagram into a new Notebook page.

Common materials and their properties

Learning objectives
QCA Unit 3C 'Characteristics of materials'
● To identify a range of common materials and know that the same material is used to make different objects.
● To recognise properties such as hardness, strength and flexibility and compare materials in terms of these properties.

Resources
'Characteristics of materials' Notebook file; photocopiable page 129 'Properties of materials' for each child; objects made from a range of materials, including metal, wood, rubber, plastic, rock, leather, wool, cotton, glass and ceramics; hand magnifiers.

Links to other subjects
Design and technology
PoS (4a) To know how the working characteristics of materials affect the ways they are used.
● Use this investigation to help the children to construct stable structures from suitable materials.
English
Creating and shaping texts
● Encourage the children to use a thesaurus to look up synonyms for describing properties of materials (*bumpy, uneven*).

Whiteboard tools
Convert handwritten words to text by selecting them and choosing the Recognise option from the dropdown menu.

 Pen tray

 Select tool

Starter
Ask the children to carry out a quick survey of the classroom (or another safe location) to identify a range of materials. Discuss why particular materials might have been used (for example, metal for chair legs, wood for floors). Write their ideas on page 2 of the 'Characteristics of materials' Notebook file.

Whole-class shared work
● Display page 3 and discuss the errors in the labelling of the objects. Establish the difference between the name of an object and the name of the material it is made from.
● Invite individual children to drag and drop the objects into the correct positions.
● Challenge the children to think of other objects made from the materials shown.
● Use page 4 of the Notebook file to challenge the children to think about what material an object is made from and identify objects that are made from the same material. The objects in the box should be dragged and dropped into groups, under the appropriate labels, on screen.
● Discuss any misconceptions and surprises. Elicit that the same material is used to make different objects and that some objects are made from more than one material (such as the well or the mirror).

Independent work
● Hand out a copy of photocopiable page 129 'Properties of materials' to each child.
● Ask the children to observe carefully and feel a number of different objects.
● In each case, ask the children to sketch the object, identify the material that it is made from and record its properties (for example, smooth, flexible, transparent, hard).
● Help less confident learners to choose and record appropriate properties from the Word Bank on the sheet.
● Extend more confident learners by asking them to compare materials in terms of their properties (for example, ask: *Which materials seem the strongest or most flexible?*)

Plenary
● Ask the children to take turns to describe an object. Invite each child to describe the object using only the properties of the material from which it is made. Can the other children identify the object being described?
● With the children's help, write the properties of each material in the space on page 5.
● Discuss which materials have common properties and which differ. Draw out why particular properties are suited to the function of an object (for example, although both plastic and glass are transparent, a ruler is made from plastic because it is more flexible and less fragile).

Absorbency investigation

Learning objectives
QCA Unit 3C 'Characteristics of materials'
● To plan a test to compare the absorbency of different papers, deciding what evidence to collect, considering what to change, what to keep the same and what to measure.
● To make comparisons and draw conclusions.

Resources
'Characteristics of materials' Notebook file; a range of different kitchen towels (up to five brands); scissors; rulers; water; food colouring; measuring cylinders, pipettes or syringes; clear plastic cups.

Links to other subjects
English
Understanding and interpreting texts
● Use this investigation to inform studies of how advertisements function and the difference between fact and opinion.
Art and design
PoS (2b) To apply their experience of materials and processes, including drawing, developing their control of tools and techniques.
● Ask the children to apply their experiences from this investigation when using watercolour paints (by mixing water and paint and applying it to absorbent paper).

Whiteboard tools
Use the Screen Shade to hide and reveal parts of the screen.

  Pen tray

  Select tool

  Screen Shade

Starter
Discuss the children's experiences of spilling liquids at home, particularly in the kitchen. Ask them how these spills are usually cleared up. Find out what they know about relevant household cleaning products and how they are advertised.

Whole-class shared work
● Display the advert for a kitchen towel on page 6 of the 'Characteristics of materials' Notebook file. Discuss the key features of the advert and how realistic its claims seem.
● Discuss how the children could go about finding the *best* kitchen towel. Establish what *best* would mean and how this could be translated into an investigation, including the resources they would need and how they could make the test fair.
● Go to page 7, and fill the criteria for a fair and accurate investigation into the three labelled boxes. You could use the Screen Shade 🔲 to cover the Word bank at the bottom of the screen, in advance, to challenge the children to think of the correct vocabulary. Write, in the relevant boxes, what they are going to keep the same (the size of the towel/amount of water); what they will change (the type of towel) and what they will measure (how much towel is needed).
● Uncover the Word bank and, together, drag and drop relevant phrases into the appropriate boxes.

Independent work
● Ask the children to cut up some small, equal-sized pieces of each of the different brands of kitchen towel.
● Using an equal quantity of water in a cup each time, ask the children to count how many pieces of each type of towel are required to soak up all the water. You may wish to use food colouring to increase the visibility of the liquid.
● Help them to record their results in a simple table.
● Support less confident learners by discussing how the fair testing will help to produce more accurate results.
● Extend more confident learners by asking them to establish some reasons as to why a certain towel performs better than another, and to predict how the next towel will perform based on such reasons.

Plenary
● Try to establish a consensus in ranking the towels in order of absorbency, completing the results table on page 8. You will need to collect all the answers and then address any differences first.
● Discuss how multiple results help to establish a consensus (or highlight inconsistencies) and draw out the children's ideas about why certain towels are more absorbent than others.

Stretching investigation

Learning objectives

QCA Unit 3C 'Characteristics of materials'
● To plan how to find out which pair of tights is most stretchy, making a fair comparison.
● To decide what to change, what to keep the same and what to measure.
● To make careful measurements of length, to present measurements as a bar chart and to draw conclusions.

Resources

'Characteristics of materials' Notebook file; photocopiable page 130 'Stretching investigation' for each child; a maximum of six pairs of tights of the same size but different thicknesses (denier): cut the legs to the same length; sets of weights; metre sticks, rulers or tape measures. (Microsoft Excel is required to view the spreadsheet .)

Links to other subjects

Science
PoS Sc4 (2d) That when objects are pushed or pulled, an opposing pull or push can be felt.
● Use this investigation to inform studies of stretching springs or elastic bands.
ICT
PoS (3a) How to share and exchange information in a variety of forms, including email.
● Ask the children to attach and send a copy of the completed spreadsheet to an appropriate recipient.

Whiteboard tools

Use the On-screen Keyboard to enter data into the spreadsheet cells. Annotate it with the Floating tools

 Pen tray

 Select tool

 Screen Shade

 On-screen Keyboard

 Floating tools

Starter

Ask the children to examine a number of pairs of tights and describe some of their properties, including any differences in thickness and stretchiness. Consider together why tights are designed in different thicknesses, known as *denier*. Ask the children whether they think the denier affects how stretchy the tights are. Write their responses on page 9 of the 'Characteristics of materials' Notebook file.

Whole-class shared work

● Discuss how the children could go about finding out which pair of tights is the stretchiest. Establish how this could be transformed into an investigation, including the resources they would need and how they could ensure a fair test.
● Go to page 10. If required, cover the Word bank at the bottom of the screen in advance by using the Screen Shade . Challenge the children to think of what they are going to keep the same in the investigation (weight); what they will change (the thickness of tights); and what they will measure (how far the tights stretch).
● Reveal tool the Word bank, and drag and drop relevant phrases into the correct boxes.

Independent work

● Hand out copies of the 'Stretching investigation' photocopiable sheet to each child.
● Ask the children to predict which tights will be the most or least stretchy (or in-between), adding *most stretchy* and *least stretchy* for the appropriate tights in the *My prediction* column.
● Ask children to secure a set weight to, or in, each pair of tights and carefully measure the length of the stretched tights. Remind them to keep their feet out of the way, or place a box or bin underneath the suspended weight.
● Ask the children to record their measurements accurately on their sheets.
● Support less confident learners by ensuring that each measurement is made and recorded accurately.
● Extend more confident learners by asking them to predict how stretchy each pair of tights will be before measuring.

Plenary

● Discuss what the children discovered.
● Inform the children that bar charts can be used to present results clearly so that comparisons can be made more easily.
● Press the hyperlinked button on page 11 to open the *Stretching investigations* spreadsheet. Use the On-screen Keyboard to enter the children's data in the table. The bar chart will complete itself automatically.
● Examine and discuss the resultant bar chart, using it to explain which tights were most stretchy. Establish if there is any link between denier and stretchiness.

Characteristics and purposes of rocks

Learning objectives
QCA Unit 3D 'Rocks and soils'
- To understand that rocks are used for a variety of purposes.
- To understand that rocks are chosen for particular purposes because of their characteristics.

Resources
'Rocks and soils' Notebook file; exercise books and pens.

Links to other subjects
Geography
PoS (3e) To identify how and why places change.
- Use this lesson to complement work on how the local built environment has changed in terms of construction materials.
Art and design
PoS (4b) To understand the materials and processes used in art, craft and design and how these can be matched to ideas and intentions.
- Identify the use of different stone in studies of sculpture.

Starter
Ask the children to point out any obvious uses of stone or rock in the classroom or nearby. Make a distinction between naturally occurring rocks, such as slate or granite, and man-made materials that contain rock, such as tarmac and concrete. Write the children's ideas and responses on page 2 of the 'Rocks and soils' Notebook file.

Whole-class shared work
- Read and discuss the sentences on pages 3 and 4. Are the children surprised by any of the facts?
- Highlight anything interesting and annotate any questions that the children have about rocks.
- Ask for any further examples of rocks used in the home.
- Encourage the children to think about what rock the objects are made from and the reason a particular rock has been used.
- Invite individual children to highlight the key words to identify all the rocks' names and associated technical vocabulary.

Independent work
- Organise the children to carry out a survey of the school buildings and playground to identify where rocks have been used.
- Ask them to note down where they identify a rock has been used and why it has been chosen (for example, steps made from granite because it does not wear away easily).
- Ask the children to consider whether the rock is natural or a man-made material.
- Encourage them to record their data in a table. Suggest column headings such as: *What is it? What is it made from? Why was this rock was used? Is it man-made or natural?*

Plenary
- Come together back in class and discuss what the children have discovered. Write their responses on page 5. Do any of the rocks have common features? Are there any rocks that they would like to find out more about?
- Display page 6 of the Notebook file and ask the children if they can remember the facts they learned at the beginning of a lesson.
- Invite individual children to come to the board and drag and drop the cards so that each phrase fits with the correct sentence starter.
- Check against pages 3 and 4 to ensure that the phrases have been correctly matched.

Whiteboard tools
Convert handwritten words to text by pressing the Right Mouse button and selecting the Recognise option from the dropdown menu.

 Pen tray

 Select tool

 Highlighter pen

Soils

Learning objectives

QCA Unit 3D 'Rocks and soils'
- To understand that beneath all surfaces there is rock.
- To understand that there are different kinds of soil depending on the rock from which they come.

Resources

'Rocks and soils' Notebook file; tall, straight-sided clear glass containers with tight lids, such as tall jam jars; good quantities of three topsoils from different locations; water.

Links to other subjects
Geography
PoS (3e) To identify how and why places change.
- Discuss how the rock or soil type in the locality has impacted historically. For example are there any local mines, quarries or china clay works?

Art and design
PoS (4b) To understand the materials and processes used in art, craft and design and how these can be matched to ideas and intentions.
- Use sand to alter the texture of paint.

Whiteboard tools
Pull down the Screen Shade to gradually reveal a soil profile.

 Pen tray

 Select tool

 Screen Shade

 Shapes tool

 Fill Colour tool

 Pen tool

Starter
Open the 'Rocks and soils' Notebook file and press the button next to Lesson 12, which takes you to page 7. Discuss the children's own experiences of digging in a garden. Find out if any of them have noticed any differences or made any discoveries about the feel or appearance of the soil as they have dug deeper. What do they think is underneath the soil?

Whole-class shared work
- Display page 8 and tell the children that they will be looking at a number of pictures that involve rock.
- Move through pages 9 to 14 of the Notebook file and, in each case, ask the children to identify where any rock is located. Draw out that, even if it is not visible, there is always solid rock underneath the surface vegetation, buildings or soil.
- Pull the tabs to reveal more information about the picture.
- Move on to page 15. Pull down the Screen Shade to gradually reveal a soil profile. Discuss the profile layer by layer from the top. Elicit that most people would not have experienced digging deeper than the top soil.
- Go to page 16 and explain that the labels have been muddled up. The children have to drag and drop them back into their correct positions.
- Display and discuss page 17. Explain that the children are going to investigate the contents of a number of soils by separating the materials within the soils.

Independent work
- Invite the children to half fill a glass container with one of the soils, and carefully add enough water so that the container is three-quarters full. (Refer to your school's health and safety guidelines when handling soils.)
- Ask the children to close the lid tightly and then shake the container well for one or two minutes, or until the soil is fully suspended in the water.
- Invite them to store their container in a dark, undisturbed place. Discuss what the children think will happen.
- Wait 24 hours and check if the soil particles have fully settled (there will be a layer of clear water on top of the settled bands of soil).
- Once the soil particles have settled, ask the children to study, draw and label their container and its contents carefully. Ensure that the children move the containers with care so that particles do not enter into the solution again.

Plenary
- Discuss the children's findings (from the bottom upwards, individual bands of settled sand, silt, clay, organic matter and water might be visible).
- Display page 18 of the Notebook file and ask the children to draw and place coloured rectangles on the containers to represent, as accurately as possible, the settled bands for the three different soils. (They could use either the Shapes tool and the Fill Colour tool to do this, or use the Pen tool, selecting different colours and thick settings.
- Discuss any differences in the banding and draw out the fact that all soils contain different amounts of sand, silt, clay and organic matter and that the quantities involved usually depend on the parent rock that is underneath the soil. Write this conclusion on page 19.

Water flow investigation

Learning objectives
QCA unit 3D 'Rocks and soils'
● To use simple apparatus to measure volumes of liquids and to measure time.
● To recognise when a test is unfair.
● To use results to make comparisons, and to draw and explain conclusions.

Resources
'Water flow investigation' Notebook file; photocopiable pages 136 'Investigation planning' and 131 'Water flow investigation' for each child; sticky labels; clocks or stopwatches showing seconds; measuring cylinders; large trays; different soil types (sand, clay, loam, and so on); two-litre plastic bottles (cut the tops off the bottles, about one quarter of the way down from the neck and make a few small holes in the base of each bottle; place the cut-off necks upside down in the top of the bottles to act as funnels). (Microsoft Excel is required to view the spreadsheet.)

Links to other subjects
Mathematics
Measuring: Choose and use appropriate units to estimate, measure and record measurements.
● Use this investigation to develop the children's skills of measuring volumes accurately.
ICT
PoS (3a) Share and exchange information in a variety of forms, including email.
● Ask the children to attach and send a copy of the completed spreadsheet to an appropriate recipient.

Whiteboard tools
Use the Floating tools to annotate the bar chart in the embedded spreadsheet.

 Pen tray

 Select tool

 On-screen Keyboard

 Floating tools

Starter
Ask the children to describe what happens to the water when a wave rolls up a sandy beach. Discuss why the sand seems to *dry out* so quickly when the wave retreats (the water quickly flows down between the sand particles). Draw a diagram on page 2 of the 'Water flow investigation' Notebook file to help the children visualise what is happening.

Ask the children about their experiences of water sinking into soil (for example, when they water pot plants). Go to page 3 and tell the children that there are six main soil types (*sandy, silty, clay, peaty, chalky* and *loamy*). Explain that they will be testing some (or all) of them to find out how quickly water flows through them.

Whole-class shared work
● Discuss how the children could find out how fast water travels through each soil type. Establish how this could be planned as an investigation, including the resources they would need.
● Using page 4, discuss how the children could make the test fair, by asking them what they are going to keep the same (volume of water); what they will change (soil type); and what they will measure (how long the water takes to flow through the soil and to start dripping from the bottle). Write these points on the page or drag the phrases from the Word bank.
● Demonstrate how to fill a measuring cylinder and read the scale accurately.
● Ask the children to complete their own copy of the 'Investigation planning' sheet.

Independent work
● Hand out copies of the 'Water flow investigation' sheet.
● Ask the children to quarter-fill the plastic bottles with the different soil types, remembering to label them and replace the cut-off necks.
● Tell the children to hold the bottles over the trays and pour 250ml of water onto the soil, ensuring that they start timing immediately. They must stop timing when the water starts dripping from the holes in the base of the bottle. Ask them to record the time on their sheets.
● Repeat this process with a number of soil types.
● Help less confident learners to measure the volume and record the timings accurately.
● Extend more confident learners by asking them to provide reasons for their predictions.

Plenary
● Discuss the children's results. Explain that bar charts can be used to present results clearly, so that comparisons can be made more easily.
● Press the hyperlinked button on page 5 to open the *Water flow investigations* spreadsheet. Enter the children's data in the table.
● Discuss the resultant bar chart, using it to explain which soil type the water flowed through the most quickly. Talk about the reasons for this (sand drains quickly because of the spaces between particles, whereas clay drains poorly due to few air spaces).
● Compare the results with their predictions.
● Use page 6 to summarise what they have learned.

Properties of magnets

Learning objectives
QCA Unit 3E 'Magnets and springs'
● To know that there are forces between magnets and that magnets can attract (pull towards) and repel (push away from) each other.
● To make and record careful observations of magnets.
● To make generalisations about what happens when magnets are put together.

Resources
'Investigating forces' Notebook file; a variety of strong magnets of different sizes and shapes, some with the poles labelled.

Links to other subjects
Design and technology
PoS (2c) To explore the sensory qualities of materials and how to use materials and processes.
● Use this investigation to inspire the use of magnets and magnetic materials in the design and construction of packaging or photograph frames.
ICT
PoS (2c) To use simulations and explore models to investigate and evaluate the effect of changing values.
● The children use simulation software to explore the properties of magnets and magnetic materials in ways that would be difficult to carry out in the classroom.

Starter
Review the children's knowledge of push and pull forces from previous years by asking them to describe or demonstrate examples of such forces (such as pushing a pencil, pulling open a door). Summarise what the children know on page 2 of the 'Investigating forces' Notebook file.

Whole-class shared work
● Use pages 3 and 4 to explain the legend of Sir Isaac Newton's discovery of the *universal law of gravitation*: While resting under a tree, Sir Isaac Newton observed an apple falling from the tree. He realised there must be a *pull* force directly towards the centre of the Earth that not only acted on apples and people, but on the Moon too.
● Compare this with the *push* force on page 5 when the ball is kicked. Use the Pen or Lines tools ◥ (select the arrows) to illustrate the direction of forces on pages 3 and 5.
● Tell the children that they are going to be investigating the properties of magnets and describing the forces they observe and feel.
● Present them with the collection of different magnets and remind them not to drop them as it damages them.

Independent work
● Ask the children to choose one pair of magnets at a time and put them very close together, observing and feeling what happens.
● Encourage the children to explore different ways of putting the magnets together.
● Ensure that all the children investigate the magnets that have the poles labelled.
● Keep page 6 on display to remind the children of their objective.
● Challenge the children to try to discuss their observations in terms of push and pull forces.
● Support less confident learners in describing their investigations and observations clearly.
● Extend more confident learners by asking them to describe what is happening in terms of the two poles.

Plenary
● Ask the children to describe what they observed with the unlabelled and labelled magnets.
● Look at the top two magnets on page 7. Ask the children what they think would happen if they were dragged closer together. Ask them to write *push* or *pull* force. Introduce the term *attract*. Delete the top grey box to reveal the answer.
● Repeat for the bottom two magnets and introduce the term *repel*.
● Repeat a similar exercise for the magnets on page 8.
● Go to page 9. Ask the children to generalise about what happens when two magnets are put together using scientific terms (*push, pull, force, attract, repel*). Use the Eraser to reveal these words hidden in the box.

Whiteboard tools
Use the Lines tool to draw straight lines on the screen. Select arrows to indicate direction.

 Pen tray

 Select tool

 Lines tool

 Delete button

Magnetic materials

Starter
Go to page 10 of the 'Investigating forces' Notebook file. Recap any previous work on the properties of magnets especially the force of attraction between opposite poles. Ensure that the children are confident at using the terms *attract, attraction, repel* and *repulsion*. Use the Eraser to reveal the key words hidden in the box.

Whole-class shared work
● Play the simple game on page 11. Drag the objects to the wall to see which are magnetic. The non-magnetic objects will disappear.
● Talk about the materials from which the magnetic and non-magnetic objects are made. Ask: *Are there any similarities between the materials?* Clarify that although an object may be attracted to a magnet, it is not necessarily a magnet itself.
● Tell the children that they are going to investigate a number of materials to discover whether or not they are magnetic (attracted to a magnet).
● Display the resources and discuss how the children could go about finding out whether each object is magnetic. Consider together how to conduct the investigation fairly (using the same magnet/same number of magnets and so on). Write the children's ideas on page 12.
● Ask the children to make clear predictions.

Independent work
● Before testing, ask the children to sort their objects into two groups: magnetic and non-magnetic, based on their predictions.
● Ask them to test each object and sort them into two groups (magnetic and non-magnetic) noting any objects that go against their predictions.
● Invite the children to discuss what they have discovered (especially any surprises) and to make an appropriate generalisation.
● Support less confident learners in their use of scientific language and what is meant by a magnetic material.
● Extend the activity by asking the children to give possible explanations for any surprises (some *copper* coins are magnetic, whereas a piece of copper piping is not, because the coins contain steel under the copper coating).

Plenary
● Display page 13 and use the children's results to write the names of the objects in the appropriate frame.
● Discuss what the results show. Establish that some objects that contain metal are magnetic and some are not.
● Ask the children to make a general statement about what the results show (that magnets, and some, but not all, metals are magnetic materials) and write the conclusion in the frame.
● To extend the learning, write the names of the metals next to the appropriate objects and ask the children to make an appropriate generalisation (iron and steel are magnetic but aluminium, brass, copper and gold are not).
● Use the multiple-choice *Magnets quiz* (on page 14) to quiz children on their understanding of the properties of magnets and magnetic materials.

Elastic investigation

Learning objectives
QCA Unit 3E 'Magnets and springs'
● To make predictions of the effect of stretching elastic bands by different amounts.
● To make comparisons and identify patterns in results.
● To draw conclusions and indicate whether the prediction was supported.
● To explain the conclusions in terms of the size of the force.

Resources
'Investigating forces' Notebook file; photocopiable page 132 'Elastic launcher' for each child, copied onto card; photocopiable page 136, 'Investigation planning' for each child; long, medium-thickness elastic bands; strips of white elastic; split-pins; modelling clay; paper; metre rulers; plastic bottle tops; scissors.

Links to other subjects
Design and technology
PoS (2c) To explore the sensory qualities of materials and how to use materials and processes.
● Ask the children to investigate objects that use materials under tension and to describe the qualities of the materials. Encourage them to think about the ways in which the materials are used.
ICT
PoS (2c) To use simulations and explore models to investigate and evaluate the effect of changing values.
● The children use simulation software to explore the properties of springs in ways that would be difficult to carry out in the classroom.

Whiteboard tools
Use the Eraser from the Pen tray to reveal hidden words. Convert handwritten words to text by pressing the Right Mouse button and selecting the Recognise option.

🖥 Pen tray

Starter
Open page 15 of the 'Investigating forces' Notebook file. Recap any previous work on the properties of springs and elastic bands, encouraging the children to use scientific terms, such as *stretch*, *compress* and *force*. Use the Eraser to reveal these key words.

Whole-class shared work
● Display and discuss page 16 and introduce the term *tension*.
● Annotate the pictures and explain that the pull force acting on the fingers is caused by the *tension* (stretch) in the elastic band.
● Ask the children to describe any objects they have seen that use materials under tension (such as catapults, wind-up toys and drum skins).
● Explain that the children are going to be investigating the elastic under tension by building an elastic launcher to launch weighted bottle tops.
● Display page 17 and demonstrate how to build the launcher from the 'Elastic launcher' photocopiable sheet.
● Give each child a copy of page 136 'Investigation planning'. Establish that the children are going to be testing how the amount of stretch (or tension) in the elastic affects the distance an object travels.
● Discuss how the children are going to carry out the investigation fairly, drawing out that they will be changing the amount of stretch in cm on the launcher's grid.
● Ask the children to make clear predictions and to complete the sheet.

Independent work
● Hand out copies of photocopiable page 132 'Elastic launcher' and invite the children to construct their own launchers.
● Tell the children to launch a bottle top weighted with modelling clay along a smooth surface, using different amounts of stretch each time (using the marked distances on the photocopiable page). Ask them to measure the distance the bottle top slides in cm.
● Ask the children to carefully record their findings on paper, using a table similar to the one on page 18.
● Support less confident learners in measuring accurately from the exact point the bottle top is launched.
● Extend more confident learners by asking them to consider any possible patterns in their results (for example, does *double the stretch* mean *double the distance*?)

Plenary
● Display page 18 and use one child's results to complete the table.
● Discuss what can be concluded from the results and if the results matched the children's predictions.
● Explain to the children that it is important to compare more than one set of results from the same investigation. Complete the tables on pages 19 and 20 with two more children's results.
● Compare the sets of results and discuss common patterns. Emphasise that by considering more results there is more chance of being able to make and confirm conclusions.
● Ask the children to make comparisons in order to write a general statement about what all the results show in scientific terms on page 21 (that the greater the tension in the elastic, the greater the distance that the object was launched).

Shadow formation

Learning objectives
QCA Unit 3F 'Light and shadows'
● To know that shadows are formed when light travelling from a source is blocked.
● To make and record observations and to present information in drawing and writing.

Resources
'Light and shadows' Notebook file; photocopiable page 133 'Shadow investigations' for each child; a selection of opaque objects, such as a comb or toy car; a cardboard tube; torches or other more powerful light sources, such as an overhead projector; large sheets of white card.

Links to other subjects
History
PoS (11b) A study of the impact of the Second World War.
● Use silhouettes in depictions of firemen fighting Blitz blazes.
Art and design
PoS (5a) Exploring a range of starting points for practical work.
● Encourage the children to use their knowledge of light and shadows in stencil or printing work.

Starter
Ask the children to identify any dark shadows around the classroom and to explain why the shadows are there. Discuss and write their responses on page 2 of the Notebook file. For a more dramatic demonstration, stand or hold an object in front of the beam from the projector, and ask the children to discuss what they can and cannot see on the whiteboard. Take care to avoid looking directly into the projector beam.

Whole-class shared work
● Display page 3 of the Notebook file and discuss what is missing from the picture (a shadow on the board).
● Ask the children to draw a black shadow onto the correct place by either drawing an outline or cloning the hand on the page, and using the Pen tool to fill it with black.
● Ask the children to explain what happens to the light from the projector on its way to the board. Invite individual children to represent their ideas by drawing on screen. Do not, at this stage, inform the children that they must draw straight lines (as children often think light bends around an object).
● Discuss the children's ideas. Next, display and discuss page 4. Establish that light travels in straight lines and a shadow is formed when light is blocked by an object.
● Discuss any misconceptions and surprises. For example, shine a torch directly through a cardboard tube and then twist the tube to one side to demonstrate that light does not bend around corners.

Independent work
● Hand out copies of the photocopiable 'Shadow investigations' sheet to each child.
● Ask the children to explore and observe shadow formation by using torches, or other light sources, and an opaque object to form shadows on white card.
● Tell the children to carefully record one of their observations (in drawing and writing) on the photocopiable sheet as directed.
● Extend the activity by asking the children to explain why a shadow is larger when an object is closer to the light source.

Plenary
● Discuss the children's observations.
● Use page 5 to test the children's learning by inviting them to drag and drop the correct words into each sentence. Emphasise that light travels from a source, not from the eyes.

Whiteboard tools
Duplicate an object by selecting it, and choosing Clone from the dropdown menu. Use the Pen tool to fill it with black to create a shadow. Use the Lines tool to draw straight lines.

 Pen tray

 Select tool

 Pen tool

 Lines tool

Shadow length investigation

Learning objectives
QCA unit 3F 'Light and shadows'
● To know that shadows change in length and position throughout the day.
● To measure the length of a shadow in standard measures.
● To make a table and line graph to show how the length of shadows changes during the day.

Resources
'Shadow length investigation' Notebook file; photocopiable page 136 'Investigation planning' for each child; a long 'shadow' stick and base, such as a rounders post; a metre stick showing cm; chalk or masking tape; a digital camera (optional); a sunny day! (Microsoft Excel is required to view the embedded spreadsheet in the Notebook file.)

Links to other subjects
Mathematics
Handling data: Answer a question by collecting, organising and interpreting data.
● Use this investigation to extend the children's knowledge of data handling, by introducing the use of line graphs to show change over time.
ICT
PoS (3a) How to share and exchange information in a variety of forms, including email.
● Ask the children to attach and send a copy of the completed spreadsheet to an appropriate recipient.

Whiteboard tools
Use the On-screen Keyboard to enter data into the table.

 Pen tray

 Select tool

 On-screen Keyboard

Starter
Go to page 2 of the Notebook file. Ask the children if they have noticed differences in the size of shadows at different times of day (some children may have noticed long shadows at sunset or short ones at noon in midsummer). Ask them why shadows might change size during the day. Tell the children that they are going to investigate exactly how the length of a shadow changes during a day at school.

Whole-class shared work
● Ask the children how they would plan an investigation to find out how the length of a shadow changes over five or six hours. They also need to think about the resources they would need. Use page 3 to make notes.
● Discuss how the children could make the test fair by asking them what they are going to keep the same (size and position of stick); what they will change (position of the Sun in sky) and what they will measure (length of shadow).
● Drag and drop the correct phrases into the relevant boxes on page 4 of the Notebook file together.
● Demonstrate how to measure distances of under and over 1m accurately in centimetres, using a metre stick.
● Ask the children to complete their own copies of the 'Investigation planning' photocopiable sheet.
● Display page 5 and encourage the children to predict what will happen.

Independent work
● Set up the *shadow stick* in a flat location that will remain undisturbed and in direct sunlight for the day.
● At half-hourly intervals, ask the children to mark the current shadow using chalk or tape and to measure and record its length and the time accurately. If possible, record this with a digital camera as well. Provide support where necessary.

Plenary
● Discuss the pattern made by the different length markings around the *shadow stick*, asking the children what they think has happened.
● Inform the children that a line graph can be used to show how shadow length changes over time. Press the hyperlinked button on page 6 of the Notebook file to open a spreadsheet to record the children's results. Use the On-screen Keyboard [image] to enter their data into the table.
● Discuss the resultant line graph, explaining how the shadow shortens towards noon and lengthens into the afternoon. Compare the results with the predictions.
● Ask the children to explain why the shadow changes length in this way (shadows shorten in the morning as the Sun rises higher in the sky and lengthen in the afternoons as the Sun sets).
● Encourage the children to explain the movement of the shadow around the stick (the Sun moves across the sky from east to west, so light and shadows are cast from different directions). Use page 7 to demonstrate this and display the children's photos of the stick and shadow, if necessary.
● Repeat this investigation in a different season and compare the results (shadow length in winter will be longer than in summer as the sun travels lower across the sky due to the Earth's tilt and orbit around the Sun).

Shadow time-telling

Learning objective
QCA Unit 3F 'Light and shadows'
● To know that shadows can be used to tell the approximate time of day.

Resources
'Light and shadows' Notebook file; photocopiable page 134, 'Make your own sundial' for each child (photocopied onto card if possible); magnetic compass; scissors; sticky tape or masking tape; a sunny day!

Links to other subjects
Mathematics
Understanding shape: Identify right angles in 2D shapes.
● Use the shapes and angles of the sundial and gnomon to identify right angles.
Design and technology
PoS (2d) To measure, mark out, cut and shape a range of materials, and assemble, join and combine components and materials accurately.
● Challenge the children to design their own sundials using more robust materials, such as wood and card.

Starter
At the beginning of the day, ask any children with watches to remove them. If possible, remove or cover the classroom clock. Before the lesson starts, ask the children to estimate the time, justifying their estimates.

Inform them that digital watches were invented less than 50 years ago and mechanical watches appeared about 500 years ago, yet the Ancient Egyptians had ways of telling the time nearly 5000 years ago. How do the children think people would have told the time before clocks and watches?

Whole-class shared work
● Discuss how each object on pages 6 to 9 of the 'Light and shadows' Notebook file could have been used to tell the time. Discuss which historical era each object is from, and its approximate age.
● Ask the children to circle the objects that rely on light and shadows (the Egyptian obelisk and sundial) and label them.
● Discuss the children's familiarity with sundials and display page 10, explaining that the dial's shadow is used to tell the time. Point out that the *gnomon* is the part of the sundial that projects the shadow, which is used to tell the time.
● Encourage them to say how the dial works, using the correct scientific and technical vocabulary.
● Tell the children that they are going to make their own simple sundials and display page 11.
● Drag the gnomon over the base to demonstrate where it fits. Use the right-angled corner to emphasise the correct orientation of the gnomon.
● Display page 12. Tell the children that they will be using a magnetic compass to make sure that their sundials are pointing north.

Independent work
● Hand out a copy of photocopiable page 134 'Make your own sundial' to each child.
● Tell the children to carefully cut out the gnomon, and cut the slit in the base as indicated.
● Help them to fold the gnomon along the line and insert it into the base, making sure it is correctly orientated. They then need to secure it underneath with a strip of tape.
● Place the completed sundials in direct sunlight and use a compass to point them northwards.
● Ask the children to estimate the time from their sundials. Compare their estimates with the correct time. If possible, repeat at a different time of day.
● Support less confident learners in making and reading their sundials.
● Extend more confident learners by asking why the time on the sundials might be different from the correct time, drawing out the limitations of the sundial.

Plenary
● Ask the children to share their experiences with their sundials.
● Encourage them to judge the accuracy of the sundials and suggest the limitations of them.

Whiteboard tools

 Pen tray

 Select tool

Opacity and transparency investigation

Learning objectives
QCA Unit 3F 'Light and shadows'
● To understand that opaque objects/materials do not let light through and transparent objects/materials let a lot of light through.
● To use their knowledge about light and shadows to predict which materials will form a shadow, and to plan how to test this.
● To compare the shadows formed by different materials and to draw conclusions from their results.
● To decide whether the results support their predictions and to use knowledge about shadow formation to explain the conclusions.

Resources
'Light and shadows' Notebook file; photocopiable page 135 'Light, shadows and materials' for each child; a collection of opaque objects/materials, transparent (plastic bottles, acetate sheets or coloured Cellophane) and translucent (fine gauze, thin nylon tights, greaseproof or tissue paper); torches or other more powerful light sources, such as an overhead projector; large sheets of white card.

Links to other subjects
Art and design
PoS (2c) To use a variety of approaches to communicate ideas.
● Use translucent and transparent materials to convey atmosphere when photographing a dream sequence.

Whiteboard tools
Use the Spotlight tool to highlight objects.

 Pen tray

 Spotlight tool

 Select tool

Starter
Position an object in front of the beam from the projector and ask the children to discuss what they can see on the whiteboard. Review any previous work on shadow formation. Take care to avoid looking directly into the projector beam. Tell the children that they will be using their knowledge of light and shadows to predict whether a collection of objects made from different materials will form a shadow when a light is shone at them.

Whole-class shared work
● Present the children with the collection of objects and discuss what each is made from.
● Display page 13 of the 'Light and shadows' Notebook file and ask the children to make their predictions. Write the names of the materials in the appropriate frames.
● Discuss how the children could ensure a fair test by asking them what they are going to keep the same (light source, distance between light, object and card); what they will change (object/material); and what they will measure (intensity of shadow).

Independent work
● Hand out a copy of photocopiable page 135 'Light, shadows and materials investigation' to each child.
● Ask the children to choose a number of objects and complete the first three columns of the sheet.
● Invite them to test the objects using the torches and white card, taking care to test in a fair manner.
● Tell the children to record their findings in the next three columns, describing the shadow produced as *dark*, *pale* or *none* and describing the object as *transparent*, *translucent* or *opaque*.
● Support less confident learners in making and checking predictions.
● Extend more confident learners by asking them to provide reasons for their predictions in terms of what is happening to the light.

Plenary
● Classify the children's findings by writing in the names of the objects/materials in the appropriate frames on page 14 of the Notebook file.
● Discuss, and then drag and drop each scientific term (*opaque*, *translucent*, *transparent*) over the appropriate frames.
● Tell the children that they are going to be using this knowledge in an underwater adventure challenge. Display page 15.
● Activate the Spotlight tool and go to the next page. Resize the spotlight to increase or decrease difficulty.
● Ask the children to move the spotlight to find and identify all the animals on page 16.
Exit the Spotlight tool and check their answers. Move the black net and the rock to reveal the two hidden creatures.
● Encourage the children to classify each material using their learning from the lesson (water is transparent, net is translucent, and rock is opaque).
● Use page 17 to summarise what the children have learned in this lesson.

A healthy meal

■ You need to design a healthy meal for a school lunch. Choose six items from this list and draw and label them on your plate. Make sure that you choose at least one item from each food group so that the meal is varied and balanced. Use the food pyramid on the whiteboard to help you.

apple	bread slice	peas	lettuce
banana	yoghurt	crisps	watermelon
broccoli	mushrooms	fish cakes	lentils
chocolate bar	lollipop	potato	crackers
fish fingers	orange	rice	carrot sticks
pear	peanuts	pasta	leeks
pork chop	baked beans	grapes	cheese slices
sweetcorn	spaghetti	boiled egg	roast chicken

Illustrations © Andy Keylock / Beehive Illustration

Animal diets

◼ Use these tables to help you carry out your animal diets survey.

Name of animal	Tick or cross
Has this animal ever eaten:	

Name of animal	Tick or cross
Has this animal ever eaten:	

Plant investigations

Growth investigation: Number of leaves

Where will the plants be kept?

How much water and when?

What will we measure and when?

Growth investigation: Water

Where will the plants be kept?

How much water and when?

What will we measure and when?

Growth investigation: Light

Where will the plants be kept?

How much water and when?

What will we measure and record and when?

Word Bank

light	height	ruler	same
dark	stem	tape measure	different
sunlight	soil	colour	amount
shady	hours	description	every
millilitres (ml)	days	health	quantity

Stem observation

■ When your teacher tells you, carefully draw the equipment in each box showing what happens to the coloured water.

Time	Time	Time

Properties of materials

Sketch	Name of material	Describe the properties of this material

Word Bank

fragile	crumbly	elastic	tough	irregular
hard	coarse	flimsy	durable	squashy
smooth	regular	delicate	inflexible	powdery
transparent	solid	weak	clear	firm
flexible	brittle	sturdy	stretchy	frail
rough	silky	stiff	bendable	glossy
soft	spongy	rigid	bumpy	shiny

Stretching investigation

Name of tights	Denier	Length before stretching (cm)	My prediction (most stretchy to least stretchy)	Length when stretched (cm)

Water flow investigation

Soil type	Time (seconds)

Remember: 60 seconds = 1 minute
120 seconds = 2 minutes
180 seconds = 3 minutes

Elastic launcher

■ Photocopy or glue your elastic launcher sheet onto card.

■ Place a ball of modelling clay underneath each X mark on your elastic launcher.

■ Make a hole by pushing your pencil through the middle of the X.

■ Measure and cut a piece of elastic to the length of 17cm.

■ Place the elastic over the line. Push a split pin through the elastic and the hole in the X.

■ Do the same for the other end of the elastic and the second X.

IMPORTANT SAFETY NOTE: Remember to use your elastic launcher safely and don't aim anything at other people.

Length of stretch
0cm
1cm
2cm
3cm
4cm
5cm
6cm
7cm
8cm
9cm
10cm
11cm
12cm

▪ SCHOLASTIC
www.scholastic.co.uk

Shadow investigations

■ Use a ruler to draw on lines of light from the light source to the board. Don't forget that some light is blocked by the object!

Draw the shadow on the whiteboard here.

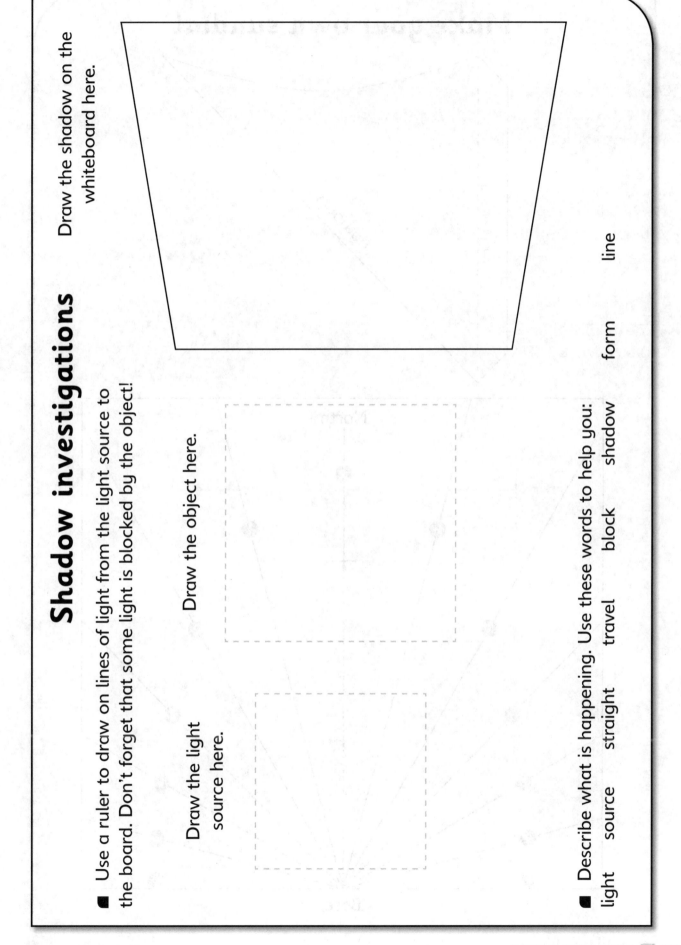

Draw the object here.

Draw the light source here.

■ Describe what is happening. Use these words to help you:

light   source   straight   travel   block   shadow   form   line

Make your own sundial

Fold along line

Gnomon

North

12

11   1

10   2

9   3

8   4

7   5

6   6

Base

Light, shadows and materials

- Complete the first three columns before you begin your investigation.
- Record your investigation results in the last three columns.

Object	Material	Prediction (all light, some light, no light)	Shadow (none, pale, dark)	Correct prediction? (yes, no)	Transparent, translucent or opaque?

Investigation planning

PLANNING

What are you trying to find out?
(A question that can be tested.)

What do you think will happen?
(Prediction)

What will you use? (Resources)

LABELLED DIAGRAM

FAIR TESTING

What will you change?
(The variable we are testing.)

What will you keep the same?
(Variables which will be kept constant.)

What will you measure and
record? (Results)

Foundation subjects

The following lessons offer ways to use an interactive whiteboard to teach the foundation subjects, using a range of whiteboard tools to target different learning styles.

Using an interactive whiteboard gives teachers and children a unique opportunity to project, annotate and save large-scale images. The children will be able to study and focus on details of historical artefacts, maps and aerial photographs, as well as audio and video resources. This in turn facilitates group discussions. In practical lessons, such as design and technology, you can film techniques and processes with a digital camera or take pictures of children's work, and then display the results on an interactive whiteboard. This allows you to annotate the images and it provides a great opportunity for assessment.

Lesson title	Objectives	Expected prior knowledge	Cross-curricular links
History			
Lesson 1: Dig this!	QCA Unit 6 'Why have people invaded in settled in Britain in the past?' • To place periods in a chronological framework. • To learn that there are some things we can learn from archaeological remains.	• Children should have used a range of sources of evidence including pictures and artefacts.	Science Sc3 (1a) To compare properties of everyday materials and objects, and relate these properties to everyday uses of the materials.
Lesson 2: Have you seen this man?	QCA Unit 7 'Why did Henry VIII marry six times?' • To answer questions using a portrait as a source. • To learn about the appearance and character of Henry VIII.	• Have used a range of sources of evidence including pictures and artefacts. • Where to place the Tudors on a timeline.	English Creating and shaping texts: Write non-narrative texts using structures of different text-types.
Lesson 3: Evacuated!	QCA Unit 9 'What was it like for children in the Second World War?' • To find out about the experiences and feelings of evacuees. • To communicate learning in an organised and structured way, using appropriate terminology.	• Children should have used written and pictorial sources to gain information. • Know about life in the time of their parents or grandparents. • Have talked about how people might have felt in different situations. • Can place WWII on a timeline and know some of the main facts about the war.	English Drama: Present events and characters through dialogue to engage the interest of an audience. English Drama: Use some drama strategies to explore stories or issues.
Lesson 4: Who said that?	QCA Unit 6A 'Why have people invaded and settled in Britain in the past? A Roman case study' • To learn there are different interpretations of Boudicca's revolt. PoS (3) Historical interpretation • To learn that the past is represented in different ways.	• That the Romans invaded a long time ago. • They should have considered the different ways the past is represented.	English Creating and shaping texts: Make decisions about form and purpose, identify success criteria and use them to evaluate their writing.
Geography			
Lesson 5: Hot or cold?	• To know which parts of the Earth are hotter and which are colder. • To see patterns in the temperatures of locations around the world.	• Have used thermometers, traditional and digital, to measure temperature. • What the temperature for a warm day might be, and what the reading on a thermometer might be on a very cold day.	Science PoS Sc4 (4a) To know that the Sun, Earth and Moon are approximately spherical. ICT PoS (1b) How to prepare information for development using ICT, including selecting suitable sources, finding information, classifying it and checking it for accuracy.
Lesson 6: Local land use	• To identify physical and human features. • To identify land use. • To use ICT to handle data.	• Have previously encountered map symbols. • Have some concept of aerial photographs, although they may not have matched them to a map of the same area yet.	Geography PoS (2d) To use secondary sources of information, including aerial photographs. History PoS (4a) To find out about the events, people and changes studied from an appropriate range of sources of information.

Lesson title	Objectives	Expected prior knowledge	Cross-curricular links
Lesson 7: Headline news	• To investigate places. • To use secondary sources. • To use and interpret maps and plans	• Newspapers should already have been used to introduce the concept of headlines. This may have been covered as part of literacy work.	**History** PoS (4b) To ask and answer questions, and to select and record information relevant to the focus of the enquiry. **Geography** QCA Unit 16 'What's in the news?' **English** Text structure and organisation: Group related material into paragraphs.
Lesson 8: Spot the difference	• To identify and describe what places are like. • To identify how and why places change, and how they may change in the future.	• The children should have experienced close observation, perhaps in science work. • It will help if the children have completed activities in puzzle books where they are asked to *spot the difference*.	**English** Creating and shaping texts **English** Text structure and organisation: Signal sequence, time and place to give coherence. **Science** PoS Sc1 (2f) To make systematic observations and measurements.

Design and technology

Lesson title	Objectives	Expected prior knowledge	Cross-curricular links
Lesson 9: What makes a good tower? (1)	• To understand and analyse how towers are built and formed. • To recognise the features of a good tower.	• The children should have prior knowledge of 3D and 2D shapes.	**Mathematics** Understanding shape: Relate 2D and 3D solids to drawings of them; describe, visualise, classify, draw and make the shapes. **Science** PoS Sc1 (2d) To make a fair test or comparison.
Lesson 10: What makes a good tower? (2)	• To generate suitable and realistic ideas to make a tower. • To communicate personal ideas clearly when working in a group.	• Experience of working with others to achieve a common goal. • Children should have had opportunities to analyse the features of good towers.	**Speaking and listening** Objective 31: To actively include and respond to all members of the group.
Lesson 11: What makes a good tower? (3)	• To display effective teamwork skills. • To reflect on the progress of their work and identify ways they could improve their work.	• Children should have had experience of team-building exercises and been given opportunities to appraise their work and evaluate reflectively.	**Mathematics** Using and applying mathematics: Solve one- and two-step problems involving numbers, money or measures, choosing and carrying out appropriate calculations. **Science** PoS Sc1 (2c) To think about what kind of equipment and materials to use; (2e) to use simple equipment and materials appropriately.

Art and design

Lesson title	Objectives	Expected prior knowledge	Cross-curricular links
Lesson 12: Investigating pattern	**QCA Unit 3B** 'Investigating pattern' • To describe some different ways that patterns are used in everyday life. • To apply their experience of materials and processes, developing their control of tools and techniques. • To explore different ways of making and creating patterns. • To compare, ideas, methods and approaches in their own and others' work.	• Children should have used a range of media to create different patterns using line and tone. • Awareness of how patterns are used in everyday life, for example in their homes for wallpaper, and how patterns are used in other cultures.	**ICT** QCA Unit 4B 'Developing images using repeating patterns' **Mathematics** Understanding shape: Describe, visualise, classify, draw and make 2D shapes.
Lesson 13: Observational drawing	• To understand how to form an observational drawing. • To understand how different types of lines can be combined and organised for different purposes.	• Experience of using a variety of different media to create pictures.	**English** Creating and shaping texts: Write non-narrative texts using structures of different text-types. **English** Text structure and organisation.
Lesson 14: Portraying relationships	**QCA Unit 3A** 'Portraying relationships' • To identify ways in which artists approach group portraits. • To suggest what the pictures show about the people in them. • To identify aspects of a group portrait and say what they think and feel about it.	• Children should have had experienced drawing a self-portrait.	**ICT** PoS (5b) Explore a variety of ICT tools.

Lesson title	Objectives	Expected prior knowledge	Cross-curricular links
ICT			
Lesson 15: Using a floor turtle	• To understand how movements can be controlled around a page. • To understand the concept of turning. • To enter simple instructions to control a floor turtle.	• Vocabulary relating to directions.	**Geography** PoS (2c) To use atlases and globes, and maps and plans at a range of scales. **Mathematics** Handling data: Answer a question by collecting, organising and interpreting data; use tally charts, frequency tables and bar charts to represent results and illustrate observations.
Lesson 16: Making an instructional leaflet	**QCA Unit 3A** 'Combining text and graphics' • To manipulate text and graphics using a word-processing application. • To write simple instructions using text and graphics.	• How to input text in a word-processing document. • A basic understanding of using formatting to change the appearance of text.	**English** Creating and shaping texts: Write non-narrative texts using structures of different text-types. **English** Creating and shaping texts: Use layout, format graphics and illustrations for different purposes. **Geography** QCA Unit 16 'What's in the news?'
Music			
Lesson 17: Animal magic	**QCA Unit 9** 'Animal magic – Exploring descriptive sounds' • To recognise how musical elements are used and combined to describe different animals. • To identify how music can be used descriptively, for example, to represent different animal characteristics. • To use instrumentation to match appropriate sounds to an animal.	• The children should have experimented with different ways in which instruments can be played and how this affects the quality of sound produced.	**PE** PoS (6b) Dance activities: To respond to a range of stimuli and accompaniment. **PE** PoS (8a) Gymnastic activities: To create and perform fluent sequences on the floor. **ICT** QCA Unit 3B 'Manipulating sound'
Religious education			
Lesson 18: Celebrating Divali	• To learn about Divali as a New Year Festival. • To look at the worship of Lakshmi, Goddess Of Wealth And Good Fortune, during the festival of Divali. • To think about how Hindus prepare to welcome Lakshmi. • To create a rangoli pattern for a Divali card.	• Why Hindus celebrate Divali.	**Citizenship** QCA Unit 5 'Living in a diverse world' **Art and design** QCA Unit 3B 'Investigating pattern'
Lesson 19: The Easter Story	• To learn about the Good Friday and Easter Sunday stories. • To think about how Christians celebrate Easter. • To explore why Easter is important for Christians.	• The stories and events that happened to Jesus leading up to his crucifixion.	**Speaking and listening** Objective 36: To use some drama strategies to explore stories or issues.
Physical education			
Lesson 20: Balancing	• To demonstrate how different parts of the body can be used to form interesting balances. • To perform balances with more consistent control and quality. • To use photographs to identify what makes a balance effective and to suggest improvements where appropriate.	Experience of developing gymnastic routines and using movement imaginatively.	**Science** PoS Sc2 (2e) To know that humans and some other animals have skeletons and muscles to support and protect their bodies and to help them to move.

Dig this!

Learning objectives
QCA Unit 6 'Why have people invaded and settled in Britain in the past?'
● To place periods in a chronological framework.
● To know that there are some things we can learn from archaeological remains.

Resources
'Dig this!' Notebook file; photocopiable page 160 'Studying artefacts' for each child; pencils; bucket of sand; objects to bury in sand.

Links to other subjects
Science
PoS Sc3 (1a) To compare properties of everyday materials and objects, and relate these properties to everyday uses of the materials.
● Prepare images of everyday objects made from a variety of materials for use in a science lesson. Gradually reveal the objects to identify them and the materials from which they are made. Include objects made from more than one material.

Starter
Establish the learning objectives on page 1 of the 'Dig this!' Notebook file. Ask the children how we learn about the past, for example, by using objects (introduce the word *artefacts*) and written records. Annotate their suggestions on page 2.

Read the word *Archaeologist* on page 3. Ask the children what an archaeologist does. Write down their suggestions. Ask: *how can an archaeologist help us to learn about the past?*

Whole-class shared work
● Explain to the children that they are going to be archaeologists.
● Go to page 4. Tell the children that a number of objects are hidden in the earth.
● Press on the layer of brown soil and gradually pull down the top of the object to reveal the first object. Ask the children what it might be. Encourage them to give reasons for their answers. Have they seen anything like it before? What do they think it is made of?
● What makes it easy or difficult to identify the object? Rotate the whole object, once it is fully revealed, to make it easier to recognise.
● Emphasise that objects are only revealed to archaeologists slowly as they are unearthed. Sometimes archaeologists do not know what the artefacts were used for.
● Continue with this process until all the artefacts have been uncovered. (The artefacts are, from earliest to latest: a teabowl; a teething rattle; a coin; a hot-water bottle; a Rubik's Cube; a mobile phone.)
● Annotate the artefacts with the name (or purpose) of the object and the material from which it is made.
● Explain that the oldest artefact would be the deepest in the soil (in this case, at the bottom of the screen). Illustrate this as a practical activity using objects and a bucket of sand: one child buries the objects, noting the order. A second child digs them up and identifies the sequence.
● Challenge the children to guess the age of the coin on page 5 of the Notebook file. Enlarge the coin to read the date.
● Hand out copies of photocopiable page 160 'Studying artefacts'. Ask the children to find that date on their timeline.

Independent work
● Ask the children to look carefully at the artefacts on page 4. Using photocopiable page 160, Ask them to draw each artefact next to the appropriate date, and write a few facts about it. Invite more confident learners to justify their decisions.
● Remind the children of the sorts of clues they could use to work out the dates, such as material and condition. Let them discuss their ideas with a partner.

Plenary
● Invite volunteers to move the artefacts to the correct place on the timeline on page 6, encouraging them to give reasons for their decisions. Press the hyperlinks to check the answers. Press the button *Back to timeline* to return to page 6.
● Are the children surprised that there are no plastic artefacts deep in the earth? Why is this? Explain that plastic was not used until around the 1930s. Which other objects would not be found at the earliest dates?
● Use page 7 to make notes and review the children's learning.

Whiteboard tools
Convert handwritten words to text by pressing the Right Mouse button and selecting the Recognise option from the dropdown menu.

 Pen tray

 Select tool

Have you seen this man?

Learning objectives
QCA Unit 7 'Why did Henry VIII marry six times?'
● To answer questions using a portrait as a source.
● To learn about the appearance and character of Henry VIII.

Resources
'Have you seen this man?' Notebook file; a range of other portraits of Henry VIII; pencils; crayons; a timeline showing the Tudor period.

Links to other subjects
English
PNS: Creating and shaping texts: Write non-narrative texts using structures of different text-types.
● Use this technique to record information and to identify key facts when writing non-chronological accounts.

Starter
Display page 2 of the 'Have you seen this man' Notebook file. Ask the children to point to the Tudor period on the timeline. Relate this to other periods of history studied, such as the Romans. Pull the tab across to check where the Tudor period is situated on the timeline.

Ask the children what they already know about Henry VIII, and list these facts on page 3, for example: *Henry VIII had six wives*. Remind the children of the names of his wives, the order in which he married them, why he married them, and their fates.

Whole-class shared work
● Explain that the children are going to use *contemporary evidence* to find out about Henry VIII. Establish that contemporary means *from the same time*. Can the children tell you why contemporary evidence might be more helpful than paintings or descriptions created at a later date?
● Tell the children that the first source is a description of Henry VIII written by the Venetian ambassador in 1515. Go to page 4 and read the text to the children, explaining any difficult vocabulary, such as *potentate* (a monarch or ruler).
● Highlight words, suggested by the children, that describe what Henry VIII looked like. Use the Spotlight tool to focus on passages.
● Go to page 5. Explain that this portrait was painted in 1540, when Henry was 49 years old. During this period in history, portraits were often very flattering.
● Ask the children to describe Henry using the evidence of the portrait. Annotate the portrait using their descriptions. Focus on parts of the portrait with the Spotlight tool.
● Read the text on page 6 with the children. Ask them to suggest what this says about the king's appearance and character. Highlight the key words in the text. Use the Spotlight tool to focus on passages.

Independent work
● Explain to the children that we know what our queen looks like because of television and photographs, but in Tudor times most ordinary people would not recognise the king.
● Ask the children to write a detailed description of Henry VIII and draw a picture of him, using the information from the three sources. Recap the information they might include, such as build, hair, and clothing.
● Encourage more confident learners to include any information about the king's character that they have deduced from the sources. Invite less confident learners to write simple bulleted facts rather than a piece of extended writing.

Plenary
● Ask for volunteers to read their descriptions of Henry, a sentence at a time, identifying the source of information.
● Compare their descriptions. What key facts have most of the children included?
● On page 7, create a class description of the king and identify the source of the information used (referring to the highlighted text and annotations made to the three sources).
● Compare the three sources and ask the children to comment on their usefulness. Are there any contradictions? Annotate the children's responses on page 8.

Whiteboard tools
Focus on passages or parts of the portrait with the Spotlight tool from the SMART Board tools menu. Set the transparency to 50% and the shape to rectangle.

 Pen tray

 Spotlight tool

 Select tool

 Highlighter pen

Evacuated!

Learning objectives
QCA Unit 9 'What was it like for children in the Second World War?'
● To find out about the experiences and feelings of evacuees.
● To communicate learning in an organised and structured way, using appropriate terminology.

Resources 🅿
BBC webpage *Audio Memories of the Evacuees* (go to **www.bbc.co.uk/history/british/britain_wwtwo** and select Evacuees in World War Two: the True Story, then Audio Memories of the Evacuees (last accessed 19 March 2007). Appropriate audio clips are: 'Long-distance Lambeth Walk'; 'Train Now Leaving Platform One'; 'Evacuation and Adventure'; and 'Leaving Home'); pictures of children being evacuated (check copyright restrictions before inserting any pictures into a Notebook file); photocopiable page 161 'Evacuation wordsearch' for each child.

Links to other subjects
English
Drama: Present events and characters through dialogue to engage the interest of an audience.
Drama: Use some drama strategies to explore stories or issues.
● Use hotseating to answer questions that the children have prepared on the subject of evacuation.

Whiteboard tools
Use the Spotlight tool from the SMART Board tools menu to focus on parts of the photographs. Adjust the transparency as required.

 Pen tray

 On-screen Keyboard

 Spotlight tool

Starter
Recap what the children already know about the Second World War. Ask questions such as: *When did it happen? Which countries were involved? What was the Blitz? What areas were most affected and why? What were the main effects of the air raids? How did people protect themselves?*

Explain to the children that they are going to use some historical sources to find out more about what it was like to be an evacuee. On a new page of the Notebook file, write the heading *What we know about evacuation* and record what the class already know. Can they tell you why children were evacuated? Do they know where they were evacuated from/to?

Whole-class shared work
● Discuss the photographs of evacuees. Ask: *What do these photographs show? What are the children wearing and carrying? How do your class think the children are feeling? Why? Why are they wearing labels round their necks? Why do some of them look happy and some look sad?*
● What clues show that the photographs are old? Ensure that the children understand that a black and white photograph is not, necessarily, evidence of age. Use the Spotlight tool 🔍 to focus on parts of the photographs.
● Record the children's observations about the photographs.
● Now play the audio clips from the BBC's webpage, *Audio Memories of the Evacuees.* Do these recordings add to the children's knowledge about evacuation?
● Add their responses to a list headed *What we know about evacuation.*
● Relate the spoken memories to the pictures of evacuees. Ask questions such as: *Does one set of information support the other? Are there any conflicts? What could be the reason? Are both sources of information totally reliable? Why/why not?* Encourage the children to realise that the audio memories were recorded long after the events, and human memories are fallible!

Independent work
● Divide the class into groups of four or five, representing two older family members and the children. Usually the father would be in the armed forces, but there would be older male relatives, for example grandfathers.
● The groups have to decide among themselves which family role each child is to play. Each child must be prepared to give brief biographical details (name, age, and so on) appropriate to the time of the Second World War.
● Ask each group to devise a role play in which the adults discuss the evacuation of the children. In the next part of the role play they have to explain to the children what will happen.
● Encourage the children to use appropriate vocabulary. Prompt them with words from your copy of the wordsearch on photocopiable page 161.
● After ten minutes, invite groups to perform their role plays to the rest of the class.

Plenary
● Address any misconceptions that may have arisen during the role play.
● Review the list of information that children have made about evacuation. Do they have any information to add as a result of their role plays?
● Give each child a copy of the 'Evacuation wordsearch' (photocopiable page 161) to complete. What other words could have been used?

Learning objectives
QCA Unit 6A 'Why have people invaded and settled in Britain in the past? A Roman case study'
● To learn that there are different interpretations of Boudicca's revolt.
PoS (3)
● To learn that the past is represented in different ways.

Resources
'Build your own' file - prepare a Notebook file using the Roman and Celtic characters from the Foundation folder under My Content in the Gallery, and a range of statements in speech bubbles similar to those on photocopiable page 162; copy of photocopiable page 162 'Who said that?' for each child; scissors; glue.

Links to other subjects
English
Creating and shaping texts: Make decisions about form and purpose, identify success criteria and use them to evaluate their writing.
● In a subsequent lesson ask the children to write the story of the rebellion in different ways, for example as a letter or news report.

Whiteboard tools
Select speech bubbles from the Shapes tool. Use the Lines tool to draw columns.

 Pen tray

 Gallery

 Select tool

 Shapes tool

 Highlighter pen

 Lines tool

🔲 On-screen Keyboard

Who said that?

Starter
● Recap facts about the Roman invasion and settlement:
  ● The Romans invaded then settled.
  ● The Celts were Pagans.
  ● There were many tribes living in Britain, each with its own ruler.
  ● The Iceni were a tribe living in East Anglia, ruled by King Prasutagus.
  ● Prasutagus was a client king; this was one way that the Romans controlled Britain.
  ● Boudicca was the wife of Prasutagus.
● Ensure that the children understand concepts such as invasion, settlement and client king.

Whole-class shared work
● Tell the story (below) of Boudicca's rebellion against the Romans, writing key points on the whiteboard.
  When Prasutagus, king of the Iceni, died, Boudicca became queen. The Romans believed that the land should have been given to them: they were not used to women and men being equal. When Boudicca refused to give the land to them, the Romans beat Boudicca and her daughters. Boudicca raised an army, and attacked and destroyed Colchester. The Celts killed all the Romans they found. Other Celtic tribes joined the revolt. They marched north to fight Suetonius. The Celtic army outnumbered the Romans by about ten to one. The highly disciplined Roman army defeated the Celts, and were ordered to kill all Celts, including women and children. Boudicca and her daughters fled. Legend has it that they took poison.
● Ask the children what the Celts would have thought of Boudicca and her rebellion. Write key words in one column under the heading *Celts*.
● Would the Romans have had the same opinion as the Celts? Why/why not? Write key words in a column under the heading *Romans*.

Independent work
● Give out copies of photocopiable page 162 'Who said that?'
● Explain that there are eight statements made by either Romans or Celts.
● Read through the statements together, explaining any difficult language. Invite the children to work in pairs and decide who made each statement.
● Ask them to cut out the statements and stick them next to the appropriate figure.
● Extend the activity by asking the children to write another statement made by either a Celtic warrior or a Roman soldier.

Plenary
● Display your prepared Notebook page (see Resources, above) showing the Roman and Celtic characters and the statements. Read through the statements again and ask a volunteer to come and move the speech bubble to the correct speaker. Does everyone agree? Discuss any differences of opinion, and use a Highlighter pen to identify the key words and phrases that indicate the speaker.
● Repeat until all the phrases have been positioned.
● Ask the children to read out their own statements without saying whether the speaker is Roman or Celtic. The rest of the class has to decide who the speaker is.

Hot or cold?

Learning objectives
● To know which parts of the Earth are hotter and which are colder.
● To see patterns in the temperatures of locations around the world.

Resources
'Hot or cold' Notebook file; atlases; copies of an outline world map (one per child).

Links to other subjects
Science
PoS Sc4 (4a) To know that the Sun, Earth and Moon are approximately spherical.
● Adapt this activity to support the work on Earth, Sun and Moon.
ICT
PoS (1b) How to prepare information for development using ICT, including selecting suitable sources, finding information, classifying it and checking it for accuracy.
● Enter the temperature data into a spreadsheet and sort the data from hottest to coldest.

Starter
Look at the set of photographs on page 2 of the 'Hot or cold' Notebook file. Discuss which photographs show hot places and which show cold. Do the children think that the same places will always be hot or cold? What influence might the weather or season have on them?

Explain that they are going to find temperatures for different locations around the world and mark them on a map of the world.

Whole-class shared work
● Hand out atlases and use the contents to find a map of the world with countries labelled.
● Discuss how to locate countries on the world map on page 3 of the Notebook file.
● Look at a world weather website. There is a hyperlink to the World Meteorological Organization website on the Notebook page. It provides the mean maximum and minimum temperatures for many places around the world. Discuss how the time of day affects the temperature.
● Ask the children which country they would like to know the temperature for. Press the link for a country and then choose one of the places listed. Decide whether to use the maximum or minimum temperature.
● Return to the Notebook file. Drag the text __ ˚C onto the map and double-press to edit it and enter the mean temperature.
● Invite a child to drag it to the correct place on the world map.
● Repeat with more countries. Direct the children to choose countries from all continents to get a cross section of temperatures.

Independent work
● In pairs, ask the children to transfer the data from the Notebook page to their own maps. Ask them to find data for more places using the website or an atlas.
● Remind them of how to locate the countries by finding the right continent, then looking at the shapes of the countries and their relationship to other countries. Ask them to find data from countries all round the world.
● To make the task easier, provide a world map with locations already labelled. The children could then find the data for these locations.
● Challenge more confident learners to repeat the process for a different season.

Plenary
● Return to page 3 of the Notebook file. Look at the temperatures on the map. Use a Highlighter pen to join together similar temperatures giving bands across the globe. Ask questions such as: *Which latitudes are hotter? Which are cooler?* Drag the words to the correct locations.
● Look at page 4 *The Sun's rays*. What shape are the Earth and Sun? Use the Lines tool or the Pen tool to draw lines from the Sun to the Earth to demonstrate the Sun's rays.
● Pull the red tab to reveal how the Sun's rays reach the Earth.
● Demonstrate that near the equator the Sun's rays are concentrated, while further from the equator the rays are more spread out.
● Revisit the objectives on page 1 and assess the children's progress. You can use page 5 to make notes.

Whiteboard tools
Double-press on text and use the On-screen Keyboard to edit it.

 Pen tray

 On-screen Keyboard

 Select tool

 Pen tool

 Lines tool

Local land use

Starter
Load the Ordnance Survey *Understanding mapping* website **www.ordnancesurvey.co.uk/oswebsite/freefun/understandingmapping.html** (last accessed 19 March 2007) to introduce the children to map symbols.
Open the 'Build your own' file and look at the map symbols supplied in the Foundation folder under My Content in the Gallery 🏛. Discuss what they mean. Explain to the children that they will be looking for examples of some of these features (physical and human) on an aerial photograph.

Whole-class shared work
● Look at the aerial or oblique photograph on page 1 of the Notebook file you have prepared. Discuss how the picture might have been taken. Pick out the key features, physical and human.
● Ask how these features could be represented by any of the map symbols in the Gallery. Invite children up to drag map symbols onto the photograph to the position of the corresponding feature.
● Continue to label aspects of the photograph with map symbols. Record the features on the 'Local land use' sheet (photocopiable page 163).
● Turn to the aerial or oblique photograph overlaid with a grid on page 2. Are there any features which cannot be represented by a single map symbol? Accept answers which indicate features covering a large area, such as fields or forest. Suggest that these features be sorted into types of land use. Allocate each type of land use a colour. Allow children to shade these areas in the appropriate colours.
● Estimate and record the number of squares shaded in each colour. Record on photocopiable page 163. What does this say about the land use in this area?
● Save the annotated Notebook pages.

Independent work
● Show the children the basic sketch map of the same area on the Notebook file, which only shows a few of the features. Relate observations from the photograph to this map.
● Return to the annotated photograph. Explain that they are going to use this information to complete their own copy of the basic sketch map. They will need to use the correct map symbols and different colours of shading to show how land is used for a particular purpose. They may discuss their work but must produce their own maps.
● Provide more or less detail on the maps to suit the children's different abilities.

Plenary
● Discuss what sort of land uses are most common in the locality. Ask: *Is this likely to change at all with time?*
● Load the Ordnance Survey map for the area from the *Get-a-map* site (see Resources, above).
● Compare it to the maps produced by the children. Ask questions such as: *What are the key differences? Why have these occurred? Does one map have to be right and one wrong? Are there different ways of presenting data on maps?*

Headline news

Starter
Tell the children that they will be looking at local news and finding out where exactly the events happened. Look at page 2 of the 'What's in the news?' Notebook file. A headline and pictures are visible, but the news story has been hidden, with a few words still visible. Discuss what the news story might say. Allow the children to guess and then use the Eraser from the Pen tray to reveal each item. Re-evaluate the responses in the light of what is revealed.

Whole-class shared work
● Look at page 3 of the Notebook file. Drag and drop the pictures to match the headlines and news stories.
● Tell the children that if these stories were in your local newspaper, you would like to know where they occurred. Introduce the idea of using maps to find out where local events took place.
● Give a brief outline of the local news story you have ready and give each group a copy of the news article. Ask the children to find details of the location in the article.
● Demonstrate how to find a location using a mapping website. Having found the location, ask the children how it relates to places they know: is it near the school or a place they know?
● Talk about the features of a news report. Record the key vocabulary and notes on features on page 4. The key question words are displayed at the bottom of the page: *Who? When? Why? Where? What? How?*
● Now record useful vocabulary relating to the particular event and its location.

Independent work
● Leaving the notes and vocabulary on the whiteboard for reference, ask the children to write a report on an item of local news. Invite them to use a word processor and to insert images if possible.
● Ask them to include the details of where the news happened. Use the finished reports to form part of a display alongside a map of the local area.
● Encourage more confident learners to organise the report with a mind to writing for a newspaper. Ask them to use paragraphs carefully for each part of the report, including an introduction and a conclusion.
● Provide children who are less confident in writing reports with sentence starters for each section. Standard phrases such as *The event happened at ____ on ____* are useful for guiding writing.

Plenary
● Look at the local map that you have inserted into page 5 of the Notebook file. Look in the local newspaper for other recent events. Discuss where they happened. Locate the places on the map and label them with the headline using the Select tool and On-screen Keyboard.
● Move on to discuss aspects of the local area that could be improved, and ask the children to write a news report to raise awareness of this issue.

Spot the difference

Learning objectives
● To identify and describe what places are like.
● To identify how and why places change, and how they may change in the future.

Starter
Outline the objectives for the session. Remind the children of the popular activity *Spot the difference*, then look at two versions of an image that has been quickly altered in a paint program. This could be a picture of a child that has been reversed or an image with something changed to a different colour. Tell the children that some images can be subtle in differences. This is going to be their challenge.

Whole-class shared work
● Look at the two digital images in the Notebook file. They are of the same place, but have been taken at different times.
● Point out large differences between the images, such as the absence of leaves on the trees, snow or frost on the ground or whether anything has been changed by people. Ask for further suggestions for obvious differences.
● Use text and arrows (from the Lines tool ◥ menu) to label the differences as the children make their observations.
● To enlarge areas of the screen for closer study, select the Area Capture (freehand) tool 🖾 and draw around the required area. Capture the image to a new Notebook page (which will be automatically inserted as the last page).
● Provide printouts of the pictures and encourage the children to highlight or annotate the points they notice.
● Invite the children to record their observations on photocopiable page 164 'Spot the difference', either in simple note form or with sketches on the back of the sheet. Encourage them to discuss why there may be differences between the two pictures.

Resources 🅿

Photocopiable page 164 'Spot the difference' for each child. Prepared Notebook file with: page 1: two digital images of the view from the window, but at different times in the day, month or year; page 2: two digital images with more subtle differences (provide printouts as an alternative to on-screen work). For inspiration, visit the website **www.tre.ngfl.gov.uk** (last accessed 19 March 2007) and search for *Seasons in the garden*. Two other images of the same view at different times placed in a presentation software package such as Microsoft PowerPoint: arrange them so that children can flick between the two images quickly.

Links to other subjects
English
Creating and shaping texts Text structure and organisation: Signal sequence, time and place to give coherence.
● Use a similar activity to stimulate descriptive writing. The two views could be ones which represent a *before and after* situation.
Science
PoS Sc1 (2f) To make systematic observations and measurements.
● Use this activity to compare photographs of different seasons. Compare the flora and weather.

Independent work
● Present the two images again and ask the children to connect the differences with simple arrows.
● Show two further images where the difference is slight. Arrange for the children to view them, in pairs, at a computer or on printouts. Show them how to move quickly between the two images to spot the differences. Ask the children to discuss the differences.
● Encourage more confident learners to elaborate on the differences they spot.
Some children may find representing the differences in pictorial form, on the back of the photocopiable sheet, more appropriate.

Plenary
● Remind the children of the objectives of the session. Discuss the obvious and subtle differences found in the first two images that they looked at. Ask for suggestions as to what could be done to improve the views.
● Encourage the children to consider the following: Do these changes require money? Are any changes dependent on changes in attitude? Are there some aspects which could not possibly be changed?

Whiteboard tools
Select arrows from the Lines tool menu.

 Pen tray

 Lines tool

 Area Capture tool

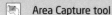 On-screen Keyboard

What makes a good tower? (1)

Learning objectives
● To understand and analyse how towers are built and formed.
● To recognise the features of a good tower.

Resources
'Building a tower' Notebook file; photocopiable page 165 'What makes a good tower?' for each child; writing materials.

Links to other subjects
Mathematics
Understanding shape: Relate 2D and 3D solids to drawings of them; describe, visualise, classify, draw and make the shapes.
● Investigate the various 3D shapes towers can take.
Science
Sc1 (2d) To make a fair test or comparison.
● Challenge the children to examine how the *Building a Tower* project is a fair test. Ask the children to tell you the elements that will be kept the same.

Starter
Open the 'Building a tower' Notebook file and go to page 2. Ask the children what they think a tower is. Write their responses on the Notebook page.

Tell the children that, over the next few lessons, they will be looking at different types of towers and that, in this project, teamwork is an essential skill needed for building a structure. Explain that this lesson will ask them to look carefully at what is needed to make a good tower.

Whole-class shared work
● Draw the children's attention to the questions on page 3.
● Ask them to look carefully at the three pictures on page 4. Allow a few minutes thinking time.
● Encourage the children to tell you the features of each tower. Ask: *What makes each tower different? What do they notice about the base of the tower? Why are some of these towers taller than some of the others?*
● Point out that, although the Tower of Pisa is a magnificent structure, it is an example of a weak tower. It does not have strong foundations and is slowly sinking into the soft soil beneath it. The latest measure to make it more stable was to remove soil from under the raised end.
● Take a vote to see which towers the children like the best. Encourage the children to give reasons for their choices.
● Talk about the similarities and differences between the towers. Trace the outlines of the towers.
● Write notes about the features of the towers in the area around the Notebook page. To increase the page size select View, then Zoom and then 100%. (Select Entire Page to return to the original viewing mode, and to hide the notes.)
● Ask the children, in pairs, to discuss the tower-related words they can see on page 5. Do they know the meaning of any of the words?
● Look at the picture on page 6. Explain to the children that in France there is a tower called the Eiffel Tower. Ask them to look carefully at the photograph. Encourage the children to explain what they notice about the legs? Why are these so strong?
● Display the different towers on page 7. Ask the children to draw the tower they like best.

Independent work
● Hand out photocopiable page 165 'What makes a good tower?' Ask them to draw the tower that they particularly like on their sheet and label the features which make it a really strong tower.
● Next ask the children to design their own tower on the back of their sheet. Explain that they will be designing and making their own tower in the forthcoming lessons. Tell them what resources they will have: art straws; string; sticky tape; sticky tack; paper clips.

Plenary
● Ask the children to share their ideas for their towers. Explain that they will be using these designs to help them design and make their own tower.

Whiteboard tools
Change the viewing mode by selecting View, then Zoom, and write in the area around the Notebook page.

 Pen tray

 Pen tool

What makes a good tower? (2)

Learning objectives
● To generate suitable and realistic ideas to make a tower.
● To communicate personal ideas clearly when working in a group.

Resources
'Building a tower' Notebook file; photocopiable page 166 'Designing a tower' for each child; paper and pencils; a scanner.

Links to other subjects
Speaking and listening
Objective 31: To actively include and respond to all members of the group.
● Ensure that all members of the groups participate in the design exercise.

Starter
Remind the children of the discussion work that took place in the previous lesson. Using a scanner, scan a selection of the towers drawn by the children on photocopiable page 165 'What makes a good tower?' As a class, look at the work. Ask the children to describe the features they particularly like about the designs.

Whole-class shared work
● On the whiteboard, load the 'Building a tower' Notebook file and look at the sequence of photographs on page 8. Ask the children to spend a few minutes thinking and looking carefully at the photographs. Invite them to look at what the photographs show and consider how the tower has been built.
● Discuss the images with the children and ask them to share their thoughts. Draw their attention to the fact that the tower has been built in stages, beginning with the foundations. Discuss why the builders begin with the foundations first and not the spire or the main body of the tower.
● Annotate the children's ideas.
● Explain to the children that good towers always begin with strong foundations to support the rest of the tower (unlike the Tower of Pisa!).
● Show the children page 9. Tell them that they will be competing to win a prize. Explain that, in their group, their task will be to try and build the tallest tower they can.
● Display page 10. Tell the children that each group will have 40 art straws, a pair of scissors and 60p to spend at the shop. Explain that the shop is very limited and only stocks paper clips, 2cm strips of sticky tape, 10cm pieces of string and 1cm squares of sticky tack.
● Emphasise to the children that they will have to spend wisely, as once their money has been spent they will not be allowed to buy anything else.

Independent work
● Ask the children to get into groups of no more than five.
● Show the children page 11. Discuss the teamwork skills they will need when working together.
● Ask the children to spend five to ten minutes considering the designs of their art straw towers. What features would they like to include? Encourage them to look for good ideas in each other's designs from the previous lesson. For example, they may wish to construct a spire because it is really tall, or a base with very strong corners, and so on.
● Ask each group to design a tower. They need to draw what the tower will look like on the photocopiable sheet.
● Return to page 10 of the Notebook file and remind the children to think carefully about the resources they need to buy with their 60p. They can write their shopping list on the back of their sheets.
● Ask the groups to label their towers to show where and how they will use their resources. For example, they may choose to join the art straws with string and use tape to secure the tower to the table.

Plenary
● Ask the different groups to share their ideas for their towers with the rest of the class.

Whiteboard tools
Upload scanned drawings by selecting Insert, then Picture File, and browsing to where you have saved the images.

 Pen tray

What makes a good tower? (3)

Learning objectives
● To display effective teamwork skills.
● To reflect on the progress of their work and identify ways they could improve their work.

Resources
'Building a tower' Notebook file; 40 art straws and a pair of scissors for each group; plastic money (50p and 10p coins for each group and sufficient 5p and 10p coins for change); sticky tape; sticky tack; paper clips; a ruler; a digital camera.

Links to other subjects
Mathematics
Using and applying mathematics: Solve one- and two-step problems involving numbers, money or measures, choosing and carrying out appropriate calculations.
● Ask the children to add up the tally totals from the board. Then ask: *Which group spent the most money? How do you know this?*
Science
PoS Sc1 (2c) To think about what kind of equipment and materials to use; (2e) to use simple equipment and materials appropriately.
● Examine with the children the most appropriate materials needed to make a tower.

Starter
This lesson will take more than the hour allocation. You can extend the lesson depending on the detail of the written work required.

Ask the children to show their group's tower design from the last lesson. Load the 'Building a tower' Notebook file and show the children page 9. Remind them of the task and outline the equipment they have (on page 10).

Independent work
● Within their groups, allow the children sufficient time to build their towers.
● Set up the shop next to the whiteboard.
● Go to page 12 of the Notebook file. This shows a table to record the resources bought by each group. There is room for up to eight groups. You can change the names of the groups by double-pressing on the text and typing with the On-screen Keyboard. Alternatively, select the Text tool A and use your computer keyboard to type.
● As the children purchase various items, keep a tally on the table.
● Encourage the children to use the different strengths of the group. The more able mathematicians could work out the change they will receive from the shop.
● Support the less confident learners, by encouraging them to think carefully about the stages they need to complete in order to build their tower.

Plenary
● Take the opportunity to include ad-hoc voting in the lesson and to assess the children's mental mathematics skills. Ask the children to identify which group: spent the most/least amount of money on the different materials; spent the highest/lowest amount in total.
● Write the letters *a, b, c* and *d* next to the column headings and ask the children to vote on the most and least used materials.
● Measure the height of each group's tower and record this on the table on page 13.
● Use a digital camera to take a picture of each tower to record each group's achievements.
● Encourage the children to evaluate their work thoroughly.
● In a follow-up lesson to the practical work, use the evaluation section at the end of the Notebook file (pages 14 to 17) to support the children in this process. If necessary, guide them through the process of recording how they built their tower, using a new Notebook file. Model sentence work and encourage the children to brainstorm ideas.
● To foster a positive evaluation process, encourage the children to adopt a *Two stars and a wish* approach. For example, name two things about making your tower, or working in a group, that you really liked; then name one thing you would wish to change or improve.

Whiteboard tools

 Pen tray

A Text tool

 On-screen Keyboard

Investigating pattern

Learning objectives
QCA Unit 3B 'Investigating pattern'
● To describe some different ways that patterns are used in everyday life.
● To apply their experience of materials and processes, developing their control of tools and techniques.
● To explore different ways of making and creating patterns.

Resources
Home- or lifestyle-themed magazines; a sketchbook for each child; photocopiable page 167 'Patterns' for each child.

Links to other subjects
ICT
QCA Unit 4B 'Developing images using repeating patterns'
● The children use a paint package to replicate the activity using the stamps available.
Mathematics
Understanding shape: Describe, visualise, classify, draw and make 2D shapes.
● Ask the children to fold a piece of squared paper in four. Invite them to draw a pattern using the squares, and then replicate the pattern in each of the four folded squares.

Whiteboard tools
Use the Creative pen to add interesting elements to patterns. Press on an object and select Infinite Cloner to create multiple copies.

 Pen tray

 Select tool

 Shapes tool

 Lines tool

 Creative pen

 Undo button

 Redo button

 Gallery

Fill Colour tool

Pen tool

Starter
Ask the children to tell you what the word *pattern* means. Allow them a couple of minutes to think of objects in their homes which are patterned. Prompt them with questions such as: *Where in your house do you have patterns?* (Curtains, carpets, and clothes, for example.) Ask them to draw an example of a pattern in their sketchbooks. Next, ask the children to explain how their pattern has been formed. Have they used blocks of colour? Are there any unusual or interesting shapes which have been used? Are any of the patterns used again? Divide the children into groups of two or three. Ask them to find different examples of patterns, using magazines, and add these to their sketchbooks.

Whole-class shared work
● Explain to the children that in this lesson they will be exploring how a simple pattern can be used and repeated.
● Open a new Notebook page and invite the children to draw examples of patterns. They can make patterns using lines and shapes, or they can draw them. Each time, discuss how the child thought about the process of making a pattern.
● Now experiment by alternating the thickness of the line for freehand patterns and use different colours to build up the design. You could use the Creative pen to add extra design elements.
● On a new page, insert a square and ask a child to draw a simple pattern within it, using any of the techniques that have been demonstrated.
● Tell the children that you are now going to use it to create a repeated pattern. Marquee select the square and the drawn pattern and select Group from the dropdown menu to convert it into one image. Clone the image and place the new one next to the original. Talk through this process and invite children to repeat it to build up a pattern.
● Press the Right Mouse button and set the background to a different colour. Discuss the effects of changing the colour. Ask: *Why is the colour as important as the shapes in patterns?*
● Use the Undo and Redo buttons to show the children the differences of changing colours.
● Alternatively, fill in the backgrounds of the different tiled squares and the patterns within them (by pressing on them, selecting Properties and using the Fill Colour option). You could also use images from the Gallery and infinite clone them to create a repeated pattern, in the style of wallpaper and wrapping paper patterns.

Independent work
● Using photocopiable page 167 and some paper, give the children time to create a wallpaper pattern of their own.

Plenary
● Share the children's work, noting positive features and areas that could be improved.
● Ask the children to evaluate their own work. Ask: *Where would you use your patterns? Which patterns do you like to look at? Which would you use in a living room?*

Observational drawing

Learning objectives
● To understand how to form an observational drawing.
● To understand how different types of lines can be combined and organised for different purposes.

Resources
'Observational drawing' Notebook file; a selection of plant life, glass bottles (under supervised use), flowers or other natural objects to share between groups of three; sketchbooks or cartridge paper, one per child; pencils.

Links to other subjects
English
Creating and shaping texts: Write non-narrative texts using structures of different text-types.
Text structure and organisation
● Ask the children to work in groups to write instructions on different ways to use lines in observational drawing.

Starter
Invite the children to use the Pen tool on page 2 of the 'Observational drawing' Notebook file to draw as many different types of lines as they can. Ask them to consider the different ways of drawing a line – straight, curvy, wavy, circular, zigzag, dotted, or any variation. Explain too, that in this lesson, they will be exploring how we can use a mixture of these lines to create an *observational drawing*.

Whole-class shared work
● Go to page 3 of the Notebook file. Tell the children that this picture is part of a line drawing. Ask them to identify the lines that have been used. Can they guess what the picture may show? Is it a scribble or could it be part of a picture? Explain that although, close up, the picture may look scribbled and untidy, when a picture is looked at from a distance, the lines blend together.
● Show page 4 to the children. Did anyone predict correctly? Ask the children to describe how lines have been used in different ways to make this drawing.
● On page 5, ask the children to look at the drawing of the cup and saucer. What do they notice about how it has been drawn? (It is just drawn with lines and no colour.)
● Press the picture to see a sequence of drawings that show the children how the lines can be built up to create the finished drawing.
● Use the outline on page 6 to model for the children how they can add tone to the basic line drawing by adding lines in different ways. Demonstrate different techniques, such as cross-hatching, scribbling, and straight or curved lines. Vary the thickness of the pen.
● Tell the children that when making observational drawings they need to observe their object and pay attention to details like shape, colour and shadows.
● Insert a photograph of a simple object into page 13 and use the Pen tool to draw the outline of the main object. Select the drawn outline and drag it to the side of the photograph. Fill it in using appropriate techniques to illustrate shading and tone.

Independent work
● Give each child some sketching paper and pencils. Place an object in front of each group. Encourage them to study their object and then draw the bare outline.
● After drawing the outline, ask the children to add darker and lighter tones to their work.

Plenary
● After completing their drawings, ask the children to show their work to the rest of the class.
● Encourage each child to point out the features they particularly like. Annotate their responses on page 14.
● Discuss the techniques they all used and how they have shown tone in their drawings.

Whiteboard tools
Upload a digital image by selecting Insert, then Picture File, and browsing to where you have saved your image.

 Pen tray

 Select tool

 Pen tool

Portraying relationships

Starter
Display page 2 of the 'Portraying Relationships' Notebook file. Tell the children that they will be looking at some pictures of groups of people and you would like them to think carefully about what each picture shows. What do they notice about these pictures? How are the people feeling? How can they tell? Give the children a minute to look at the picture on page 3. Repeat this with pages 4 and 5.

When you reach page 6, invite the children to share their thoughts about the photographs. You could use the opportunity to include voting in the lesson to encourage their responses.

Whole-class shared work
● Allow the children some thinking time to consider the word *portrait*. Ask them for their ideas. What do they think a portrait is?
● Look at the pictures on pages 7 to 9, allowing the children a few minutes to think about each one. What do they think of the picture? What can be seen in the picture? How has it been drawn?
● Encourage the children to see that all the pictures that you have shown to them portray relationships. Look at details such as expressions, gestures, the relative sizes of the figures and any background details.
● Ask for volunteers to talk about the image they chose. Encourage them to talk about what relationships are portrayed and why they made this decision. Prompt the children with the questions on pages 7 to 9.
● Explain to the children that they will be drawing their own group portrait. Choose one of the previous images, or insert an alternative picture of a group portrait, depicting friendship, love or family on page 10.
● Explain to the children that when they draw their group portrait, it is important that they look carefully at the proportions of each section of the body. Draw on top of the picture that is on the whiteboard to create a bold and simplified version of the portrait.
● Use the Spotlight tool ⟨icon⟩ to focus the children's attention.
● The pictures are all locked so they can be drawn over, and the annotations can be selected and then dragged over a plain part of the Notebook page. This will help them to see how faces can be drawn.
● Annotate the picture with any details that show how the relationship is being portrayed.

Independent work
● Ask the children to think about a relationship that is important to them and then to draw a group (or two-figure) portrait that illustrates this relationship. It may be helpful to use the children's own pictures of family and friends to aid them in their portraits.
● Encourage the children to sketch the picture first, thinking about the arrangement of the figures, clothes, expressions, gestures and background setting. They should also consider their preferred media: crayons, paints, pencil and so on.

Plenary
● Go to page 11 and invite the children to show their work, reflecting on the elements they like within their portraits. Ask: *Which sections of your portrait do you like? What did you enjoy? If you could choose a different type of media to make your portrait in, which would you choose?*

Using a floor turtle

Starter
Program a floor turtle to follow a set of directions. Ensure that the children understand that after each instruction a Go command is needed to make the floor turtle move. When using a Logo programme, the Enter button takes the place of the Go button.

Demonstrate the floor turtle following the route. Invite the children to explain how the turtle *knows* where to go. Explain that the turtle remembers the instructions that a person gives it and then follows those instructions in order. Ask the children if they can think of any other machines or devices that carry out instructions when they are programmed to do so (such as video recorders, microwaves and timed security lights). Write their suggestions on page 2 of the 'Which way should I go?' Notebook file.

Whole-class shared work
● Go to the map of *Monkey Ville* on page 3 and tell them what the map shows. Explain that they have come to visit the village in their car and they will have to drive to different places.
● Ask the children to tell you how you would get the car to move from the start to the end of the road.
● Discuss the need for measurement (squares), and also for a Go command to start each movement. Ask: *How can we get our car to turn?* Discuss with the children the need for degrees when measuring amounts of turn and explain that 90° is a quarter turn.
● Ask a child to come and move the car to the end of the road (before the road turns left) ensuring that the class count the number of squares they move as they go.
● Demonstrate to the children how to turn the car by pressing on it and then dragging the green dot. Ask the children to tell you which way they turn.
● Use the right-angle shape to demonstrate that the car has to make a right-angle turn to go around a corner.
● In pairs, ask the children to work out how they would drive the car from the start to St John's Church car park. Invite a pair to demonstrate how they would get to the car park, and to say their instructions out loud as they go.
● Using the *My Directions* pad (on the Notebook page) write the instructions as the children give them.
● If the children need more practice, work out other routes between different points on the map.

Independent work
● Give each child a copy of photocopiable page 168 'Using a floor turtle'. Ask each child to design a map of their own, writing their directions for another person to follow.

Plenary
● Scan in a child's piece of work and insert it on page 4. Using the car and working as a class, follow the instructions on the directions pad.

Making an instructional leaflet

Learning objectives
QCA Unit 3A 'Combining text and graphics'
● To manipulate text and graphics using a word-processing application.
● To write simple instructions using text and graphics.

Resources
Computers for pairs or small groups of children (ensure that SMART Notebook is already running and minimised); word-processing application; pencil and paper.

Links to other subjects
English
Creating and shaping texts: Write non-narrative texts using structures of different text-types.
Use layout, format graphics and illustrations for different purposes
● Write notes linked to work in other subjects.
Geography
QCA Unit 16 'What's in the news?'
● Use ICT to present information about what is happening in our local area. Use a map of the local area as a focal point and investigate geographical features or local news in the area. Ask the children to produce short reports that link to particular places on the map, which combine information with pictures.

Whiteboard tools
Use the Area Capture tool to take screenshots. Minimise Notebook so the Floating tools can be used with other applications.

  Pen tray

  Screen Shade

  Floating tools

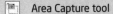 Area Capture tool

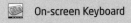 On-screen Keyboard

Starter
Ask the children to locate the icon on the computer's desktop for the word-processing application. Invite them to open the program by double-pressing on it. Review what the children know already about the application. For example, do they know how to: enter text; change the text; insert a picture; draw shapes?

Tell the children that they will be making instruction leaflets to explain how to combine text and graphics. Ask them what will be needed (such as a heading, instructions and pictures) and how the leaflets should be presented. Write their ideas on a blank Notebook page.

Whole-class shared work
● With Notebook minimised, use the Screen Shade to focus on the toolbars in the word-processing application. Ask the children what the symbols may mean. Why are symbols used? Highlight relevant symbols and toolbars.
● Type the following on a blank page: *Instructions on how to combine text and graphics.* Ask the children how they can make the text look like a heading. Encourage them to experiment with different fonts, colours, sizes and other text effects.
● Discuss how the instructions will need to be bulleted or numbered. Do the children know how to do this? Guide them to find the Numbering and Bullets symbols on the toolbar.
● Discuss how pictures are useful in instructions because they help the user to check that he or she is following the instructions correctly. Use the Print screen key on the keyboard to take a picture of the whole screen or use the Area Capture tool to take a picture of part of the screen, and then paste the image into the document.
● Show the children how the image can be manipulated by dragging the edges to change its size. If they press once on the image, the Picture toolbar should appear, which will allow them to crop the image, change its outline, and use the text wrap options.

Independent work
● Ask small groups or pairs of children to make an instruction leaflet to explain one of the following:
  ● How to format the text to get headings, sub-headings and bulleted or numbered points.
  ● How to create *screenshots* (images of the finished products, once the instructions have been followed) and to insert them into text.
  ● How to insert WordArt (from the Insert picture menu).
  ● How to create captions in text boxes to accompany pictures.
● Encourage the children to consider clear and simple instructions, and to think about where they should use screenshots.

Plenary
● Invite one or two groups to explain their instructions to the rest of the class.
● Encourage the class to feed back on whether the instructions were useful or if they could be improved. Show them how to save their work into an appropriate folder.
● Print out and distribute the different instructions to the rest of the class.

Animal magic

Starter
Play the musical game of *Switch!* with the children. Ask the class to keep a steady four-beat pulse by tapping on their knees. Encourage them to keep the pulse steady and not to rush. Then ask them to copy the rhythm shown on the first page of your prepared Notebook file, clapping along with them to keep the rhythm.

When the children are keeping the rhythm, call out *Switch!* and at this point press the next screen button: the children have to switch to that rhythm. After repeating this rhythm a couple of times tell the children to return back to the first pulse. Work through the different four-beat rhythm patterns.

Whole-class shared work
● Tell the children that you are going to play some music that describes different types of animals. Play 'Trust in me' from *The Jungle Book*. Tell the children that the music is used to show the characteristics of an animal.
● What do the children think the animal might be? (A python.) Prompt them with questions such as: *How does the music help us to picture this animal in our heads? What type of animal do you think it is? How can you tell?*
● On a blank Notebook page, place a picture of a snake from the My Content folder in the Gallery . Around the image, annotate the children's thoughts about this animal's characteristics.
● Play Nikolai Rimsky-Korsakov's *The Flight of the Bumblebee* (but don't say the name of the piece) and ask the children which animal this makes them think of and why.

Independent work
● Ask the class to work in small groups to create sounds and melodies to describe an animal. Tell the children to think of an animal with distinctive movements that the rest of the class will recognise.
● In their groups, ask the children to select a few instruments that will make the sound of the animals they have thought of.
● Encourage the children to think of words to accompany the sounds to convey the animal. Remind them of the way the words are sung in 'Trust in me'.

Plenary
● Ask each group to perform their compositions. Record the compositions. Ask: *Can you guess the animal? What helped you to guess?* Encourage the children to use the musical terminology when explaining their answers.
● If a microphone is available, use Windows® Sound Recorder to add the children's compositions as sound recordings next to pictures of their chosen animals in a Notebook file.
● Extend this activity by adding narration and movement. Digitally record the children's movements of their chosen animal, and use ICT software to combine the images or video footage with the music to create a multimedia presentation.

Celebrating Divali

Learning objectives
● To learn about Divali as a New Year Festival.
● To look at the worship of Lakshmi, Goddess Of Wealth And Good Fortune, during the festival of Divali.
● To think about how Hindus prepare to welcome Lakshmi.
● To create a rangoli pattern for a Divali card.

Resources
'Celebrating Divali' Notebook file; Divali cards (which should include pictures of Lakshmi); 'Celebrating Divali' Notebook file; A4 card folded in half; paper (plain and squared or dotted); coloured pencils; glue. (Microsoft Word is required to view the embedded story of Lakshmi in the Notebook file.)

Links to other subjects
Citizenship
QCA Unit 5 'Living in a diverse world'
● If possible, visit a local mandir to see how the Hindu community celebrates Divali, or invite a Hindu from the local community to talk about what Divali means to them.
Art and design
QCA Unit 3B 'Investigating pattern'
● Encourage the children to study the different elements of rangoli patterns.

Whiteboard tools
Use the Spotlight tool to focus on a picture. Set the transparency to 50%.

 Pen tray

 Spotlight tool

 Select tool

 Lines tool

 Shapes tool

 Fill Colour tool

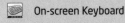 On-screen Keyboard

Starter
Establish the learning objectives on page 1 of the 'Celebrating Divali' Notebook file. Go to page 2 and ask the children why we send cards at special times. Lead them to talk about the festival of Divali (page 3). Give examples of Divali cards to the children and encourage them to talk about why people send Divali cards. Use the Eraser to reveal the key words if the children need support.

Whole-class shared work
● Move on to page 4. Explain that it shows Lakshmi, the Goddess Of Wealth And Good Fortune. Hindus worship her during Divali because they hope that she will bring them good fortune in the coming year. Use the Spotlight tool 🔦 to focus on aspects of Lakshmi: her many hands indicate her powers as a goddess; the lotus flower signifies purity; coins are falling from one of her outstretched hands.
● Hindus draw a rangoli pattern on the entrance to their homes during Divali. This is to welcome Lakshmi into their homes, to bring them good fortune. It is also a sign of welcome to visitors. They often use coloured flour or rice paste.
● Tell the class a story about Lakshmi and Divali. Press the hyperlinked button towards the top of page 4 to view a story about Lakshmi and the washerwoman. This story can be used in subsequent lessons on literacy, or as the basis of a script for a short play for Divali.
● Examples of rangoli patterns are shown on page 5. Ask the children what they notice about the rangoli patterns. What shapes or pictures are used? Most rangolis are geometric patterns made from dots, lines, squares, circles and natural symbols such as the lotus.
● Go to page 6 and invite the children to build up a rangoli pattern by taking turns to add lines or shapes, or to draw a symbol. There are some shapes at the bottom of the page to start them off.
● Use colours to fill in spaces and encourage the children to think about appropriate colours for a Divali festival (bright colours would be better than black or grey).

Independent work
● Ask the children to create a rangoli pattern for a Divali card. Children who need more support in creating symmetrical and geometric patterns can use squared paper to guide their drawings.
● Encourage the children to colour their patterns using appropriate colours. Monitor them as they work, and offer guidance and support as required.

Plenary
● Discuss how the children have created rangoli patterns in different ways. Hand out the folded A4 cards and ask them to cut out and stick their patterns on the front to make a Divali card.
● Encourage them to write appropriate greetings on the front and inside the cards using the prompts on page 7.
● Discuss other appropriate New Year's greetings and add these to the page.

Learning objectives
● To learn about the Good Friday and Easter Sunday stories.
● To think about how Christians celebrate Easter.
● To explore why Easter is important for Christians.

Resources
'The Easter story' Notebook file; classical music, such as Samuel Barber's *Adagio For Strings*; photocopiable page 169 'Role on the wall' for each pair; paper and pencils; images relating to the Good Friday and Easter Day stories, such as palm crosses, a crucifix, an empty cross, Easter eggs, flowers, picture of an Easter garden.

Links to other subjects
Speaking and listening
Objective 36: To use some drama strategies to explore stories or issues.
● The technique of writing external events and facts outside a character's outline and the feelings and emotions within the outline can be applied to any character study. Ask a volunteer to assume the role of one of the characters from the Easter morning story for a hot-seating exercise. Decide as a class on some questions that could be asked of that character. Use a digital camera to film the interview.

Whiteboard tools
Drag a finshed sequence to another page via the Page Sorter.

 Pen tray

 Select tool

 Pen tool

 Area Capture tool

 Page Sorter

The Easter story

Starter
Look at images and artefacts relating to the Good Friday and Easter Sunday stories, accompanied by some classical music. Talk about what they mean and separate them into the two parts of the story of Jesus' last week: Good Friday and Easter Sunday. Ask the children which parts of the story they would consider to be sad or happy. Write their ideas on page 2 of 'The Easter story' Notebook file.

Whole-class shared work
● Use a Children's Bible or picture book to tell the story of Jesus' last week.
● Go to page 3. There is an outline of a person on the page. Tell the children that this is a drama technique called *Role on the Wall*. Explain that it helps them to see how people are feeling: we write facts and events around the outside, and how that character is feeling inside the outline.
● Choose one of the key moments in the story of Jesus' last week, up to Good Friday. Tell the children that they will be thinking about how one of the characters was feeling about Jesus. For example, how Peter or Judas felt when they betrayed Jesus, or what the disciples felt when they saw Jesus carrying the cross.
● Write the name of the person (such as Peter or Judas) above the figure outline and also write his or her relationship to Jesus. Around the outside, write the facts we know about Jesus from the things we have read.
● Ask the children what their chosen person might have been feeling. Select a different colour and write their suggestions inside the outline (as these describe the feelings within a person).
● If there is time (or in a subsequent lesson), compare the feelings of Judas with the feelings of Jesus or one of his friends. Ask the children how they would feel if they did something behind someone's back. How would they feel if the same thing was done to them?
● Repeat the *Role on the Wall* process with a scene following Easter Sunday on page 4. Ask, for example: *What did Peter feel when Jesus appeared before the disciples?*
● Open *The Easter story* interactive activity on page 5. Invite the children to correctly sequence the events from the Easter story. Press the red button to see the captions for the Easter story activity.
● Use the Area Capture tool to take a snapshot of the finished sequence and drag it onto page 5 via the Page Sorter.

Independent work
● Split the children into groups of six (maximum) and ask them to illustrate one scene from the Easter story and to write a few sentences about what the illustration shows. Provide adult support for the less confident learners.
● Let more confident learners or mixed-ability pairs use photocopiable page 169 to apply the *Role on the wall* technique to one of the people in their scene.

Plenary
● Review the correct sequence of the Easter story with the children. Ask one or two groups to recount the story using their illustrations and captions. Discuss the captions, adding notes to page 6, if necessary.

Balancing

Learning objectives
● To demonstrate how different parts of the body can be used to form interesting balances.
● To perform balances with more consistent control and quality.
● To use photographs to identify what makes a balance effective and to suggest improvements where appropriate.

Resources
Digital camera and connection leads; gymnastic mats, one for each child; low-level equipment such as benches or the top of a horse-box; calm music, such as the *Inspector Morse Theme*, composed by Barrington Pheloung.

Links to other subjects
Science
PoS Sc2 (2e) To know that humans and some other animals have skeletons and muscles to support and protect their bodies and to help them to move.
● Ask the children to carry out research into how joints in their bodies work and what movements they allow the bones to perform.

Starter
Ask the children to warm up by skipping around the space. When you call out a letter of the alphabet, the children have to stand in a pose that makes the shape of that letter.

Whole-class shared work
● Tell the children that when you clap, they must move into a still position that involves balance.
● Allow them to hold this position for up to a minute. Share ideas about what balance is and how we balance. Why are some balances easy to hold and others very difficult?
● Explain that balance is achieved when weight is evenly distributed, so they will find it difficult to balance if they lean too much to one side. They are balanced if they can stay in a still position, and not topple or wobble.
● Tell the children that you will be asking them to do *point balances*. Point balances relate to the points of the body touching the floor, so a one-point balance could be balancing while standing on one leg only.
● Ask the children to perform balances for: one point; three points; four points; two points; five points; and finally six points.
● As they perform their balances, take digital pictures of them from different perspectives. Remember to obtain permission from parents before taking any photographs of the children.

Independent work
● Working in groups, the children should do a point balance together. Choose any number of points; if there are more people, more points of the body can be used to create the balance.
● Lay out the mats and a selection of low-level equipment. Ask the children to explore the equipment in pairs, performing different point balances.
● Introduce the idea of *mirror balances* (the children mirror each other's positions).

Plenary
● Sit the children in a circle. Play some calm music and practise different mirror balances by playing *Follow My Leader*. One child performs a balance, and the rest of the class copies the action.
● Challenge the child leading to link three different balances together. Explain to the children that when they link a set of balances together and perform them, one after another, it is called a sequence.
● Back in the classroom, display the digital photos on an interactive whiteboard. Look at a variety of balances. Prompt the children with questions: *Which balances are the most popular? Which ones are unusual? Which were the easiest or most difficult balances to perform?*
● Ask the children to annotate the photographs with features they like and areas they would improve upon. This is a useful assessment exercise that allows the children to see how their balances look from different perspectives, and it is an opportunity for the children to share ideas and to critique each other.

Whiteboard tools
Add photographs to the Notebook file. Select Insert, then Picture File and browse to where you have saved the images.

 Pen tray

Studying artefacts

◼ Draw the artefacts that match these dates and write a few facts about them.

	— **2005**
	— **1982**
	— **1945**
	— **1893**
	— **1880**
	— **1795**

Evacuation wordsearch

■ Find these words related to evacuation during the Second World War. The words can be read from left to right or from top to bottom.

evacuation	suitcase	shelter	cities
evacuee	label	homesick	safety
war	train	towns	danger
gas mask	country	bomb	siren
blitz	letter	blackout	doodlebug

y	d	o	o	d	l	e	b	u	g	k	a
d	v	w	a	r	d	g	l	j	u	h	w
e	v	a	c	u	a	t	i	o	n	o	r
f	a	c	s	c	n	s	t	n	d	m	s
j	s	o	a	i	g	h	z	b	e	e	u
h	i	u	f	t	e	e	g	o	r	s	i
g	r	n	e	i	r	l	a	m	t	i	t
l	e	t	t	e	r	t	s	b	o	c	c
a	n	r	y	s	e	e	m	n	w	k	a
b	z	y	r	t	t	r	a	i	n	s	s
e	v	a	c	u	e	e	s	b	s	f	e
l	w	p	b	l	a	c	k	o	u	t	u

Name _____

Who said that?

◤ Cut out the captions. Match the correct captions to the Roman or the Celtic soldier.

The Romans	The Celts

Boudicca should not lead the Celtic army because she is a woman.	Boudicca is leading the Celtic army against the Roman tyrants.	Boudicca is a rebel.	Boudicca is a brave Celtic queen.
Boudicca is a coward because she killed herself.	Boudicca is such a great leader that lots of Celtic tribes support her uprising.	The Romans are wrong to damage sacred sites.	The Romans are kind and fair rulers.

◤**SCHOLASTIC**

www.scholastic.co.uk

Local land use

■ Keep a record of the occurrences of the various features. Include either the colour of highlighter used for each type of land use or the map symbol used to represent each feature.

Feature/ land use	Map symbol	Colour of highlighting	Occurrences or tally of squares

Spot the difference

■ Look closely at the two pictures on the whiteboard.

What things are the same?

_____

_____

_____

What things are different?

_____

_____

_____

Why do you think they are different?

_____

_____

_____

■ Now consider the next two pictures.
When do you think these pictures were taken?

Picture 1 was taken in	Picture 2 was taken in
_____	_____

Do you think one picture was taken first? How can you tell?

_____

_____

What makes a good tower?

◧ Draw a picture of a tower you particularly like. Remember to use a ruler to draw your straight lines.

◧ Label the features which make a tower strong.

My favourite tower

An architect is a person who designs buildings. Imagine you are a famous architect. Design your own tower on the back of this sheet.

Illustrations © Andy Keylock / Beehive Illustration

Designing a tower

◼ Use this sheet to help your group when designing their tower. Look carefully at the pictures below. Decide on the type of base your group's tower will have.

  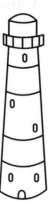

Draw your group's tower here.

The members of my group are:

Patterns

Here are some examples of patterns:

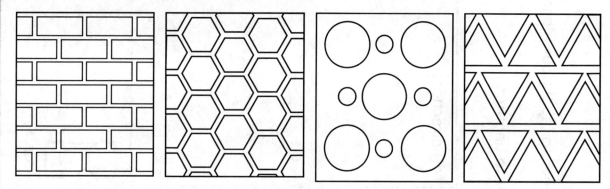

▬ Cut out these shapes. Use them to create patterns. Experiment with different colours, or by placing them in different positions.

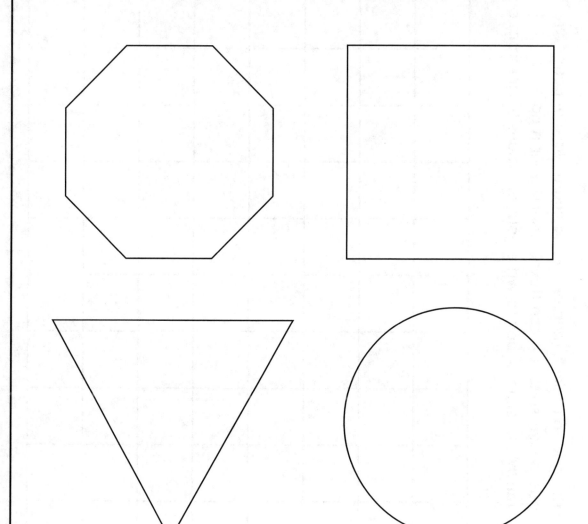

Using a floor turtle

- Use this grid to make a map of an imaginary place of your own. Remember to label your places clearly.
- Cut out the car so that it can travel around your map.
- Use the 'My directions' box to write your directions to get from one place to another.

My directions

car

Role on the wall

Who is the person? _____

What is the story? _____

◼ Write what was happening to this person, or the events in the story, outside the body outline.

◼ Write what the person might have been feeling inside the outline.

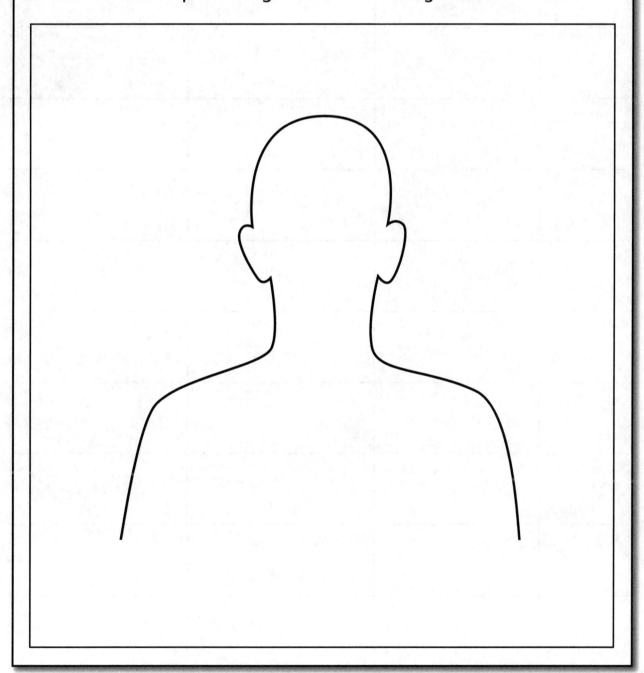

Whiteboard diary

Teacher's name: _____

Date	Subject/ Objective	How was the whiteboard used?	Evaluation

Whiteboard resources library

Teacher's name: _____

Name of resource and file location	Description of resource	How resource was used	Date resource was used

Using your SMART Board™ interactive whiteboard

This brief guide to using your SMART Board interactive whiteboard and Notebook software is based on the training manual *SMART Board Interactive Whiteboard Masters Learner Workbook* © SMART Technologies Inc.

Your finger is your mouse

You can control applications on your computer from the interactive whiteboard. A press with your finger on a SMART Board interactive whiteboard is the same as a click with your mouse. To open an application on your computer through the interactive whiteboard, double-press the icon with your finger in the same way that you would use a mouse to double-click on your desktop computer.

The SMART Pen tray

The SMART Pen tray consists of four colour-coded slots for Pens (black, red, green and blue) and one slot for the Eraser. Each slot has a sensor to identify when the Pens or the Eraser have been picked up. You can write with the Pens, or with your finger, as long as the pen slot is empty. Likewise, if you remove the Eraser from the slot you can use either it or your hand to erase your digital ink.

The Pen tray has at least two buttons. One button is used to launch the On-screen Keyboard and the second button is used to make your next touch on the interactive whiteboard a right-click. Some interactive whiteboards have a third button, which is used to access the Help Centre quickly.

The On-screen Keyboard

The On-screen Keyboard allows you to type or edit text in any application without leaving the interactive whiteboard. It can be accessed either by pressing the appropriate button in the Pen tray, or through the SMART Board tools menu (see page 173).

A dropdown menu allows you to select which keyboard you would like to use. The default Classic setting is a standard 'qwerty' keyboard. Select the Simple setting to arrange the keyboard in alphabetical order, as a useful facility for supporting younger or less confident learners. A Number pad is also available through the On-screen Keyboard.

The Fonts toolbar appears while you are typing or after you double-press a text object. Use it to format properties such as font size and colour.

On-screen Keyboard

Floating tools toolbar

The Transparency layer

When you remove a Pen from the Pen tray, a border appears around your desktop and the Floating tools toolbar launches. The border indicates that the 'transparency layer' is in place and you can write on the desktop just as you would write on a transparent sheet, annotating websites, or any images you display. The transparency layer remains in place until all the Pens and the Eraser have been returned to the Pen tray. Your first touch of the board thereafter will remove the border and any notes or drawings you have made.

Ink Aware applications

When software is Ink Aware, you can write and draw directly into the active file. For example, if you write or draw something while using Microsoft Word, you can save your Word file and your notes will be visible the next time you open it. Ink Aware software includes the Microsoft applications Word, Excel, PowerPoint; graphic applications such as Microsoft Paint and Imaging; and other applications such as Adobe Acrobat. Ensure that the SMART Aware toolbar is activated by selecting View, then toolbars, and checking that the SMART Aware toolbar option is ticked.

Aware tools

When you are using Microsoft Word or Excel, you will now notice three new buttons that will be either integrated into your current toolbar (as shown on the left), or separated as a floating toolbar. Press the first button to insert your drawing or writing as an image directly into your document or spreadsheet. The second button converts writing to typed text and insert it directly into your document or spreadsheet. Press the third button to save a screen capture in Notebook software.

When you are using Microsoft PowerPoint on an interactive whiteboard, the SlideShow toolbar appears automatically. Use the left- and right-hand buttons on the SlideShow toolbar to navigate your presentation. Press the centre button to launch the Command menu for additional options, including access to the SMART Floating tools (see page 175), and the facility to save notes directly into your presentation.

SlideShow toolbar

SMART Board tools

The SMART Board tools include functions that help you to operate the interactive whiteboard more effectively. Press the SMART Board icon at the bottom right of your screen to access the menu.

- SMART Recorder: Use this facility to make a video file of anything you do on the interactive whiteboard. You can then play the recording on any computer with SMART Video player or Windows® Media Player.
- Floating tools: The features you use most are included in the Floating toolbar. It can also be customised to incorporate any tools. Press the More button at the bottom-right of the toolbar and select Customise Floating Tools from the menu. Select a tool from the Available Tools menu and press Add to include it.
- Start Centre: This convenient toolbar gives you access to the most commonly used SMART Board interactive whiteboard tools.
- Control Panel: Use the Control Panel to configure a variety of software and hardware options for your SMART Board and software.

See page 175 for a visual guide to the SMART Board tools.

Using SMART Notebook™ software

Notebook software is SMART's whiteboard software. It can be used as a paper notebook to capture notes and drawings, and also enables you to insert multimedia elements like images and interactive resources.

Side tabs

There are three tabs on the right-hand side of the Notebook interface:

Page Sorter: The Page Sorter tab allows you to see a thumbnail image of each page in your Notebook file. The active page is indicated by a dropdown menu and a blue border around the thumbnail image. Select the dropdown menu for options including Delete page, Insert blank page, Clone page and Rename page. To change the page order, select a thumbnail and drag it to a new location within the order.

Gallery: The Gallery contains thousands of resources to help you quickly develop and deliver lessons in rich detail. Objects from the Gallery can be useful visual prompts; for example, searching for 'people' in an English lesson will bring up images that could help build pupils' ideas for verbs and so on. Objects you have created yourself can also be saved into the Gallery for future use, by dragging them into the My Content folder.

The Search facility in the Gallery usually recognises words in their singular, rather than plural, form. Type 'interactive' or 'flash' into the Gallery to bring up a bank of interactive resources for use across a variety of subjects including mathematics, science, music and design and technology.

Attachments: The Attachments tab allows you to link to supporting documents and webpages directly from your Notebook file. To insert a file, press the Insert button at the bottom of the tab and browse to the file location, or enter the internet address.

Objects in Notebook software

Anything you select inside the work area of a Notebook page is an object. This includes text, drawing or writing, shapes created with the drawing tools, or content from the Gallery, your computer, or the internet.

(ii)

Manipulating objects: To resize an object, select it and drag the white handle (i). Use the green handle (ii) to rotate an object. To adjust the properties of a selected object, use the dropdown menu.

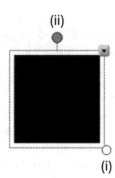

(i)

- Locking: This sub-menu includes options to 'Lock in place', which means that the object cannot be moved or altered in any way. Alternatively you can choose to 'Allow Move' or 'Allow Move and Rotate', which mean that your object cannot be resized.
- Grouping: Select two or more objects by pressing and dragging your finger diagonally so that the objects are surrounded by a selection box. Press the dropdown menu and choose Grouping > Group. If you want to separate the objects, choose Grouping > Ungroup.
- Order: Change the order in which objects are layered by selecting 'Bring forward' or 'Send backward' using this option.
- Infinite Cloner: Select 'Infinite Cloner' to reproduce an object an unlimited number of times.
- Properties: Use this option to change the colour, line properties and transparency of an object.
- Handwriting recognition: If you have written something with a Pen tool, you can convert it to text by selecting it and choosing the Recognise option from the dropdown menu.

Tools glossary

Notebook tools
Hints and tips
- Move the toolbar to the bottom of the screen to make it more accessible for children.

- Gradually reveal information to your class with the Screen Shade.

- Press the Full screen button to view everything on an extended Notebook page.

- Use the Capture tool to take a screenshot of work in progress, or completed work, to another page and print this out.

- Type directly into a shape created with the Shapes tool by double-pressing it and using the On-screen Keyboard.

	Pen tray		Lines tool
	Next page		Shapes tool
	Previous page	A	Text tool
	Blank Page button		Fill Colour tool
	Open		Transparency tool
	Save		Line properties
	Paste		Move toolbar to the top
	Undo button		
	Redo button		Capture tool
	Delete button		Area Capture tool
	Screen Shade		Area Capture 2
	Full screen		Area Capture 3
	Select tool		Area Capture (freehand) tool
	Pen tool		
	Highlighter pen		Page Sorter
	Creative pen		Gallery
	Eraser tool		Attachments

SMART Board tools
Hints and tips
- Use the SMART recorder to capture workings and methods, and play them back to the class for discussion in the Plenary.

- Adjust the shape and transparency of the Spotlight tool when focusing on elements of an image.

- Customise the Floating tools to incorporate any tools that you regularly use. Press the More button at the bottom right of the toolbar and select Customise Floating Tools from the menu.

Press the SMART Board icon at the bottom right of your screen to access the **SMART Board tools** menu (shown right).

The **Start Centre** (shown below), is reached through the SMART Board tools menu.

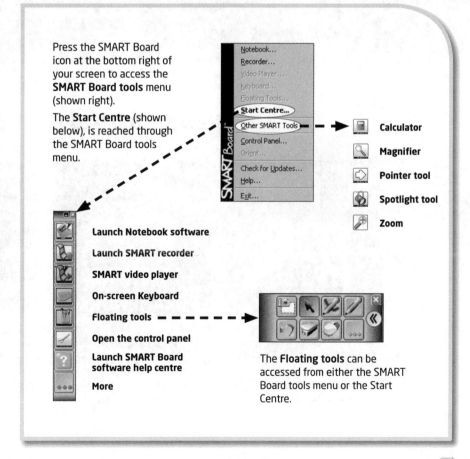

Launch Notebook software

Launch SMART recorder

SMART video player

On-screen Keyboard

Floating tools

Open the control panel

Launch SMART Board software help centre

More

The **Floating tools** can be accessed from either the SMART Board tools menu or the Start Centre.

Calculator

Magnifier

Pointer tool

Spotlight tool

Zoom

SCHOLASTIC

Also available in this series:

ISBN 978-0439-94536-3

ISBN 978-0439-94537-0

ISBN 978-0439-94538-7

ISBN 978-0439-94539-4

ISBN 978-0439-94540-0

ISBN 978-0439-94541-7

ISBN 978-0439-94542-4

New for 2007-2008

ISBN 978-0439-94546-2

ISBN 978-0439-94523-3

ISBN 978-0439-94508-0

To find out more, call: 0845 603 9091
or visit our website www.scholastic.co.uk